MARITAL
THERAPY

Frederick G. Humphrey

University of Connecticut

Prentice-Hall, Inc.   Englewood Cliffs, New Jersey 07632

Library of Congress Cataloging in Publication Data

Humphrey, Frederick G.
    Marital therapy.

    Includes bibliographical references and
index.
    1. Marital psychotherapy.   I. Title.
RC488.5.H83   616.89'156   82-5423
ISBN 0-13-556076-4   AACR2

Editorial production, supervision by Helen Maertens
Cover design by Karolina Harris
Manufacturing buyer: Ron Chapman

To My Wife

Printed in the United States of America

10   9   8   7   6   5   4   3   2   1

ISBN 0-13-556076-4

Prentice-Hall International, Inc., *London*
Prentice-Hall of Australia Pty. Limited, *Sydney*
Prentice-Hall of Canada Inc., *Toronto*
Prentice-Hall of India Private Limited, *New Delhi*
Prentice-Hall of Japan, Inc., *Tokyo*
Prentice-Hall of Southeast Asia Pte. Ltd., *Singapore*
Whitehall Books Limited, Wellington, *New Zealand*

CONTENTS

PREFACE

As a university professor who has been teaching marital therapy for the past eighteen years, and as a long-time practitioner in the profession, I have constantly searched for a comprehensive, pragmatic manual on marital therapy that would be useful to both practitioners and students. Such a manual, in my experience, simply has not been available. Books oriented toward students preparing to enter the profession have usually been highly theoretical but lacking in practicality. The few books written for the experienced marital therapist usually possess, in my estimation, rather narrow therapeutic orientations.

In recent years, while serving as an officer of the American Association for Marriage and Family Therapy, I was frequently in touch with therapists all over North America. These contacts led me to wish that I could distill my own teaching and clinical experience into a manual that would be useful to all marital therapists. When Ted Jursek of Prentice-Hall called me for suggestions about who could write a manual for practitioners, I immediately suggested that I believed I could do the job as well as anyone. Ted "called me" on that—and the work began.

What I am seeking to convey in this book is the knowledge that I have gained from working with thousands of troubled marriages over the past thirty years. These years include my earlier work in psychiatric social work as well as my later work in the practice and teaching of marital therapy. The book represents the foundations I received from my own teachers and supervisors—persons such as Emily Mudd, Hilda Goodwin, Kenneth Appel, and Stanley Hirsch—as well as what I have learned from clients, students, associates, and other sources. I end the book with observations concerning the impact on one's personal life of being a professional marital therapist. My own experiences from over thirty years of marriage, which included sharing the responsibilities with my wife of raising our three children, have also had an impact upon my professional work which is reflected in the writings. The manual, therefore, includes more than the pragmatics of marital therapy; it also presents a philosophy concerning how we marital therapists are privileged to help individuals and couples learn to cope with one of the greatest and most difficult relationships that our society provides for us. While the therapeutic stratagems I write about are designed primarily to help couples solve marital conflicts, they also address the issues of helping individuals to maximize their potential for growth. These changes often lead to the dissolution of dysfunctional marriages. This is a fact of contemporary life that marital therapists must face and come to grips with. Couples in the 1980s no longer march to only one drummer. It is our task to help them make decisions about the future of their marriages and then to help them cope with the consequences of these choices, both positive and negative.

Ideally, I would have liked to add more to the book. On the advice of the publisher, I am deleting sections on contemporary marriage and on personality and counseling theories. This information is available elsewhere as indicated in the references. The net result, therefore, is a book of direct value to practicing therapists and to advanced graduate students. If those who purchase it find it useful to read—and to periodically reread certain sections again when they are faced with specific issues in their practice—then I will have accomplished my goal.

Special thanks to the reviewers of the book, Ralph H. Earle, James E. Kilgore, Lynn Balster Liontos, Thelma F. Dixon Murphy, William C. Nichols, Donald S. Williamson, and Wayne Winkle.

Frederick G. Humphrey

PART ONE
PRINCIPLES AND PROCESS OF MARITAL THERAPY

CHAPTER ONE
PRINCIPLES
OF MARITAL THERAPY

HISTORICAL PERSPECTIVES

Marital therapy as a distinct professional treatment modality is truly a twentieth-century development. Its origins, however, are as ancient as the institution of marriage itself. Societies down through the ages have designated certain individuals, or groups of individuals, as appropriate persons to offer advice and to help partners in marriage conflict. Relatives of both the husband and the wife have fallen into this category and remain, even today, as frequent sources of advice and counsel to couples. In more recent times, members of several professions, particularly theology and medicine, have frequently been sought out for marital help. Both clergy and physicians ordinarily have contacts with family members at significant times in the life cycle of all persons—birth, marriage, illness, and death—thus it has not been uncommon for people to turn to members of these professions for help with many types of personal and family problems. Frequently, a sense of rapport with these professions already existed before problems arose—hence, it logically followed that persons would seek the advice of physicians and clergy in times of crisis. The fact that schools of theology and of medicine only rarely offered their students special training in marriage, sexuality, marital therapy, and the like seemed to be of little concern to the average citizen. In more recent years, many—particularly those from lower socioeconomic groups—have also turned to social workers for marital help. For decades social agencies have been working to strengthen family life by offering financial, housing, and job assistance and, more currently, by dealing with broken marriages in the courts, child custody services, and other social agencies. Many other professions continue their more or less traditional role of assisting couples and individuals in situations of marital distress. These include psychologists, attorneys, guidance counselors, public health and psychiatric nurses, and a variety of other mental health personnel. Indeed, all professional persons who have anything to do with human beings sooner or later find themselves called upon to deal with the marital stresses of their clients and patients. The modern practice of marital therapy has grown out of these more traditional professions. Even today the vast majority of contemporary marital therapists have received their initial clinical training in a specialty other than marital therapy.

Marital therapy, as a new and specialized body of knowledge and techniques, dates back to the 1920s and 1930s. Pioneering work may be said to have started with Abraham and Hannah Stone at the Community Church in New York City in 1929. Neither of the Stones was a member of the clergy, but the Church sponsored their work in marriage and sexuality. Shortly thereafter, two more centers were started: Paul Popenoe's American Institute of Family Relations in California and Emily Mudd's Marriage Council of Philadelphia. Both of these latter groups were established to offer counseling help specifically with marital problems, a service that made them uniquely different from the all-purpose functions served by the family agencies of that time.

Unique Features of Marital Therapy

From its inception, one of the unique features of marital therapy has been its emphasis upon the marital system itself. It has often been said that "the marriage is the patient"—not the persons in the marriage. This attention to the marital system, an emphasis which predated by over two decades the more recent focus on entire family systems, comprises one of the major identifying marks of a marital therapist—particularly as compared to an individual psychotherapist. Three other characteristics were—and remain—common to most marital therapists: psychodynamic understanding of the personalities and their interaction in the marriage, an emphasis upon current real-life problems, and a systematic use of conjoint interviewing techniques. Earlier therapists, especially those with their roots in theology, usually placed strong emphasis upon the permanence of marriage. They frequently imposed their own personal values onto their clients, especially in regard to divorce and infidelity. Today this approach is considered unethical according to professional codes of practice.

Development of Professional Associations

Outside of the marital therapy field, but closely allied to it, developed the study of marriage as a unique relationship within the broader confines of family sociology. In the 1920s and 1930s a pioneer marriage and family life educator, Ernest Groves, began offering functional courses in marriage to American college students. The 1930s saw the establishment of what has become known as the Groves Conference on the Family and also of another group, primarily academic in nature, the National Council on Family Relations. Leaders from these two groups were amongst those who established the American Association of Marriage Counselors

(AAMC) in New York City in 1942. The formation of the AAMC marked the formal establishment of marital therapy as a distinct professional field. In 1970, reflecting the growing trend by its members to conceptualize the marital relationship as an integral part of the family system, and to develop the treatment unit to include parents and children of married couples, the AAMC became the American Association of Marriage and Family Counselors (AAMFC). In 1978 the AAMFC, in turn, became the American Association for Marriage and Family Therapy (AAMFT), dropping the word "counselors" in favor of the more accurate and contemporary term "therapy." Other groups have been formed in recent times as identification groups for marital therapists, such as the Academy of Psychologists in Marital and Family Therapy. In 1977, the American Family Therapy Association (AFTA) was formed by a group of professionals whose interests were focused primarily on the total family as the preferred unit of therapy. The U.S. Commissioner of Education in 1978 recognized the AAMFT's Commission on Accreditation for Marriage and Family Therapy Education to perform the task of accrediting training programs in marriage and family counseling, rejecting the notion that marital therapy was a subspecialty of family therapy or that family therapy was a subspecialty of marital therapy. While professional associations, academics, and purists may debate these definitions and terms for many years into the future, people will continue to marry and to experience difficulties in coping with each other in the marital relationship. This book is addressed to a discussion of these marital problems and how marital therapy clinicians may best treat them.

MARRIAGE—AN IMPERFECT INSTITUTION

Marriage has never been, and never will be, a perfect social institution. In the past, partners in troubled marriages could often look to an early termination of the relationship through death of one of the partners because the human life span was so short. For centuries, serial monogamy was thus a common phenomenon for any persons living past their third or fourth decades of life. Even when marital conflict existed, the powerful social pressures of religious teachings, extended-family members, and the State forced couples to suffer in silence rather than to openly admit to marital problems or failures. In the modern American family, by contrast, the situation is quite different. First marriages usually occur when the partners are in their twenties; thus the partners face a potential lifetime together of over a half-century! This presents a challenge never before faced in the entire history of the human race. In addition to this potential extended marital life span of several decades, married people today are faced with increasingly individually oriented value systems—ones that place *individual* development and happiness above marital stability and fulfillment. Additionally, Western societies continue to demand only minimum qualifications to marry. These usually include the requirements that the potential marital partners be of the opposite sex, not be too closely related to each other, be of a minimum age (as young as 14 in some states), not have active syphilis, and have functioning sexual organs. George Bernard Shaw wrote that "When two people are under the influence of the most violent, most insane, most delusive and most transient of passions, they are required to swear that they will remain in that excited, abnormal, and exhausting condition continuously until death do them part" (Shaw 1963, p. 335). Shaw may have stated his case somewhat vigorously, but the fact remains that our society places maximum expectations upon marriage and yet demands only the barest minimum of qualifications of those who wish to marry. Marital therapists, therefore, are often confronted with requests for help from individuals who are, by many definitions, psychologically, socially, educationally, or physically lacking in the very attributes that research has demonstrated are correlates for marital success. In view of these facts, marital therapists must be highly pragmatic persons who are capable of both setting and accepting limited therapeutic goals for their patients.

THERAPEUTIC GOALS IN MARITAL THERAPY

Open, Honest Communication

One of the first symptoms listed by the majority of marital therapy patients is the absence of effective and positive communication between partners. Thus, one of therapists' first treatment goals, that of establishing or rebuilding marital communications, is usually thrust upon them by the clients' situations and demands. This poses a formidable paradox, for resolving marital problems in the absence of effective communications is almost impossible. On the other hand, communication has often been overstressed in the literature to the extent that the naive therapist may feel communication cures *all* marital ills. Good communication, in fact, may guarantee a divorce if it clearly carries the message "I hate you and want out of this marriage." This type of open, honest communication may be highly desirable in divorce therapy when it presents a reality of client feeling, but this should not be confused with "therapeutic magic" that presumably manages to dispel and undo years of rejection and neglect of a partner's needs. Effective *selective* communication, as will be elaborated upon later, rates high priority as a goal for successful marital functioning.

Value Congruency

Americans marry for love—and the romantic idea of love implies that the partners feel as one in heart, body, soul, and values. Value congruence is expected to be at its peak when a marriage takes place. Engaged couples who have strong differences in value systems—whether about money, sex, religion, children, sex roles, or whatever—might be expected to terminate their relationships instead of marrying. The urge to marry, however, is often so strong that defense mechanisms preclude any such rational decisions. Negative feelings and anxiety over major value differences are repressed or denied—only to crop up in full force after a period of stress-creating domesticity. Other couples appear to marry with excellent agreement between their fundamental life value systems but gradually, over a period of months or years, these values may grow apart. For example, the "liberated" male who marries an ardent feminist and who, at the time of the marriage, appears to share his wife's views on women and motherhood, may later reveal more traditional male values and expect the wife to be the primary housekeeper in the marriage. Such obviously discrepant values can only eventuate in a clash that rapidly escalates in open marital warfare. Lack of value congruence between the partners thus frequently engenders another major therapeutic goal for the couple and the therapist—that of negotiating to see if value congruency can be achieved between the spouses.

Conflict Resolution

Very few couples ever consult a marital therapist without first having reached a high level of conflict between themselves. Conflict resolution, in many spheres of the marriage, thus becomes another common therapeutic goal in marital therapy. The romantic myths upon which so many marriages are established suggest that marriage could and should be one long series of friendly, loving encounters between a husband and wife. Such idealism flies in the face of the realities of raising children, balancing budgets, contending with different sexual rhythms, and a host of other conflict-producing "normal" dilemmas of married life. Yet the only "education" most adults ever receive in conflict resolution takes place in the arena in which their own parents have fought—perhaps abetted by the insidious television classroom, in which violence is the main staple of "entertainment" offered. One does not have to be a therapist in a battered women's shelter to realize that marital therapists must perpetually work to help couples learn to resolve their conflicts in a more mature and constructive way than that which posits that "might makes right."

Making the Decision:
Divorce or Not?

The basic goal in marital therapy for many couples entails utilizing the skills and knowledge of the therapist to arrive at a major decision—whether to continue the marriage or obtain a divorce. Indeed, the therapist's office is often the last stop a couple makes before consulting a divorce lawyer. Some therapists may rebel at being expected to assist in such a monumental decision, feeling it to be both unethical and impossible to share their professional judgments on these extremely sensitive and idiosyncratic matters. Such feelings, however, overlook the valuable service a skilled therapist can provide when a couple is faced with this difficult decision—or, as often happens, in helping a rejected spouse face up to the reality of the partner's unilateral decision to divorce. The old image of the marriage "counselor" as a person inevitably dedicated to saving the marriage, rejecting divorce as an alternative in all cases regardless of the circumstances, is fading. Today, more and more couples are realistically utilizing therapists earlier in the psychological separation and disengagement process—specifically so they can plan most constructively for their own and their children's futures.

Setting Goals

Clinicians are also interested in *how* therapy goals are set, as well as in the goals themselves. In general, marital therapists pursue goals that are similar to those of "individual-oriented" psychotherapists, with the obvious exception of the continuous concern of the marital therapist upon the interpersonal implications of each client's feelings and behaviors. Psychodynamically oriented marital therapists encourage the development of insight into one's own as well as one's partner's psychodynamics. They support the individual growth of the partners as well as the growth of the couple. Marriage, in its most positive aspects, may result in a synergistic growth process, with both partners becoming stronger, more productive, and more satisfied than would ever have been possible without the stimulus and support of their mate. At the same time, therapy often has to focus on decisions that might substitute personal growth for unusual marital or family solidarity. A frequent and increasingly complex issue of this nature is the question of one partner accepting an occupational promotion that requires moving to another state. With dual careers now the norm for millions of couples, this problem is being encountered with increasing frequency in therapists' offices.

Emotional Support

The last major therapeutic goal to be commented upon here is that of rendering emotional support to one's clients. Couples undergoing marital troubles report that the simple, accepting support of the therapist in times of crisis is an important aspect of therapeutic benefit for them. Many therapists devalue the importance of their own psychological support and imply that this creates excessive dependence of the clients upon the therapist. Misapplied, it may do just that. But for the vast majority of clients, psychological support, appropriately given, can be of immense value. The greater the clients' pain and the greater their feelings of isolation and confusion, the more they will value the therapist's reassuring presence and concern. Psychotherapy has been described by Schofield as the "purchase of friendship" (Schofield 1974). Mundane as it sounds, this is precisely what legions of clients seek from their marital therapists. In many professions, great emphasis has been placed upon the role of extending psychological support to one's clients during periods of crisis. Regretfully, however, those professions dealing exclusively with psychotherapeutic issues, including marital therapy, often appear to treat this therapy goal more as a negative than as a positive way of helping.

Summary

Modern marital therapists, it may be said in summary, share with their clients the goals of the alleviation of stress and conflict in marriage as well as the maximum development of each marital partner as an individual human being. Therapists value marriage as an institution and support it fully—but also recognize that marriage is not suited for everyone, nor is everyone necessarily suited for the marriage he or she may currently be in. Therapists should treat every case and every client as unique. Consequently, therapy goals for any specific couple cannot be rigidly set in advance. Goals must be evolved between the therapist and the couple throughout the entire span of therapy, with all participants in the therapy process keeping open the possibility that changes in purpose and direction may be necessitated as shifts in feelings and events experienced by the couple develop.

METHODOLOGIES OF MARITAL THERAPY

Marital therapy is defined as *a psychotherapeutic process by which a therapist treats married individuals in order to assist them in resolving conflicts with their partner as they move into, cope with, or move out of their marriage.*

Separate Therapists for the Partners: An Early Theory

Interviewing techniques are the essential method by which the therapist renders this professional help. Earlier therapists, strongly influenced by psychoanalytical techniques, often favored individual sessions exclusively, with the husband and the wife each having a separate therapist. Transference and countertransference considerations, it was believed, precluded the advisability of having one therapist treat both spouses simultaneously. However, what proponents of separate treatment failed to recognize was that marital therapy differs in numerous ways from intrapsychic individual psychotherapy and psychoanalysis. One of these differences is the marital therapist's *focus upon the realities of the current time period.* Couples in crisis cannot spend months or years working through childhood problems while their marriages crumble about them. Additionally, a marital therapist's *focus on the marriage relationship,* as contrasted to the analyst's primary stress on the individual psyche, requires a knowledge of and immediate access to both marital partners' feelings and behaviors. Moreover, an important limitation of separate individual therapy is that the separate therapists' countertransferences and professional jealousies can lead to rivalry between the therapists and this, in turn, is communicated to the marital partners. The net result often leaves the partners fighting the *therapists'* battles instead of facing their own problems. In addition, even minimum communication between separate therapists is a time-consuming, expensive practice; consequently, lines of communication and cooperation often break down, with the final result that neither therapist feels any special concern for the marriage itself.

Concurrent Individual Therapy

A similar treatment procedure, concurrent individual therapy by the same therapist but always utilizing separate interviews, is a procedure that is rarely utilized exclusively. This method has the advantage of the therapist having almost immediate access to both partners so that reality testing may be more readily obtained and communication enhanced. It also allows confidential discussion of "secrets," a valuable asset to therapy that will be discussed in Chapter Three ("Extramarital Relationships"). It should ordinarily be restricted to the intake sessions, however, or used on an alternating basis with other treatment modalities, especially conjoint sessions.

Conjoint Interviewing

By far the most desirable method of marital therapy is that of conjoint interviewing, which consists of having the therapist interview the husband and wife together in the same session. This has the advantage of turning the therapy session into an "in vivo" experience in which the partners react to each other in the therapist's presence in ways characteristic of their responses in home-like situations. Reality testing is enhanced, distortions are more self-evident, and clarification can immediately occur when needed. Inasmuch as blaming the other is a frequent strategy utilized by many partners to reduce guilt and self-blame, conjoint sessions help minimize this tactic—or at least permit a more objective assessment of its validity and the treatment thereof. Therapists with a communications focus find conjoint sessions invaluable in modeling behavior, role playing, and negotiating. With both partners present, the therapist can promote increased accuracy in "reading" nonverbal clues and can also make instant interpretations that both partners hear and can challenge if they feel the need to do so. The therapist can lend strength or support to constructive ideas and actively discourage destructive behaviors or plans. This last point vividly illustrates that marital therapy requires an active, involved role for the therapist. Perfect neutrality between the therapist and each partner is neither necessary nor desirable. As long as the couple's goal is to maintain the marriage, the therapist supports and actively encourages all gestures, behaviors, and verbalizations that lead in that direction. When one or both of the partners have clearly reached the decision to separate or divorce, conjoint sessions continue to be useful to help both partners face this reality and to plan for such things as child custody, visitation, financial arrangements, and so forth. Private individual sessions should also be held from that point on, either on a regular or on an "as-needed" basis, in order to focus on the more individualistic goals and needs of each partner.

Further advantages of conjoint interviewing are that this technique often makes it easier for both the therapist and the partners to schedule appointments; it may be a less expensive form of treatment; and, according to various research studies, it is usually rated as the most effective form of therapy for couples who remain married (Cookerly 1973, 1976). However, the *exclusive* usage of conjoint interviewing should be discouraged. During the intake session(s), it is absolutely vital that each partner be interviewed alone and confidentially at some point, to allow the therapist to achieve a clear understanding of each person's feelings, experiences, and plans. For example, in a significant number of marital cases, one or both partners is involved in extramarital affairs. These individuals are usually unwilling to share this important fact if their marital partner is present; moreover, even if the affair is known to both partners, it is not reasonable to expect the spouse having the affair to openly discuss it when the marital partner is sitting there consumed with hurt and anger. Another classical restriction on conjoint interviewing exists when one partner is highly ambivalent about continuing the marriage. The presence of the other partner raises the ambivalent person's defenses by creating a higher level of anxiety; this can effectively block or slow the working through of a resolution of the dilemma.

Group Marital Therapy

Conjoint group marital therapy for couples has been growing in popularity in recent years. Clinics, overburdened with more cases than they can currently handle for conjoint therapy, frequently offer various types of marital group therapy in the attempt to service more people. If it is utilized exclusively, the group approach can offer therapy to more persons at reduced costs. Similarly, this can be a major source of income to the group therapists themselves. The merits of the group approach, as opposed to the individual or conjoint methods, include expanded opportunities for modeling behavior, the positive value of group support, the realization by clients that others share similar problems, and, finally, the potential assistance of other group members offering new insights into a given couple's situation. This last possibility can increase the likelihood that there will be more therapeutic interventions, so that each couple, in effect, receives the attention of "multiple therapists"—the other group members. On the negative side, group marital therapy shares some of the same limitations existing in conjoint therapy; it reduces the attention the therapist can give any specific couple. Therefore, group sessions are usually led by two therapists, and it is imperative that they be highly compatible in their therapeutic goals and philosophies. Finally, group therapy is frequently rejected by large numbers of couples who resist the reduced confidentiality and who want a more personalized approach to their problems; this is a factor minimized in the literature, but highly relevant to conducting therapy. Therapists who perform group therapy exclusively must have large numbers of potential couples available to them in order to compensate for the significant proportion of people who resist the group approach; if they do not, they may have to arbitrarily insist on this modality regardless of the couples' feelings.

Numerous combinations of marital group therapy exist, including having one marital partner in group therapy and the other in individual therapy; having both partners in groups of married individuals but having spouses in separate groups; having both partners together with other couples in a group; and combining conjoint marital group therapy with alternating or occasional individual or conjoint sessions. For those wishing to deepen their understanding of these procedures, there are numerous texts available on group therapy in general.

Bibliotherapy as Adjunctive Therapy

Earlier writings in the marital therapy field stressed the use of *bibliotherapy*, the utilization of reading materials by couples. Many therapists and clinics continue to offer this as an adjunctive therapeutic service. They maintain lending libraries of appropriate books on marriage, sexuality, parenting, and so forth. Given the dearth of marital and family life education offered persons before they marry, this type of service helps couples increase their knowledge and understanding of what they are experiencing. Caution must be exerted, however, against the impulse to treat serious marital problems by an over-reliance on reading materials. Where the therapist ascertains that clients are being handicapped by lack of factual knowledge, the lending of helpful literature may help—and rarely hurts. Therapists should always review the material, in advance of loaning it out, in order to assure that its "message" fits the therapist's own understandings about what each particular couple may need and be able to use constructively.

Treatment of the Family Unit

Treatment of the entire family unit must also be considered by marital therapists. While the majority of cases treated by therapists are primarily concerned with issues between the husband and the wife, the presence of older or younger generations within the home may dictate inclusion of these members into the therapy program. Additionally, other family members not in the home—whether parents, siblings, or grown children—may be involved under appropriate conditions. The choice of whether the therapist performs therapy primarily or exclusively with the marital pair or broadens the interview unit to include other family members is heavily influenced by his or her training, as well as the therapist's philosophical and psychological orientations. Those therapists who describe themselves as family systems–oriented may choose to include other family members regardless of the presenting complaints of the couple. Recent years have seen a rapid expansion of the "family therapy" approach, discussion of which is beyond the scope of this volume. However, large numbers of "family therapists" only utilize the whole family unit for purposes of assessment and then move on to perform marital therapy almost exclusively with the couple. These practitioners will find the marital therapies described here valuable for the bulk of their work: that of dealing with what is ordinarily the most significant and most pressing part of the family system—the marital unit.

THE DYNAMICS OF MARRIAGE

The Dictates of the Unconscious

Contrary to romantic myth, marriages are not made in heaven—rather, they are made in the unconscious of the husband and the wife. Choosing a marital partner is not an entirely rational process. It is an extremely complex social-psychological process. Even though the participants themselves often *think* they can explain why they are marrying their partner, the most subtle and compelling reasons for their choice, in reality, stem from the unconscious levels of their minds. Brides and grooms, when asked why they are marrying, are prone to reply rather simply that they are "in love" with their partner. This statement, describing their strong positive attraction for the other, is romanticized at best and misleading at worst.

Sager believes that marital contracts exist on a minimum of three levels: (1) a conscious, verbalized level wherein persons tell their partner about the type of relationship they consciously expect to experience with the other; (2) a conscious but unverbalized level in which the individuals know what they hope and expect to give and receive in the relationship—they do not, however, share this information with the other lest complications occur; and (3) an unconscious and, hence, unverbalized set of expectations for the relationship (Sager 1976). Here we can see the reasons many marriages are in trouble from their very beginnings—they are based upon needs that people are afraid to even articulate to their partner, or needs that have been repressed because they are unacceptable to the ego.

The Socialization Process

Human beings are social creatures. They seek union with others. Marriage is but one of numerous social institutions wherein society accepts, supports, and influences the way this unification is to be carried on. Through the complex socialization process, the young developing child takes on many aspects of his or her culture—including the aspiration to marry. This process occurs on both a conscious and an unconscious level as the child introjects the values of the parents, relatives, and of the members of the larger society. From the time children receive their very first toys and are read their earliest nursery stories, they are taught to think of themselves as potential husbands and wives, mothers and fathers. Very few persons ever question these powerful, mind-influencing teachings. By the time average boys and girls reach late adolescence or young adulthood, they are deeply ingrained with the "need" to marry. Around the world different cultures impell their young into marriage at different ages, frequently at younger ages in simpler, less developed countries and at older ages in more complex societies. Regardless of these age variations, however, powerful unconscious libidinal urges are assisted by socialization practices in pushing young people to obtain sexual gratification in the conventional fashion—by marrying. More recently, with better and more widely available contraception methods and with the declining influence of repressive antisexual religious doctrines, age at first marriage in North America is being postponed, especially among the more educated. Those young people who hold off marriage, however, frequently illustrate the instinctual push toward union and sexual gratification by living together without marriage. While they may escape some "marital" troubles by staying legally unmarried, they are prone to most of the usual problems of marriage. In addition, they frequently lack the support of other family members, a fact which, while it may strengthen their determination to succeed, may also rob them of energy as well as sustenance from the family that might otherwise be directed toward solving the conflicts that inevitably occur.

Emotional Maturity,
Personality Needs

In the process of growing up, young people reach the chronological age for marriage without necessarily reaching an equal level of emotional maturity. Marriage is a very demanding institution, one that requires a high level of personal, social, and psychological readiness. However, the more immature a couple is, the more vigorously they will often proclaim their readiness to wed—because of an unconscious rejection of this very need to be mature before entering marriage.

In addition to social and sexual pressures to marry, all persons seek to act out a wide variety of personality needs by marrying. These cover all types—from the need to dominate to the need to be dominated, from excessive needs to be accepted to complicated needs to be rejected. Ideally, these personality needs complement each other, as happens, for example, when a person with a dependent personality marries someone with a strong need to control and guide others. But what may happen, as experienced marital therapists testify so often, is that the initial positive complementarity of personality needs frequently changes over time. The harmonious balance in these needs systems remains only as long as each person changes in both the appropriate direction and magnitude that the spouse's needs may require. The frequent marital complaints that the partner has changed "since we married" or "after the baby was born," and similar reasons, bear grim testimony to this fact. These problems vividly illustrate the concept of marital systems.

MARITAL SYSTEMS

Marital partners do not relate to each other as isolated entities but rather as parts or elements of a complex network of interconnections with each other and with other persons. These interconnections occur on behavioral, social, and psychological levels. Just as our solar system contains numerous constellations or subsystems of stars and planets that, in toto, make up one complete grouping or system called the universe, so too is the marital system made up of many groupings or subsystems that combine together to form the larger marital system. These subsystems are interdependent, dynamic and constantly in flux (although often quite fixed in specific areas). Because of their interrelatedness, changes within any one subsystem affect all segments of both that subsystem and of the total marital system. In order to understand their clients' behaviors and feelings fully, marital therapists must be knowledgeable about each couple's unique marital systems and how they influence and control each person's feelings and behaviors. The first and primary system that concerns marital therapists is the *intrapsychic* or *intrapersonal* system of each spouse. Each partner has his or her own Id, Ego, and Superego, the determinants of human actions, feelings, and abilities. These interlocking parts of the psychic apparatus must function in harmony with one another or the individual will be neurotically hampered in his or her capacity to relate to others in positive, constructive, adult ways. The next marital system is the *interpersonal* one; and the marital dyad, for most people, represents the most important aspect of their interpersonal relationships with others. Failure to make the marital dyad central, such as occurs when intergenerational loyalties for one's children or parents receive preferential treatment over loyalty for one's spouse, can create severe friction within the marriage. The *family* system, which includes one's children, one's siblings, and one's parents, as well as extended family members, qualifies as the next most important segment of a married person's interpersonal system. Finally, the broader *cultural* system of each marital partner exerts an important influence—consciously and unconsciously—on his or her marital roles. The cultural system includes a client's sex, race, religion, ethnic group, socioeconomic status, and occupation.

These systems—the intrapsychic and all types of the interpersonal ones—are in a constant state of motion. They push and they pull. They compete for the person's attention, energy, and loyalty. In obedience to the basic laws of force in nature, a push in any one direction results in a pull of equal magnitude in the opposite direction. The wife who worries about her obligation to herself as a person may find herself in conflict with her own mother, who taught her that wives should always subjegate themselves to their husbands. Or this pressure may arise not from her mother directly, but from her unconscious identification with her mother's values, which she may still be struggling to discard now that she herself is a mature adult. Similarly, husbands in our masculine-oriented society frequently report conflict between their wishes to be tender and loving with their wives and the "socially expected" behavior of playing the strong, aggressive, "macho" male role.

OTHER INFLUENCES ON MARITAL SYSTEMS

Directly influencing couples' abilities to perform their marital roles is the degree of mental, physical, family, and financial health they possess. The average marital therapist works primarily with the intrapsychic and interpersonal conflicts of so-called "normal" couples—but that does not minimize his or her need to be sensitive to the limitations that may be imposed on the marriage by these other factors.

Mental health.   Marital and family conflicts rank high in all studies of psychiatric patients. For decades, a major ground for divorce in most American courts was mental cruelty—the mental pressure engendered by marital friction was ruled sufficiently destructive to a couple to constitute a legal reason for termination of a marriage. Strong emotions—anger, hate, fear, depression, loneliness, rejection—always accompany conflict, and marital conflict is no exception. Hence, persons who do not have reasonably satisfactory mental health find it difficult or impossible to cope with even the normal strains of resolving the inevitable conflicts that arise when two people live together continuously.

Physical health.   On a similar level, the physical health of couples is a matter of great importance to their marital adjustment. Couples expending large amounts of time, energy, and money on chronic medical conditions almost invariably experience declines in marital satisfaction. Often the medical condition becomes the central focus in their lives, causing the interpersonal relationship between the spouses to assume a secondary role.

Children.   The presence of children has traditionally been assumed to be a deterrent to divorce, strengthening a positive bond between the marital partners. However, in the majority of divorces today, minor children are involved, making this myth no longer tenable. Being parents means fulfilling a vast array of demanding roles—roles that at times are dull and unrewarding. Divorce statistics bear grim testimony to these facts, but these pressures of parenthood are usually overlooked—or outwardly rejected—by traditionalists and those who constantly push for the "necessity" of parenthood.

Financial health.   The financial health of a marriage also has a direct relationship to the stability and happiness of a couple. Divorce and separation have always been highest among the most financially impoverished families. Often, poor families suffer from a constellation of handicaps—medical, mental, occupational, housing, and educational. In assisting families with these multiple problems, therapists are advised to follow the priorities employed by social caseworkers: attempt to assist in improving the families' standard of living and community assets before focusing on the psychodynamic aspects of their relationship problems.

Intrapsychic mechanisms.   Marriages are not only *contracted* on the basis of many factors in the unconscious of each of the partners—they are also *maintained* there—for better or for worse. This means that every marital therapist must have a sound understanding of the human psyche, its composition, its levels of functioning, and its mechanisms of defense. The marital relationship is second only to the relationship with one's parents in respect to the intensity of psychological forces that are constantly at work between the individuals in the relationship. Ideally, marriage is a synergistic state in which both individuals become stronger, more fully actuated, and more fulfilled than would ever be possible if they were single. In reality, however, marriage partners are often the recipients of the other's projections, displacements, and needs for power and control. Consequently, intrapsychic forces must constantly be at work to maintain each person's integrity, self-esteem, and healthy ego functioning. Therapists who ignore these intrapsychic mechanisms—or are inadequately trained to recognize them—risk continued frustration of their efforts to treat marriages because they do not deal appropriately with basic individual neurotic conflicts. On occasion, the presence of excessive intrapsychic conflict dictates a period of individual therapy before marital therapy can become effective or, if the therapist is appropriately trained, concurrent individual psychotherapy and marital therapy may be conducted simultaneously.

SUMMARY

Marital therapy, it has been shown, is a contemporary psychotherapeutic field of practice within the broader confines of family therapy. It has grown out of earlier professions and has now reached the point where it possesses its own body of knowledge, theory, and therapeutic strategies. Knowledge of intrapsychic and interpersonal psychodynamics is essential to therapists and forms the base upon which the special marital treatment techniques have evolved.

Marital therapists strive to assist individuals and couples in resolving their conflicts as they prepare for, cope with, and sometimes terminate their marriages. We next turn our attention to the actual process by which therapy takes place.

CHAPTER TWO
THE PROCESS
OF MARITAL THERAPY

REFERRALS

The Initial Contact

Therapy begins the instant a client contacts the therapist's office for an appointment. The manner in which clients are treated over the telephone may be a significant factor in the establishment of positive rapport with the therapist—or in the couple's failure to keep the initial appointment. The call for help usually comes at a time of special tension for the couple. It is important that the person answering the phone (therapist, receptionist) handle the caller's initial anxiety with tact, allowing that person sufficient time to ventilate some of this anxiety while at the same time obtaining necessary information.

Facts desired at this time include the couple's names, addresses, schedules of available time, phone numbers, and the name of the person or agency who referred them. Emphasis should be placed on the expectation of seeing both the husband and the wife for the first appointment. Wives tend to make the initial request for an appointment more frequently than do husbands, reflecting the male's cultural bias against seeking help. When the husband places the initial call to the therapist, however, experience shows that the chances are greater that the appointment will actually be kept. If the therapist or receptionist detects that the caller is extremely ambivalent about the appointment—or if it appears that the therapy appointment is being requested to serve as a threat or power play—consideration may be given to suggesting that the caller discuss the potential appointment further with his or her spouse. If this is done and the person later calls back for a definite appointment, the risk of a broken or canceled first appointment is lowered, and the likelihood that valuable interviewing time will be fully utilized is increased. This caution may take courage for the neophyte in private practice whose practice is slow and whose income is marginal; in such cases, the temptation may be high to offer to see everyone immediately. However, a few hours lost because of overeagerness and insecurity on the therapist's part will usually convince the wise professional that proper scheduling procedures pay dividends in terms of increased time utilization. This also helps clients, particularly if a clinic has a waiting list, because they will be seen earlier if time lost to "no-shows" is minimized.

Sources of Referrals

Referrals for marital therapy come from a wide variety of sources. *Former clients* who are satisfied with the therapist's or agency's services constitute one of the soundest referral sources. They already know what to expect—and what not to expect—of therapy and so they also serve a valuable screening function. Most adults in our population have been to a physician or to a dentist, but relatively few have ever been to a marital therapist. Being referred by someone with actual first-hand experience in therapy lends positive support to the potential clients' quest for help.

Professional persons also constitute valuable referral sources. Particularly helpful are medical practitioners: internists, pediatricians, obstetricians-gynecologists, psychiatrists, family practitioners, and nurse practitioners. In the course of their daily work with patients, all of these professionals uncover a variety of marital conflicts that are best handled by the marital therapist.

Attorneys, particularly those with a large family law practice, are also in a position to make referrals. However, they often do not meet clients until after a decision to divorce has actually been made; thus the interest in marital therapy tends to be reduced. Even so, lawyers can refer such persons for any "divorce therapy" they may require.

Clergy of all denominations constantly meet couples in marital stress; only rarely, however, do they refer them to professional marital therapists. This results from the fact that many religions advocate religious counseling instead of specialized nonsectarian marital therapy. This situation is altered when the marital therapist is also a trained pastoral counselor; the referring clergyperson may believe that such a therapist will at least work with the couple within a "religious" frame of reference.

Social service agencies of all types constitute another potential source of referrals. Such people as domestic relations officers, public health nurses, school counselors, rehabilitation counselors, police officers, youth workers, family planning counselors, and so forth are often in contact with couples whose marriages are in distress. It is incumbent upon the marital therapist to keep all of these various sources informed about his or her availability, specialized services, fees, and referral procedures.

Finally, there is a significant proportion of *"self-referrals"*—couples who see the therapist's or clinic's name in the phone book or hear about one through some extraneous source. Therapists report varying experiences concerning the consistency with which self-referrals actually become ongoing therapy cases. It appears that they are as reliable about keeping appointments as are other couples referred through different sources, providing the precautions listed above are followed when the request for the first appointment is made.

Treatment Involves Both
Marriage Partners

In marital therapy, one should treat both the husband and the wife. This expectation should be made clear to both of them at the time of the first contact. Treating one spouse alone for even two or three sessions magnifies the absent partner's resistance to therapy and unnecessarily increases his or her anxiety. This caution bears less weight when one partner is unavoidably absent on a temporary basis due to business travel or an incapacitating illness. Even in these instances, however, the therapist should only proceed with the clearly announced expectation that both partners will participate together in therapy at the earliest feasible time.

What if one spouse refuses or cannot receive treatment? In some instances, a marital partner may absolutely refuse to enter treatment or may never be able to attend sessions. This constitutes a handicap to the therapist's potential effectiveness. It reduces the opportunity for reality testing. Moreover, alliances between the therapist and the client being treated may be perceived by the absent spouse as contrary to the best interests of the marriage. Perhaps above all, the refusal of a spouse to participate in marital therapy may represent that person's lack of motivation to resolve conflicts or even to continue the marriage. The therapist may proceed with treating the person who does come alone for therapy, but it is vital that the exact reasons for the partner's continued absence be ascertained. If these reasons are unavoidable (in cases of imprisonment, or foreign military duty, for example), the absence does not necessarily symbolize marital rejection. However, if the absent spouse is clearly able to attend sessions but consciously and deliberately rejects them, this suggests a level of isolation, distrust, anger, or rejection that often represents a poor prognosis for the future of the marriage.

GENERAL PRINCIPLES
CONCERNING FIRST
APPOINTMENTS

Marital therapists differ widely in the amount and type of information that they request from clients at the first appointment. This is partially due to different psychological orientations of therapists. Those with a traditional psychoanalytical approach, with its emphasis upon past experiences, may feel the need for several history-gathering sessions with each client before "treatment" commences. In contrast, therapists whose main concern is primarily with the clients' present reality may believe that a single session provides time for an adequate assessment of problems, client motivations, and therapeutic goals. Therapists whose basic training has been in psychology often request more than one evaluation or intake session so that they may administer psychological exams to their clients.

The Process of Intake and Evaluation

Regardless of the therapist's specific orientation, however, intake and evaluation must be regarded as a process. It begins with clients' initial calls for appointments, continues with the evaluation sessions themselves, and ends with a decision by the clients to enter marital therapy, to accept referral for some alternative type of help, or to do nothing. Normally these first appointments are crucial to the establishment of (or the failure to establish) a positive rapport with the therapist or agency.

Immediate verbal recognition of clients' feelings. To establish this initial positive rapport, it is essential that the therapist immediately verbally recognize the clients' feelings about being at the session. This allows the clients to experience the therapist as a caring person, someone who is interested in them and their feelings, and as one who wants to understand them. Cold, distant, "professional detachment" on the part of the therapist in the early minutes of a first session is frequently interpreted by clients as rejection, disinterest, or disapproval. Marital therapists who have received their original training in the medical field may be especially vulnerable to projecting these negative messages to clients, since both their personality structures and their medical training may foster a detached attitude. Clients are very sensitive to such an attitude, and it is likely to cause them to respond negatively.

Establishing the "facts." Marital therapy involves working with couples who may be experiencing a vast array of both intrapsychic and interpersonal problems. However, certain problems—conflicts over money, children, communication, sex, and extramarital affairs—appear with predictable regularity. Research by the author and his colleagues suggests that at least half of professional marital therapists' cases involve the last complaint, extramarital sexual affairs (Humphrey and Strong 1976). If a therapist is going to be able to render proper and adequate treatment, it is essential that he or she know what the "facts" are about the marriage and how each partner consciously perceives these "facts."

Need for initial individual sessions. In the case of extramarital problems alone, it is much less likely that accurate data will be shared if both marital partners are present throughout the entire evaluation session(s). Intake sessions are always times of increased stress for clients, and their psychological defense mechanisms can be expected to be functioning at a peak level under these circumstances. The absence of one's marital partner from the interview room lowers this stress temporarily and permits the client to share his or her feelings and experiences more openly, candidly, and without fear of retaliation or misunderstanding on the part of the spouse. It is for these reasons that it is imperative that marital therapists *always* see both the husband and the wife for one or more individual sessions during some part of the assessment process. Clients should be promised confidentiality about what they share in these individual sessions, and this promise should be made in the opening minutes of the interview. This enables both partners to begin to build up the necessary trust in the therapist as an individual who knows "all" about them and as one who accepts them as they "really are" (which may not coincide with the image they have been attempting to convey to their spouse).

Need for conjoint sessions.   While individual, confidential sessions are an essential part of the intake evaluation process, so too are conjoint sessions. During the conjoint sessions, the therapist can experience the couple "in vivo." He or she can check out impressions formed about the marital interaction from the individual sessions, and can share recommendations to both spouses with minimal danger of distortions occurring.

Ordinarily, the husband and wife are requested to come to the therapist's office together for the first appointment; during this session each one is then seen individually, and finally they are interviewed conjointly. This takes at least two interview hours if each person is seen individually for 30 to 45 minutes and the conjoint session is allocated another 30 minutes.

Background information and questionnaires.   If background information sheets and/or marital adjustment scales are utilized, the couple should be advised to arrive at the office sufficiently in advance of the scheduled appointment times to perform these tasks. Here again, the marital therapist's psychological orientation and/or training generally determines whether clients will be requested to fill out questionnaires about themselves and their marital adjustment or whether the therapist will choose to gather whatever information he or she needs during the interviews themselves. Being able to look through a paper-and-pencil type checklist or evaluation sheet before sitting down with the clients may enable the therapist to focus in on specific problem areas more quickly than he or she could do otherwise. At the same time, however, clients may resent the extra time they have to spend filling out information sheets while anxiously waiting to see the therapist. Some practitioners minimize this latter complaint by mailing questionnaires to the clients in advance of the appointment. In this case, the clients fill them out at home and mail them to the office before their first appointments. While a clinic or therapist performing special research tasks may find detailed client information schedules essential, the average therapist will have to make the decision for him- or herself concerning what practice to follow.

CONDUCTING THE ASSESSMENT INTERVIEWS

Assessment sessions are held to obtain information about the clients, to share information and recommendations with them, and to begin formally the process of therapy. Therapists may choose to follow a specific procedure or outline during the sessions or they may opt for an unstructured mode of interviewing. The following sections address specific areas that need clarification and together comprise a general guideline that provides an overall framework for the assessment interviews with both partners, separately and conjointly. The partners are first each seen individually by the therapist and then the assessment is concluded by a conjoint session with the partners together. During the individual sessions individuals are asked the questions listed in the following sections, and they are asked to answer them both for themselves and for their partners. This supplies therapists with individuals' feelings and judgments and also with their *perceptions* of their partners' responses. This information alerts therapists to potential misperceptions, conflicting attitudes and expectations, and sometimes deliberate distortions of facts.

Clients' Feelings about Being There

Are they anxious? Angry? Worried? Asking about these feelings allows the clients to vent their anxiety, lets the therapist immediately verbalize a recognition of clients' tense feelings, and reveals some of the clients' psychological defense mechanisms. For example, clients who say they are in no way troubled about being in the office may be consciously lying, may be repressing their anxiety, or may be stating a simple fact. The therapist usually finds it necessary to reserve judgment on which of these phenomena are occurring until other parts of the mosaic begin to fit together.

Referral

Who referred the couple? Why were they referred at this particular time? What is the *clients' understanding* of the reasons for the referral? What is the nature of the clients' relationship to the referral source? The answers to these questions often tell the therapist whether the clients have come willingly, with a clear understanding of what therapy may be about, and whether the potential for positive rapport has been aided by the referring person speaking well of the therapist. Conversely, the response to these questions may reveal resistance, misunderstandings, or even devious reasons for coming. One husband openly stated that he had come to see the therapist only to impress the divorce judge with his "sincere efforts" to try to save the marriage. When this was revealed, he and the therapist discussed it openly. He was given further opportunities to explore and examine what he was doing but he was totally uninterested. All he truly wanted was to be able to tell the court that he had consulted a marital therapist—and he still wanted a divorce!

If the clients are referred by past or present therapists who do not perform marital therapy themselves, it is ethically appropriate—and therapeutically wise—to obtain the clients' written permissions to contact the referring person for his or her recommendations and findings concerning the clients. This both increases the marital therapist's knowledge of the clients and renders a courtesy to one's referring colleague. Good professional relations are an essential aspect of maintaining a practice, and acknowledgments of referrals constitute an effective mechanism for aiding in this process. If it is learned that the clients plan to continue their therapeutic sessions with the referring therapist—or with a separate one—it is essential that the marital therapist's own role be clarified in the clients' plans and a determination made as to whether separate concurrent therapy with someone else is feasible or not.

In addition to obtaining each partner's version of how and why they were referred, it is helpful to inquire about how they believe their spouse feels about the referral. This inquiry provides further diagnostic data about perceptions, communications, and mutuality of goals between the husband and the wife.

Clients' Concept
of the Marital Therapy Process

Getting both partners' impressions of exactly how *they* think the therapist can help them adds to the information obtained concerning the referral source and reveals whether the clients have realistic expectations of therapy or not. Because so few people have ever consulted a professional marital therapist before, they tend to have little knowledge of the therapist's role. They may expect the therapist to judge them, to take sides, to be a referee, or to put them on a couch and "analyze" them. If the clients' perceptions of marital therapy are incongruent with the therapist's own concepts, these differences should be immediately revealed and, it is hoped, resolved. Realistically, of course, not one of them—husband, wife, or therapist—has a firm idea about how the therapist may be able to help until the separate interviews with each spouse and the conjoint intake session(s) have all been completed. The therapist can describe his or her usual therapeutic modalities early in a session, but a marital therapy outcome prognosis can rarely be made until all aspects of the total situation have been explored.

Previous Therapy

If information concerning previous therapeutic treatment was not elicited in discussing the referral, this question should be posed next. Particularly relevant here is previous individual or marital therapy. It is helpful to know who the therapist was, what the presenting problems were, what the course of therapy consisted of, and what the final outcome of such therapy was. This information may be particularly important when the previous therapy was for a psychiatric problem and the marital therapist is not qualified in that specialty. As was true in the case of referrals, it is helpful to know more about this earlier therapy; in fact, both ethical and legal considerations may exist to make the inquiry mandatory. The latter situation—a legal requirement—may exist when the marital therapist is not also a licensed physician or psychologist. For example, state statutes may restrict the practice of psychotherapy for mentally ill persons to professionals such as licensed physicians and psychologists. A client's refusal to sign a permission form to enable the previous therapist to release information to the marital therapist should be regarded as resistance on the part of the patient, dislike of the former therapist, or even a possible clue that a psychiatric condition may still be active. In this latter instance, the marital therapist may decide to refuse to treat the client or, if there appear to be mitigating circumstances causing the client to refuse to have the previous therapist contacted, the marital therapist may request the client to see a consulting psychiatrist for an objective assessment of the client's current mental status and treatment needs. In that case, the therapist should abide by the consultant's findings and recommendations concerning whether or not to proceed with marital therapy.

If the client reports having received previous marital therapy, the therapist may judge the requirement to contact the previous therapist as somewhat less compelling than when a legal issue exists, such as that indicated in the previous paragraph in the case of the treatment of mentally ill persons. At the same time, it would appear somewhat presumptuous to assume that one cannot learn anything of value from a former therapist. In this matter, as is so often true in marital therapy, the therapist will wish to make a final decision on the matter in the context of the total situation in which the couple find themselves.

Basic Identifying Data

If the therapist does not utilize a written questionnaire for the client to complete in advance, it is appropriate and helpful to gather this information in the course of the assessment sessions. Minimum information to be collected at this time would include the names, sex, and ages of all members of the marital unit's household; dating, engagement, and marital history (or histories); occupational and health histories; and the existence of any unusual situations that may be influencing the marital adjustment, such as pregnancy, a drug dependence problem, legal problems, and so forth. In addition, before the assessment sessions are completed, it is advisable to obtain a brief family history of both the husband and the wife in order to obtain a basic understanding of each individual's family of origin and the circumstances under which their socialization into marital and family life occurred. Most of this information will flow forth naturally in the course of the first session, but a brief outline listing the desired material may be utilized to help remind the therapist of any missing sections.

Major Problems in the Marriage

One of the fundamental purposes of the first session is to determine whether or not the wife and husband are indeed suitable candidates for marital therapy. Therefore, one of the prime purposes of this interview should be to focus on finding out what the problems may be, and what is needed to resolve them. Questions are utilized to elicit this information. What do the clients believe are the problems? When did they start? What was occurring in the couple's life then? How has the marriage been affected? What efforts has each of the partners made to resolve the problems? Is either partner involved in an extramarital affair? What does each partner think needs to be done to resolve matters? How do they believe the therapist can help them now?

These questions are not asked on a one, two, three basis as if one were merely conducting an information-gathering interview. Instead, they should flow naturally, as part of the interview process. The therapist asks, the client responds, the therapist comments on the affective meaning to the client, and the therapist reflects back, guides, and directs the client as may be necessary to keep the process moving. While information is being shared, the client usually experiences a release of tension and a decrease in anxiety. The person may begin to clarify issues and feelings, to communicate better to the partner about their needs, and to make decisions about him- or herself and the marriage. In a sizable number of instances, a single group of assessment sessions may accomplish so much understanding and reconciliation between the partners that further therapy sessions are unnecessary. While the therapist may be cautious about such "instant" marital health, clients should always be accorded the right to decide whether or not they need or wish to contract for regular therapy sessions.

The Conjoint Conclusion
to the Assessment Sessions

After the clients have finished their individual evaluative sessions, they should next be interviewed conjointly. In this conjoint session, the therapist will experience them for the first time as a couple. Often while interviewing the first spouse, the therapist will form certain ideas about the partner. Then, when that person is seen, the therapist may begin to question and rework his or her initial judgment. When the therapist experiences the partners directly, instead of through their perceptions of each other, diagnostic impressions usually become clarified. The therapist sees some of the couple's predictions and ideas about each other validated, but he or she also sees and begins to understand their distortions, projections, and denials about each other. For this reason, the conjoint session is invaluable in revealing the realities of the clients' feelings and problems.

A few minutes spent jointly discussing the problems ordinarily reveals the couple's readiness to work on their problems—or their unwillingness to do so. Abstract comments such as "We don't communicate" may be vividly portrayed—or revealed as individual misperceptions rather than actual existing problems. If the husband and wife reach a decision to go ahead with therapy, plans are made for this before the session ends. Frequently, however, one or both are indecisive about committing themselves to therapy. In this case, it is helpful to either plan another intake session or encourage the clients to return home and telephone in their decision later. By allowing this additional time, the therapist minimizes the possibility of their breaking the next appointment if their initial decision to commence therapy was made too impulsively and was not well considered. If they decide to proceed with therapy, the final step in the session will be the establishment of fees and interview times, and the completion of any other administrative and informational details that are needed. Ordinarily, these assessment sessions are all held during one visit to the therapist's office. Each individual session and the conjoint session are allocated approximately 30–45 minutes, and the total process takes about two hours.

As soon as these three interviews are completed, the two individual sessions and the conjoint one, the therapist should record his or her impressions. In private practice, this may have already been sufficiently accomplished in the notes the therapist takes. In a clinic setting, where another therapist is often assigned the case at this initial point, the summary helps the new therapist become immediately aware of the main issues involved. Performing this same exercise in private practice forces the therapist to both sharpen his or her conceptual thinking and to write down diagnostic impressions that can be verified or refuted later on, hence increasing the therapist's sensitivity and awareness of his or her competence.

ONGOING THERAPY

Basic Principles

Therapist directs and guides content and tempo of sessions. After the completion of the intake sessions, regular therapeutic interviews are established. These are ordinarily spaced at weekly intervals and consist of both conjoint and individual sessions. In these meetings, the therapist will utilize many traditional psychotherapeutic concepts plus the specialized ones that have been developed to meet the unique requirements of marital therapy. Each session allows clients ample opportunity to ventilate their pent-up feelings—such as anger, joy, sorrow, or anxiety—and to derive the cathartic benefits from doing this. Many clients, fearing rejection if they articulate their deepest feelings, make massive use of denial. With them, the therapist "invites the negative" by verbalizing the probable feelings they are repressing. This enables them to "own," to identify, to articulate, and to share with their spouse the strong feelings they have—feelings which until now they have been too anxious to acknowledge. Sometimes the therapist may directly articulate the feared emotion: "You are mad as hell at her for doing that!" In other instances, if the client is too fragile to accept such directness, the therapist may pose the statement more tentatively: "I assume you probably felt very angry at her about that." This gives the client the opportunity to "own" the emotion if he or she is psychologically ready to do so or, on the other hand, to reject the emotion at that time and feel "safer" and less overtly anxious about it. The therapist always controls the pace or tempo of the interviews. He or she moves the individual or couple along when they bog down in trivia and, at the other extreme, slows down the pace when pressures and emotions are flying at a speed which one or both partners cannot tolerate or handle psychologically.

Therapist maintains focus on major issues and uses partialization. The therapist can "partialize" the problems for the couple. People with marital difficulties frequently feel overwhelmed by the breadth and the magnitude of their dilemmas. The therapist can break their situation down into manageable issues or "partialize" it. Instead of trying to resolve all the issues at once, the husband and wife can cope more adequately by dealing with them singly. At the beginning of each interview, the therapist allows the couple to set the agenda for that session. Until the therapist knows what is uppermost in the couple's minds and feelings at that moment, he or she should not proceed further. Clients who are anxious or disturbed about a specific issue cannot ignore that issue and should not be required to immediately deal with therapist-mandated subjects. At the same time, the therapist has the responsibility to maintain the focus on the major issues that the clients have been attempting to resolve throughout the course of therapy. Keeping the focus of a therapeutic session on the major issues is a continuing responsibility of all therapists. Clients frequently act out their resistance to facing their problems by seducing therapists into irrelevant discussions about such things as the weather, the news, recreational events they have just attended, and a host of other matters that they unconsciously hope will keep attention away from anxiety-producing subjects.

Therapist confronts clients with firmness and empathy. Therapists listen; they are supportive; they are empathetic. Clients are almost always feeling some pain and discomfort in their lives and they expect their therapist to help them get relief from these painful feelings. At the same time, the therapist must also confront the clients with their behaviors, their attitudes, and the messages they convey to others. This is done through words and tone of voice in a manner designed to help the client "hear" positively what is being presented; if the therapist utilized a harsh, attacking, or argumentative manner in such confronting behavior, it would only breed defensiveness in the clients. This is not to question the firmness of the therapist's confrontations. Firmness is different from attacking; firmness is a caring insistence that the issue be aired; attacking, on the other hand, attempts to hurt or injure the client for possessing the issue.

Therapist concentrates on feelings, behavior, and recurrent issues. Therapy continuously and repetitiously concentrates on the feelings of the couple. At the same time, behaviors are also important to the dynamically oriented therapist, both for what they accomplish and for the feeling messages that they convey to others. Therefore, the therapist always looks behind the obvious or the overt behavior for the latent meaning and feeling that a given act may possess. Persons in marital conflict are frequent users of projection, displacement, and blaming. The therapist should help clients to recognize what they are feeling so that they can move on to resolving the issue or feelings if at all possible. In marital therapy, as in most psychotherapeutic modalities, the therapist always supports the principles of positive mental health and positive interpersonal relationships. Obviously, this assumes that individuals should learn to understand their feelings and act on them in a mature and responsible manner.

Years ago Leon Saul introduced the concept of the "red threads" that therapists find woven into the fabric of their clients' lives and therapy sessions. By being alert for these "red threads," therapists can enable clients to move more quickly to the healing business of facing and addressing recurrent issues. The persistent reappearance of particular issues in the therapy sessions is evidence that they are both significant and unresolved. Raising them to a conscious level gets them "out into the open" so the couple and the therapist may work on them.

Therapist's personal style. Every therapist has a unique style, one that is congruent with the therapist's own personality. An Albert Ellis is not, should not, and could not be a Carl Whitaker. It is incumbent upon every therapist, as part of the professional preparation, to do whatever possible—including undergoing personal psychotherapy, if indicated—to maximize the positive attributes that assist him or her in establishing rapport with clients. Clients almost invariably appreciate warmth, caring, and humor in their therapists. At the same time, the way the therapist conveys these attributes must be congruent with the clients' expectations of him or her. This is true for vocabulary, behavior, and general communicated attitudes about marriage and family life. Therapists who insist on "being themselves," communicating and behaving without taking into consideration the clients' expectations and needs, risk both offending the clients and losing the opportunity to be helpful to them. In addition, this disregard for the clients' feelings suggests either a blatant parallel disregard for ethical principles or a gross lack of training and professionalism on the therapist's part.

Therapist clarifies issues.   Challenging or confronting clients assists them in facing reality. Frequently they know a given fact or feeling intellectually, but resist facing it on a "real-life" level. The firm and positive use of the therapist's authority role aids these clients in coming to grips with the real but troubling feeling. Sometimes people, seeking insight into their behaviors and attitudes, can be assisted by being actively challenged to break through into new knowledge and acceptance about themselves and/or their partners. On occasion, the technique of "pseudo-stupidity" assists this process. Here, the therapist deliberately acts as if he or she is "stupid" and cannot understand the client. This forces the client to rephrase or restate his or her statement or feeling repeatedly until the "dense" therapist understands. In the process, clients themselves ordinarily achieve a clearer and better understanding of the specific issue—which is the therapeutic goal in this strategy. It should be obvious that this technique should not be overdone. However, it can be a useful device, during both individual and conjoint sessions. In the latter instance, it has the additional value of making the issue crystal clear to the partner and it may be used specifically for that purpose.

Therapist makes specific recommendations when appropriate.   Behaviorally oriented therapists utilize specific and elaborate instructions to their clients on various behaviors and actions to take. Psychodynamically oriented therapists ordinarily are cautious about specific recommendations, believing that most behaviors, to be truly meaningful, must stem from the client's own will, not that of the therapist. However, all therapy involves a certain amount of teaching and education. It is both appropriate and valid for the therapist to recommend actions that are congruent with the therapeutic goals of the couple and that stem from the therapist's theoretical and practical knowledge of human behavior and relationships. It is true that ultimately the clients themselves must be accountable for their actions, and they must make their decisions out of their own unconscious as well as their conscious motivations. Therapists can often constructively influence the development of more positive attitudes and behaviors, however, by making appropriate recommendations to the couple. The concept of absolute therapist neutrality has rarely been more than an ideal in individual psychotherapy. In marital therapy, absolute therapist neutrality is both impossible and inadvisable. The therapist must frequently take stands and make recommendations, but these must always be made with the best interests of both clients in mind.

Psychological insight is a common goal that virtually all psychodynamically oriented therapists hold for their clients. While marital therapy, in contrast to individual psychotherapy, is less concerned with major changes in intrapsychic personality structures, it does recognize the importance of clients becoming aware of their major drives, concerns, and feelings in order that they can understand themselves better and, especially, understand the "inner dimensions" of their relationship to their marital partners. Frequently, for example, people will unconsciously transfer particular feelings toward their spouse as the same feelings they held for their parent of the same sex. Awareness of this transference enables the client to begin to see his or her partner as a unique and separate individual instead of as a psychic ghost from his or her family of origin.

SPECIALIZED CONCEPTS
AND TECHNIQUES
IN MARITAL THERAPY

In addition to possessing specialized knowledge about marital and family dynamics, human sexuality, and individual psychodynamics and therapy, marital therapists need to be knowledgeable and skilled in respect to concepts and techniques that are unique to marital therapy. Marriage, as discussed earlier, involves a minimum of two human beings who are relating to each other within a variety of psychological, social, cultural, and biological systems. While the emphasis in this book is primarily upon the marital relationship, the therapist must constantly be alert to the myriad of other interpersonal systems with which each partner is involved—those with their children, parents, siblings, fellow workers, friends, neighbors, extramarital partners, and so forth. In addition, the therapist must be knowledgeable about the particular values and customs of clients' religious, racial, ethnic, occupational, and socioeconomic groupings. These may all have profound influences upon individuals' expectations of marriage. These values and customs are themselves frequently grounds for marital conflict, especially if the marital partners stem from widely divergent backgrounds. In treating marital dysfunction, the therapist must constantly be alert to conflicting or special issues that originate from one or both partners' various systems and deal with the implications these may have for the individual and for the couple.

Establishing Effective Two-Way
Communication

Communication—or more accurately, poor or ineffective communication—is a common major issue in marital conflict. Consequently, one of the unique tasks in marital therapy is to strive to enourage and build effective communications between the partners. This task involves (1) identifying communications that each partner desires to share, (2) assisting each in transmitting these feelings or wishes to the spouse, and then (3) aiding the latter in acknowledging them. The process may be conceived of as what occurs when two portable transceiver radios—"walkie-talkies"—are operated. Each sender must produce clear messages and transmit them in a clear and mutually understood language. Excessive "static" must be eliminated, or it will interfere with the transmission. Each set's receiving apparatus and circuits must be functioning properly to "hear" the message. This means, for example, that husbands must "transmit" clear messages to their wives (no double-talk); "static" (e.g., crying kids) must be absent or controlled so that the message completes the passage to the wife accurately; and wives must concentrate on hearing the husbands' messages (not "tune out" by escaping into their reading).

Teaching, modeling, and demanding good communication patterns. To be able to help a couple with communication problems, the therapist must initially concentrate on the *process* of communication between the husband and wife. Only after a positive two-way *process* has been successfully established can attention be effectively concentrated upon the *content* of the messages. Some couples find it exceptionally difficult to overcome years of poor communication patterns, but they must succeed in this endeavor before marital readjustment can be accomplished. This requires the therapist to teach and model good communication patterns, and also to demand that the couple concentrate on both verbal and nonverbal methods of communicating. Particularly to be avoided—or eliminated—are those habit patterns in which one partner forces his or her mate to play the role of "mind reader." Men who are involved in the physical sciences, in engineering, and in other logical and "rational" occupations appear to be especially vulnerable to these undesirable traits. Their personalities and their training combine to aid them in their occupations—where reasoning and predictability are valuable traits—but these same characteristics influence them to expect their wives and their children to also act "reasonably" and "predictably" in all instances. With these expectations, they see little or no need to repeatedly communicate their feelings and wishes. Therapists must assist these handicapped individuals to understand the importance of communication, to develop the courage to appropriately share their thoughts and feelings with their partners, and to develop new and positive ways of handling communications.

Even when such a person begins communicating, there may be a complementary problem in the spouse's responses. Having become used to the *lack* of communication, one often finds that the spouse of the previously noncommunicating partner unconsciously creates a "negative receptivity" to any messages. This person may "broadcast" signals on a conflicting wavelength, and such signals divert or drown out the partner's new efforts at communicating. Again the marital therapist must help such offending "nonreceivers" to develop insight into how they are sabotaging the process, explore the reasons for their doing so, and then work to help them develop new patterns of *assisting* communications rather than blocking them.

Obstacles to communication are many, ranging from maladaptive childhood training and negative family models to pressures from other systems onto the couple, such as the incessant demands of small children for time and attention. Social, cultural, and psychological patterns that interfere with effective communication usually yield to effective therapeutic remedial efforts, but some barriers to communication, such as time and health problems, require the couple to realistically aim for the best compromise methods of coping that can be achieved under the circumstances. Complete success may be an unattainable goal for some marital units.

Encouraging selective communication. Many couples today have heard a great deal about the importance of communicating, and the marital therapist may sometimes meet advocates of the "let it all hang out" ethic. Like children running wild in a candy store, adults who subscribe to this idea accept it as a license to bombard their mates with every thought that enters their head—regardless of the impact this may have on the partners and on the relationships. These clients need to be shown that the key to effective communication in marriage is not "total" communication but rather *selective* communication. This style of communicating encourages the sharing of all significant feelings with the partner, but refrains from burdening them with trivia and with potentially destructive messages that may offend sensitivities, demean the partner, and set up barriers to partner receptivity. The therapist may find it useful to admonish clients to "communicate unto your partner as you would have him or her communicate unto you."

The Therapist as Catalyst

In the process of establishing effective communication between partners, marital therapists perform a role that they maintain throughout the entire process of therapy—that of being a catalyst for growth for the individual partners and for the relationship. When couples are sufficiently motivated to come for therapy, this usually implies that each partner is consciously searching for something more constructive in the relationship—or at the very least, something better for himself or herself. All psychotherapists seek to be catalysts for individual growth; the marital therapist, in addition, seeks to assist those forces that will lead to the growth of the marriage. For those couples that will stay together, this growth results in a strengthened, more intimate, and more satisfying relationship. Even in cases in which the husband and wife choose to divorce, a certain amount of growth in the partners may need to occur before the spouses can allow the relationship to end. Many couples are caught up in longstanding, conflict-ridden marriages that are slowly destroying each person. In these instances, the therapist must help to move the relationship out of its unwholesome stalemate position and develop it to a level at which both partners can allow it to dissolve. If both of the partners can participate relatively equally in this process, each can leave the marriage with a greater sense of self-confidence and integrity. Unfortunately, this is not always possible.

Teaching Negotiation Skills

Until fairly recently, marital therapists were usually called marriage counselors. The term "counselor" denotes one who gives guidance, direction, or advice. The word "consultation" which stems from the word counsel, however, is sometimes defined as an *interchange of opinion*. This is what both old-style counselors and contemporary therapists do when they treat couple dysfunction by assisting the couple in negotiating compromises between themselves. Successful marriage requires a congruence of the partners' goals, philosophies, feelings, and behaviors. Because each marital partner is a separate, unique individual with a separate, unique history and background, husbands and wives need to acquire and sustain the capacity to give in, to compromise, and to adjust to each other—if their union is to succeed. This is especially true in modern egalitarian marriages in which male dominance has been rejected in favor of mutuality between the partners.

By the time they come for therapy, many marital partners have either lost their capacity to negotiate and compromise or their willingness to do so—or both of these. The therapist, therefore, must work to bolster each partner's ego to the point where each can once again give in to the partner on certain issues while still maintaining their own psychic equilibrium and personal integrity. Others never possessed these capacities. The therapist's work with these individuals will necessarily proceed slowly and will require considerable additional focus on them as individuals. The therapist must also assist couples in developing the necessary skills to negotiate compromises in order that each person can reasonably satisfy his or her own idiosyncratic needs. For numerous couples, the process is less complex. They have the necessary strengths and skills to adjust to each other's needs but they have unconsciously displaced certain angers and hurts into a stubborn pattern of refusal to give in. In these instances the therapist seeks to provide them with insight into the motivation for their behavior. This opens the potential for them to work on the "real" issues instead of continuously acting out their anger.

Interpreting Maladaptive Behavior

Resolving conflicts that have been unconsciously displaced into patterns of stubborn refusal to compromise is but one of numerous instances in which the marital therapist treats dysfunctional marriages by interpreting maladaptive behavior so that clients can develop insight into their marital dynamics. Therapists must constantly look behind the obvious, behind the concrete behaviors, in order to ascertain the preconscious and unconscious motives that determine feelings and behavior. The therapist who has not been trained to do this or who fails to "respect" the underlying dynamics behind clients' behaviors and feelings, risks allowing his or her clients to persist in their unsatisfactory or maladaptive actions.

This is not to suggest that marital therapists must necessarily always interpret *all* behavior and feelings so that the partners will develop *total* insight into themselves and their spouses. Often only a modest amount of insight is sufficient to enable the couple to begin to alter their own, and/or their partner's feelings, by specific actions.

Enlisting the aid of a "spouse therapist." The marital therapist has a unique advantage over the individually oriented therapist. In certain instances, through the process of providing insight and understanding, he or she can, in effect, enlist one spouse to provide a therapeutic and growth-producing milieu for the partner. This is done by helping that person understand the partner's special needs and then, by capitalizing upon the motivation that love and caring provide, encouraging that person to consistently relate to the partner in a "therapeutic" fashion. Initially, many clients resist this concept and practice, insisting that they came to therapy to "cure" their marriage, or themselves, but certainly not to "treat" their spouse. When this occurs, the therapist can educate the client by pointing out the benefits that will accrue to *both* partners when either one is helped to improve self-concept, ego strength, and self-respect. And, because of the reciprocal interdependence that is inherent in all marital systems, improvement in any part of the system will also benefit the "spouse therapist." This therapeutic approach is limited to those couples where one of the partners possesses average or above average ego strength and marital commitment and the other partner is not a severely neurotic person with only limited capacity to grow and change.

Because the therapist works conjointly and concurrently with both partners, he or she is ordinarily in a position to encourage positive actions by both partners or, at the very least, to increase each partner's insight into the marital dynamics. If both the husband and the wife want the marriage to succeed, the therapist exploits this fact by supporting all actions and expressions of feelings that will enhance the marital relationship. There is no place for "therapeutic neutrality" in these instances. Everything that helps the marriage is championed by whatever means and techniques best suit the couple and the therapist.

Working through ambivalent feelings. A great proportion of marital therapy deals with clients' ambivalent feelings—about themselves, about their partners, and about their marriage. In these instances, therapeutic neutrality must be maintained and the therapy hour should be guided to focus upon helping the client resolve these ambivalences. The chief strategy utilized in these instances is to promote insight and develop a reality orientation for the client so that he or she can attempt to make choices that are in harmony with the majority of his or her conscious and unconscious feelings and needs.

In severely troubled marriages, this working through of ambivalent feelings frequently leads one of the partners to seek a divorce. Here the focus of the sessions should shift, with the therapist affirming the right of the person to seek a divorce while, at the same time, assisting the rejected partner to face the reality of divorce and the disruption of the marriage. Understandably, this position of being "in the middle" is often very uncomfortable for marital therapists. They must develop their capacity to cope with it, however, in order to continue their practice. Conjoint sessions are often extremely stressful, with the "rejected" partner venting his or her hurt and anger onto their spouse or even onto the therapist. At the same time, conjoint sessions are very valuable in helping the couple, or at least one partner, to face up to the reality of the problems.

The Therapist's Educational Role

Psychotherapists have often tended to neglect or reject the educational aspects of therapy, considering them to be inappropriate to the process. The marital therapist cannot and should not overlook clients' frequent need for more education—especially about marriage, sexuality, parenthood, and other areas directly connected to one's marital role. The majority of persons who marry in the United States receive no formal family life and sex education—and their ignorance is amply demonstrated in their failure to comprehend what is expected of them as a man or woman, husband or wife, father or mother. Therapists may share relevant information on these issues during treatment sessions or they may choose to recommend specific reading materials for study at home. Knowledge does not resolve conflicts by itself, but it helps to increase each partner's capability to respond in an intelligent and enlightened fashion to the many complex facets of married life.

A very common complaint heard in the marital therapist's office is "My partner does not understand me." Education and knowledge may lessen such complaints. However, this issue is not always what it seems to be. The spouse may understand his or her partner quite well—but may be choosing to ignore that person's wishes. In this case the therapist must concentrate on the process of rejection and not be side-tracked into futile efforts to "educate" the partners so they can "understand" each other better. Some therapists spend a great deal of time and effort with patients on developing listening skills, conflict management skills, negotiation skills, and so on. Although these techniques may be effective in many cases, therapists need to be cautioned against the excessive use of educational "gimmicks"; when their use overshadows or eliminates the vital focus upon the underlying psychodynamics within and between the partners, the effect can be poor therapy.

Helping Couples Accept
Present Reality

Marital therapy, in contrast to individual psychotherapy, is primarily concerned with present events. To some extent, the past is explored in order to gain an understanding of the present, but the focus in marital therapy is primarily on the here and now, the clients' present realities. Developing insight into the adolescent traumas of one's partner, for example, may increase one's tolerance for that person's neurotic shortcomings, but probably more important to the success of the marriage is the development of *current acceptance of the partner as she or he truly is now.*

"We didn't have time to get to know each other." Frequently, in marriages of short duration, one hears that problems exist because the partners did not know each other well before marriage and are now dissatisfied with each other. Enforced separation due to work, college, and military service, coupled with a short court-ship, may well be a realistic cause of failure to get to know the prospective partner intimately.

"I thought I could love him in spite of it all." A second reason given for current dissatisfaction in young marriages is that some fault or defect was perceived during courtship but its obstacle to marital satisfaction was rejected by the "love conquers all" theory. "I loved him (her), so I felt I could easily overlook that trait which I now find terribly upsetting," these clients say. Love does *not* conquer all and once the normal disillusionment phase of marriage sets in, "love" often evapo-rates in the face of continued dissatisfaction. These couples need to concentrate on developing mature love for each other.

"I thought I could change her." A third major reason many persons, married for one to five years, give for not accepting their partners *as they are* is rooted in the egocentric delusion that they will be able to change their partner's objectionable habits or characteristics after marriage. Spouses of alcoholics are classic examples. These individuals may perceive their partner's "defects" before marriage realisti-cally—but then unrealistically think they have the right, and the ability, to some-how magically change that person after they are married to them.

These and similar examples of current dissatisfaction with one's marital part-ner are reasons why the marital therapist must continuously focus on present reali-ties. If love and respect are gone or if one partner has decided to terminate the marriage, the therapist must quickly ascertain these facts and proceed with helping both the husband and the wife deal with the issue of separation and termination. This does not mean that the therapist fails to seek change in the clients. While pro-fessional marital therapists have long since rejected the goal of keeping all marriages together at any cost, they nevertheless are ethically bound to aid couples seeking solutions that will potentially best help all the persons involved—husbands, wives, and children. In the type of marriage that is so troubled that it lands first in the marital therapist's office and then in the divorce court, it is often impossible for marital conflict to be resolved to the complete satisfaction and well-being of all con-cerned. Even in cases with "negative" outcomes, however, the therapist's consistent emphasis upon present realities can help the family members to survive a breakup with stronger psychological coping mechanisms, with fewer permanent regrets, and with more positive attitudes toward the future.

The Therapist as Agent of Change

In some instances, marital therapists function as agents of change. Their inter-cession opens up new ways of thinking, of perceiving, or of responding. They are catalysts who accelerate the process of discovery, negotiation, and of making new efforts. Frequently the couple may reject the therapist's suggestions for change by claiming, "We already tried that and it didn't help at all." In these instances the therapist must persistently urge or even demand that they try again if, in his or her judgment, a renewed effort seems worthwhile. A gratuitous side effect of simply *entering* marital therapy is often increased hope, improved motivation, and more openness on the part of both partners at the same time. Efforts that have failed in the past may prove successful once therapy commences because the husband and wife are now mutually united in trying to make their relationship better. Before entering marital therapy, couples may have failed frequently in their individual efforts to improve the system because they were "out of sync" with each other. The therapist, by synchronizing and unifying their efforts, can serve as a choreographer who melds a complex collection of separate issues into a flowing, dynamic, and well-coordinated whole.

Nurturing the Marriage

One weakness of individual therapy for persons experiencing marital distress has been the frequent failure of both therapists and their individual clients to place much emphasis upon the needs of marriage itself. Marriage is a demanding institution. It is a special, complex form of human relationship. It is greater than the sum of its component parts. If neglected by either or both partners, the marriage will suffer. Each partner has his or her own ego, his or her own psyche; their essential narcissism is a normal feature of human beings. Each person looks out for himself or herself—and this is an expectable state of affairs. But who looks out for the *marriage*—for the give and take, for the attention, for the priorities that must necessarily be granted to it—unless the marital partners themselves do? One answer should be that in therapy the marital therapist temporarily performs this role.

Marriage is hard work! Immature couples frequently believe that love conquers all—and that for love to endure, even in marriage, no special efforts need to be made by the "participants." This false belief must be aggressively challenged by the therapist. He or she must repeatedly perform the role of *amicus curiae,* "friend of the court." The therapist must remind, educate, and challenge the partners to perform their necessary roles in keeping the marriage itself alive and healthy.

In keeping with this common illusion that love conquers all and continues forever without effort, some couples are lulled into a state of false complacency by the fact that marriage is both a civil and a religious institution. The partners are guaranteed certain rights and expectations within the marriage, so what's the need to work hard to make things go right? In reality, each partner frequently has to put his or her own needs temporarily aside in order to give to the partner and thus to preserve the relationship. At the same time, in a sense, each individual partner must protect him- or herself from the marriage and from the partner. Each must demand to be heard; individual needs must be satisfied; personal integrity must be preserved. The marital therapist, therefore, is frequently called upon to help the individuals decide what they "owe" to themselves, to their partners, and to the relationship. A marital unit that continues only at the cost of the respect or the needs of one of the partners is destined for eventual failure. And, as has been mentioned, therapists should have no part of the dehumanizing belief that all marriages must be preserved no matter what the cost. When a marriage reaches a point at which one individual's self-respect and self-esteem are being irredeemably sacrificed, it is the responsibility of the therapist to encourage movement towards separation and/or divorce.

The Therapist as Active Participant

The preceding material illustrates another special trait of the marital therapist—namely, the need for that person to be dynamically active in the therapeutic process. Contemplative or purely reflective-type therapeutic modalities simply fail to answer clients' needs. Many clients report previous unsatisfactory work with therapists who "just sat and listened." As noted in the section on the initial interviews, such therapist passivity is frequently experienced as coldness, distancing, and rejection.

Change ordinarily occurs much faster in marital therapy than in individual therapy. The presence and interaction of the two partners puts pressure upon the therapist to make decisions quickly and to actively take part in the therapeutic process. Being active and involved, however, should be distinguished from dominating, controlling, or "preaching," none of which have any justifiable role in marital therapy.

INDIVIDUAL NEEDS
AND SESSIONS

Emphasis so far has been on treatment issues and modalities that relate primarily to both marital partners. Stress must also be placed upon individual concerns and individual sessions for clients. If the couple has agreed upon the continuation of the marriage and neither have any special "secrets" or major intrapsychic problems, conjoint sessions may be the routine method of interviewing utilized by the marital therapist. However, the majority of "typical" marital cases are more complicated. With at least half the therapy cases in the United States involving extramarital affairs, it is essential that individual, confidential sessions be always offered to these couples. In addition, many clients have issues they prefer not to work on in their partner's presence, such as some sexual conflicts and specific earlier life events. Individuals faced with resolving highly ambivalent feelings toward their spouse also report greater freedom and ability to be objective when they are seen individually as well as conjointly.

It is advisable to commence marital therapy by routinely seeing the couple in alternating individual and conjoint sessions. If the conjoint session is held first each week, the therapist can frequently utilize the content and interaction of this session with great intensity in individual sessions which follow immediately thereafter. Later the individual sessions can be discontinued if there is no further need of them. It is highly important to preserve the confidentiality of individual sessions and to treat "prying" on the part of the other partner for just what it usually indicates—a lack of trust in the partner and in the therapist. Most clients, realizing that they are as protected by the confidentiality of the therapist as their partners are, have no problem whatsoever with this issue. These individual sessions have the additional value of allowing the therapist to focus on special intrapsychic issues for each partner that, if handled in the conjoint session, might well evoke feelings of rivalry, boredom, or hostility in the other.

PACING AND GUIDING INTERVIEWS

In all the aforementioned treatment strategies, whether within the context of individual or conjoint sessions, the marital therapist is actively entering the marital system itself in order to effect change. The focus of the content may vary from session to session and even within any one session. It may be on communication, on earlier events that effect current issues, on conflicts, on pleasures—there is no predicting in advance what the couple's specific needs may be at any given moment. As therapy continues, each new session starts with the therapist's determination of where the clients are that week—in their feelings, in their activities, and in their marriage. If volatile issues immediately emerge, these will become the main focus of the session. If it has been a "routine" week, the therapist can quickly move the focus to the main issues that are disrupting the marriage.

Frequently clients resist "getting down to business," and a fair amount of tact and firmness may be necessary to bring this about. If clients persist in their resistance, this should be treated directly and efforts made to resolve the blockage. In marital therapy, as in individual therapy, it is impossible to predetermine precisely how "fast" therapy can and should move. If clients are pushed by the therapist beyond their capacity to tolerate the stress or if they feel threatened by a breakdown of their defenses, they may regress or even flee therapy entirely. Therapists must constantly remain sensitive to how *each* partner is moving. During conjoint sessions if the therapist misjudges one person's capacity to handle the therapeutic issue of the moment, it frequently follows that the spouse will intervene in a protective manner. This again illustrates the helpful technique of conjoint interviewing. Toward the end of each session, the therapist and the person or the couple, depending on who the interview unit is at that moment, should begin to summarize what has occurred and to look ahead toward the next session. This results in a natural ending for the session and, at the same time, gives a sense of continuity to the ongoing process of marital readjustment.

EMERGENCIES

Marital therapy frequently does not commence until the situation between the couple has reached crisis proportions. During the course of therapy, further crises may often occur. One partner discovers the other's extramarital affair . . . divorce papers may be unexpectedly served . . . someone gets fired from his or her job—any number of sudden, unexpected events can occur that threaten either or both partners. In these instances provisions should always be made for enabling the couple to contact the therapist on an emergency basis, day or night. In clinics, hospitals, and group practices, this emergency duty is often rotated among the various staff therapists. Solo private practitioners, however, usually have no such alternates and must make themselves accessible or arrange for someone else to cover their crisis calls if they are unavailable. Marital crises occur less often than medical crises but, like the latter, often seem to happen late at night or on weekends. Many of these emergencies can be adequately handled over the telephone but on occasion office or home visits may need to be conducted. Marital clients in general, in contrast to "pure" psychiatric patients, usually have fairly strong abilities to cope on their own or to temporarily get by with the help of close friends or family members. However, when true emergencies arise the therapist should be able and willing to intercede on short notice.

PERSONAL QUESTIONS
DIRECTED TO THERAPISTS

Throughout the process of marital therapy, questions will invariably arise about the therapist's own personal life. Is the therapist married? Does he or she have children? Is he or she divorced? Each therapist should handle these questions according to his or her own philosophy and degree of comfort. Many such inquiries are not so much attempts to learn about the therapist as they are strategies to divert the session away from the clients. However, clients, like all human beings, are curious. Who is this "expert" who is treating us? What does he or she know about family life? Does he or she have a good or a lousy marriage? Usually clients make the assumption that if their therapists are married, they must be perfect spouses. The reality is that therapists probably have marital adjustment records that are no better and no worse than those of other citizens. If the therapist is married, divorced, widowed, or single, he or she may choose to discuss this with clients if this will help them understand their own situation better, assuming the material being shared is relevant.

Many therapists have family pictures in their offices and others, including the author, have their offices in their homes. In these instances one could hardly expect clients not to comment or to raise questions about the therapist's own life. When this is shared appropriately with them, it both satisfies the questioner's curiosity and presents the therapist as a real human being, ordinarily aiding in rapport and trust. Persons under stress often feel "different" and peculiar. It is frequently reassuring for them to learn that their therapist, too, may have lived through such moments. At the same time, it must be stressed that excessive references by the therapist to his or her own marital stress periods may impart a negative impression upon the clients. It is not uncommon for clients who have been in therapy elsewhere to reveal that they have terminated that therapy because they considered that therapist to be so maladjusted in life that he or she could not be a helping person. Thus, it appears rather obvious that therapists who communicate with their clients about their own personal life should do so in a selective fashion—sharing that which is relevant, human, and constructive, and refraining from sharing things that may be inconsequential or that may gratify the therapist's needs, but not those of the client.

THE ENDING PROCESS

Marital therapy is a process. It has its beginning, its middle phase, and its ending. In general, marital therapy is "short-term" therapy. It ordinarily lasts from a few weeks to a few months. It is frequently undertaken in efforts to achieve specific goals. When these are approaching fruition, the therapist should plan to reduce the frequency of sessions in a gradual process. However, marital therapy endings, in contrast to endings during individual therapy, may be prone to terminate prematurely because one of the partners decides to stop, even though the goals have not been met; this means that the unified work that the couple has done as a unit ends abruptly. At this point two alternatives exist: continue therapy with the remaining partner or terminate with both. If therapy continues with only one of the partners, the focus of the sessions invariably changes. It may shift to helping this continuing client adjust to the limited gains that had been achieved, to considering whether or not to remain in the marriage, or to highly individualized concerns that are typical of regular individual psychotherapy. The decision to terminate with both partners because one of them ends prematurely usually occurs as the result of negative pressures from the absent spouse on the one remaining in therapy, or because of resignation to the marital status quo. In these instances therapists should offer the remaining partner more therapeutic time if he or she desires and needs it but, at the same time, must accept that person's decision to terminate if that is his or her wish.

Planned, positive endings in marital therapy occur when the clients have jointly decided that the crisis is over, maximum growth has occurred, and they no longer "need" the therapist. Couples are invariably ambivalent about ending. In spite of increased competence in their marital interactions, they have the normal anxieties about separating from the therapist to be "on their own." Support and reassurance that such feelings are to be expected often alleviate much of this anxiety. In addition, the couple may be assured of the therapist's availability in the future if they wish to return for additional help. The transference feelings of dependence may be lessened by reducing the frequency of therapy visits from weekly to alternate week sessions and then, if desired, one or two monthly "checkups." This gradual weaning process enables the couple to increasingly test and trust their new-found strengths before they actually end all visits. The marital therapist, like members of other helping professions, should always have as a goal the elimination of the couple's need for therapy. A return to marital health, similar to the return to physical health after a disabling illness, signifies the successful completion of the therapist's work. Long-term, continued dependence on the therapist frequently constitutes both a therapeutic failure and an unethical exploitation of the clients' resources.

REFERRALS ELSEWHERE

At any point in the process of marital therapy, it may be desirable and necessary to refer one or both members of the marital unit to other sources of help in addition to the marital therapy. This situation usually occurs because of revealed needs for medical, legal, or other types of assistance. It is incumbent upon every therapist to be knowledgeable about other types of specialized services in their communities that their clients may need. If there is not an adequate centralized referral service available (such as Council of Social Agencies' "Infolines"), the therapist should compile his or her own data file of local resources. One advantage in doing this is that it enables the therapist to develop a feedback system so that he or she may evaluate and keep track of the quality of various services. Judgments about the therapist will be formed by clients in accordance with the quality of help to which they are referred. In addition to the comfort of knowing that clients are being referred to competent help, the therapist benefits from the positive feelings clients will generalize back to the therapist. Conversely, if referrals are made and the clients are not happy with the quality of service being rendered elsewhere, they are likely to assume that the therapist is not really interested in them—or that the therapist lacks the competence to judge other services. Either feeling will adversely affect the marital therapy.

Frequently couples consult a marital therapist when what is more realistically needed is traditional psychiatric care. Marital therapists are inappropriately consulted because they are seen as "safer" since they deal with "ordinary people—not crazies." Referring such individuals for psychiatric consultations or care requires great tact and sensitivity to the clients' feelings. The more psychiatrically disturbed a client is, the more he or she may resent and resist such a referral. Unless the marital therapist is also a qualified psychiatrist or psychologist, however, it would ordinarily be inappropriate to attempt to treat such persons. All professional people are ethically required to respect the limits of their own competence, and the marital therapist is no exception. Other referrals such as to a family physician or to a lawyer may engender some feelings of abandonment by the therapist but not to the extreme degree ordinarily felt in relation to a psychiatric referral.

In all cases of referral, it is vital that the therapist receive signed permissions from the clients to release confidential information to the referral person or agency. Refusal of one or both clients to grant this permission presents an obvious stumbling block to the referral. Except in emergency situations in which the life of someone is threatened, therapists are legally bound to respect the confidentiality of their clients. Such refusals are ordinarily rare in occurrence but, when they do occur, must be handled with extreme caution because of the various repercussions that could ensue.

In making referrals, therapists should communicate clearly and concisely to the referral person or agency the pertinent facts and information necessary to understand the client's problems. At the same time, especially if the therapist does not know the referral person or agency well, caution is advised against going into excessive detail or speculations about the client. Not all professional persons and agencies can be guaranteed to treat the shared information with absolute confidence and respect, hence this need to be highly selective. Some therapists prefer to share data over the phone, instead of committing it to writing, since they believe this lessens the possibility of distortions or misunderstandings. Some, however, believe that written reports are best. Therapists should be selective in what they share, offering more details to those they have learned they can trust to handle the information well, and being extremely parsimonious when they are unsure about how the material will be utilized.

SUMMARY

Marital therapy is a specialized process that renders therapeutic help to couples as they move toward marriage, cope with a wide range of problems within it, or move out of marriage and into divorce. Specialized treatment techniques are required to assist these individuals, with conjoint interviewing of both spouses being the most common and effective form of treatment. The therapy process commences with both individual and conjoint assessments by the therapist of the couple's problems, strengths, and needs; it is completed by a series of interview sessions lasting from a few weeks to several months. The ending of therapy occurs when the goals of the couple have been achieved or when further progress is no longer possible. Problems that cannot be treated by the therapist are referred to appropriate sources of help elsewhere.

In the first part of this book we have reviewed the general principles and the process of marital therapy. In Part Two we will examine in detail the therapeutic management of the major types of problems seen and treated by marital therapists.

PART TWO

THE
THERAPEUTIC
MANAGEMENT
OF MARITAL
PROBLEMS

CHAPTER THREE
EXTRAMARITAL
RELATIONSHIPS

BACKGROUND

The most common issue marital therapists encounter in their practice is probably that of the extramarital relationship, in which one or both of the partners are involved with someone outside the marriage. Such relationships usually, but not always, involve sexual activities—the familiar extramarital sexual (EMS) affairs. In a study undertaken by the author and a colleague at the University of Connecticut in 1976, a representative sample of clinical members of the American Association for Marriage and Family Therapy said that approximately half of the cases they were treating involved an EMS situation. That study also confirmed the author's impression from his own years of performing marital therapy. EMS affairs represent severe threats to marital happiness and stability (Humphrey and Strong 1976). The system of marriage in North America is heavily influenced by religious teachings that almost universally condemn EMS. Laws governing marriage and sexual conduct further attempt to enforce these teachings. Socialization and dating patterns usually lead young couples to anticipate absolute sexual fidelity from their marital partners.

Yet at the very same time, EMS affairs are glorified by the news media. Politicians, movie stars, and various other public figures are envied and admired for their sexual exploits outside of marriage. Professional organizations composed of various mental health therapists debate the ethics of whether sexual relationships between therapists and clients may comprise an ethical form of "treatment" by the therapists. The mass media blatantly use sex—without regard to the marital status of the participants—to sell movies, perfumes, liquor, cars, soap, and all sorts of nonerotic items. All these contribute to paradoxical messages about extramarital sex. "Don't do it—it's evil." "Be open—be modern—live for today—do it!" Absolutely no person or couple is immune to these tantalizing, if conflicting, messages. The admission of "born-again Christian" President Jimmy Carter to feelings of lust toward women other than his wife helped the public recognize that sexual feelings are rarely felt exclusively toward one's marital partner, and that no one person may be expected to be exempt from these feelings—regardless of his or her position in life. In addition, many persons question whether lifelong exclusive monogamy is a "natural" institution, given the seventy- to eighty-year life span of modern Westerners. People were unable or unwilling to always keep their vows of sexual fidelity even when life spans averaged only one or two decades of sexual adulthood and when serial monogamy due to death of a partner was the norm. How can today's married couples be expected to remain faithful for the fifty years of marriage that they theoretically face? Modern travel, especially by cars and airplanes, as well as modern lifestyles which often require extended periods of absence from the home, permit affairs to be carried on with greater secrecy and anonymity than was ever true in the past. All these factors contribute to conditions which increase the likelihood of one or both partners in a marriage having an affair.

REASONS FOR EXTRAMARITAL SEX

Sexual Causes

Various facets of modern marriage itself add to the pressures on sex in marriage. Women are still being encouraged to stay "pure" (i.e., nonsexual) until marriage. They are then expected to shed twenty or so years of negative sexual conditioning and to act and feel "sexy" with their husbands. Meantime, young men are socialized premaritally under a dominant theme of "get all (the sex) you can get." Once married, these opposing attitudes held by husbands and wives about sex quickly collide. Couples argue over the frequency of intercourse, over nudity, and over techniques and coital positions. Modern wives are expected to be superwomen—great mothers and homemakers and to simultaneously have exciting jobs and careers outside their homes. All these pressures can be enormously fatiguing to these wives—and fatigue is one of the primary factors that affect females' erotic interests adversely. The net result of these combined forces is likely to be frequent bitter marital arguments over sex. In desperation or disgust, many wives ultimately tell their husbands to "go get it" somewhere else—and the husbands do precisely that, rationalizing that their wives have encouraged them to do so. Today, marital therapists report increasing numbers of the reverse types of situation—"tired" husbands who tell their wives to take their sexual interests elsewhere, with the wives then acting out these "invitations."

The Cup of Coffee Syndrome

EMS affairs frequently result from attractions that are initially quite "innocent" and asexual in nature. They may begin with the "cup of coffee" syndrome in which two persons, each married to someone else, begin to relax over a cup of coffee—at work, after church choir rehearsals, when their respective partners are playing tennis and these two are at home splitting the babysitting chores, and similar situations. Soon they develop the "habit" of meeting regularly; they share more and more details of their lives and feelings; they develop a dependence on these coffee talks. Finally, sex enters as the next level of involvement.

Actually, EMS affairs cover wide variations of sexual and emotional involvements. Some are almost exclusively sexual pursuits with little "love" being felt by either partner. At the other extreme, an affair may be totally devoid of any actual acts of intercourse but may involve deep levels of loving feelings. On the continuum between these extremes are the intense affairs that involve both love and sex between partners in EMS relationships.

Alternative Lifestyles

EMS affairs may represent attempts by couples to adopt "alternate lifestyles" that are "beyond jealousy and sexual possessiveness." Therapists don't meet couples who successfully accomplish these goals, but they are expected to treat the failures and the rejects that result from these idealistic activities. Not infrequently, such cases will involve married couples indulging in "swinging," or mate-swapping activities, where one of the partners enjoyed and accepted the game but the other partner—most likely the wife—found it unacceptable and disturbing.

Affairs vary widely in their length. Couples may appear for therapy after a single act of marital infidelity, but more commonly the affair, or affairs, have been going on for months or even years. The length of the affair, however, cannot necessarily be equated with the depth of feeling that exists between the EMS participants themselves or between the marital partners. Clients repeatedly demonstrate that human beings have a potential capacity to love and to engage in sexual relations with more than one partner. Around the world polygamy is the most commonly preferred system of marriage—even if it is not the most commonly occurring system. Many EMS clients state that bigamy would be the only ideal solution to their situation, because they love both their spouse and their EMS partner. Love, however, is certainly not the only reason reported by clients for engaging in EMS.

Sexual Diversity

When patients reporting an EMS relationship are asked what they believe led to its development, they provide a wide number of explanations. Many, as in the "cup of coffee" syndrome, say it "just happened." Some describe themselves as just plain curious. They had never engaged in coitus with anyone except their spouse and wondered what "it" would be like with someone else. Just as human beings so often seek variety in their diets, their clothes, their choice of recreational pursuits, and so forth, so too may they be interested in a variety of sexual activities and partners. Married persons, like others, read the widely available "sex" magazines and manuals and want to try out new techniques. An inhibited or reluctant spouse is frequently poor competition for an exciting and adventuresome EMS partner when it comes to experimenting with novel sexual behavior.

Boredom

Marital sexual frustration or boredom is frequently listed as another reason for EMS. Performing the same act with the same partner in the same way at the same time under the same conditions (at night, in bed, with the lights off, after the kids are asleep, when both are in the mood, with the husband on top, and so on) can—and does—easily lead to this boredom. An unimaginative spouse, often unaware that he or she is being secretly "rated" by the partner, is weak competition for a sexy, daring, adventuresome EMS lover.

Unhappiness

Marital partners who are unhappy in their marriages, even if their sexual adjustments have been satisfactory, may become emotionally vulnerable to sexual approaches from others. They yearn to be noticed, to be appreciated, to be "understood." In many subtle ways they communicate their unhappiness to others—including members of the opposite sex—and this often leads to sexual involvement through the familiar sequence of sharing, listening, feeling rapport, closeness, mutual dependence, caring, and then sexual expressions of these feelings. Individuals who have been conditioned to equate love with sexual intercourse in their marriages will naturally wish to express their caring for adults outside the marriage in a similar—that is, sexual—manner.

Need to Be Needed

One of the least understood motivations for EMS relationships is the fact that intercourse, per se, may be only secondary to more pressing motivations for persons engaging in affairs. Many human beings suffer from low self-esteem, personal insecurities, and profound feelings of inadequacy. To be accepted, needed, and valued by another person is enormously gratifying to such individuals—and an EMS relationship ordinarily appears to provide many of these satisfactions. Many persons are unsure of their own sexuality and their marital sexual adjustment may have only reinforced these anxieties. The husband who repeatedly accuses his wife of being frigid may literally be driving her into the arms of a warm, supportive lover.

Emotional Disturbance

Occasionally, EMS affairs are a symptom of a psychiatric illness in which an individual's judgment is grossly defective. These types of marital therapy cases, however, are not too common in the marital therapist's office, unless he or she is functioning primarily as a psychiatrist or a psychologist and seeing a large proportion of emotionally disturbed persons in his or her practice.

Propinquity

Propinquity is another major factor in starting an EMS relationship. Married persons, like everyone else, are constantly put in regular, close contact with adults other than their spouses. These include co-workers, other persons in commuter car pools, neighbors, persons who serve together on PTAs, church, and synagogue committees—the list is endless. In contemporary Western life, almost everyone has several "significant" others with whom they interact almost daily—and all of these must be regarded as members of the "pool of eligibles" from which one may draw an EMS partner.

Reactions to EMS

It is impossible to catalog all the reasons why EMS relationships develop. In addition to those already listed, the marital therapist will be told that affairs occurred to allow one partner to "get even" with the other's infidelities; were assertions of one's "rights" as individuals; evolved because a spouse was frequently unavailable for sex; because of "seduction"; because others were drunk or high on other drugs; and on and on. Sometimes the reasons given by married persons for the EMS soften the blows to their marital partner's feelings when the latter learns of the affairs. If the spouse who is not participating in the EMS believes that his or her partner had some justifiable reason for doing what he or she did, that person may find it less disturbing. (For example, a man who knows he was extremely preoccupied with work pressures and irritable at home in the time before his wife started an affair may blame himself for the wife's affair.) Wives who have been thoroughly indoctrinated with the double standard of sexual fidelity—one for the woman (complete fidelity) and one for the man (occasional sexual indiscretions are "normal")—may be less upset by their husbands' affairs—both consciously and unconsciously—than wives who hold to single standards of fidelity. Husbands, on the other hand, only rarely tolerate their wives' affairs. This differing reaction of husbands and wives has been borne out: evidence shows that when men charge their wives with adultery, they almost always go through with the divorce. When women bring similar charges against their husbands, however, they frequently drop the divorce action and reconcile.

INITIAL EVALUATIONS
IN TREATMENT

In Chapter Two, it was emphasized that initial evaluations in marital therapy should always—*without exception*—include a minimum of one separate confidential interview with each spouse. This is recommended, in part, because of the large proportion of cases therapists may be expected to treat which will involve EMS activities. It should be a routine part of therapists' examinations during these individual interviews to simply inquire, "Have you or your partner ever been involved with someone outside of your marriage?" Individuals who have not been involved frequently laugh at this question and then share their fantasies about doing so. These "admissions" should lead to further exploration of such impulses and their meanings to the persons and to their marriage.

It is advisable for therapists to inform clients in the very opening minutes of the individual sessions that whatever they say will be kept strictly confidential. Unless therapists inadvertently convey other messages that lead clients to question the veracity of such a promise, this will help free persons to divulge their EMS activities as well as other secret or highly emotionally charged subjects that they do not want their marital partners to know about.

SECRECY

The Ethical Issue

If an extramarital sexual relationship has been revealed to the therapist, two significant questions must then be asked: Does the marital partner know about this other relationship and What is the emotional meaning of the relationship to the husband, to the wife, to the extramarital partner, and to the "other person's" own spouse? Therapists have argued both ways on the question of whether or not EMS clients should be encouraged or even required to reveal the relationship to an otherwise unsuspecting spouse. This is partially an ethical issue, a question that deals with whether or not therapists have the right to require their clients to do or say anything against the latters' wishes. If therapists subscribe to a code of ethics that respects clients' rights of self-determination, then obviously information cannot and should not be forced out into the open. Marital therapists functioning in a religious setting, especially if they are clergy, will ordinarily be expected by clients to adopt a position on this matter that is congruent with the teachings of their particular faith. This often means that clients who are involved in EMS activities deliberately avoid therapists identified with religious institutions; they do so because they wish their therapists to have a "nonjudgmental" approach to their problems. Therapists who represent themselves to the public as nonsectarian, however, clearly have an obligation to be precisely that and to refrain from imposing their own moral codes upon their clients. This is an especially important issue in treating EMS cases.

Results of Revelation—
Constructive or Destructive?

In addition to the ethical issues surrounding the question of revealing an EMS relationship to one's partner, there is a tactical question—what is to be gained by sharing this hitherto unknown information? Will the marriage be strengthened? Will the "confessor" have his or her guilt assuaged? Or will all hell break loose in the marriage? It is predicted that the latter will occur. The revelation of an unknown EMS activity is likely to immediately traumatize the marital partner, generate high levels of anger and distrust, and virtually insure that a mammoth void—one that may never be bridged—will be formed between the marital partners.

TREATMENT OF THE
PARTICIPATING SPOUSE

Exploration of the Reasons for EMS

Therapists must realize that sexual fidelity is one of the most deeply held values in the institution of marriage, at all levels of consciousness, and it must be regarded as an extremely sensitive issue. Instead of encouraging the client to share immediately his or her secret EMS relationships with the marital partner, therapists should proceed, during regularly scheduled individual sessions, to explore the meaning of the relationship to the partner who is having it, to the person(s) with whom he or she is conducting the EMS relationship(s), and the probable meaning the EMS relationship would have to the marital partner if he or she knew about it. Ultimately, the decision about continuing or discontinuing EMS relationships rests upon the shoulders of the participants themselves. It is not common in marital therapy to find clients who can continue EMS relationships over long periods of time without revealing it to their marital partners or without its detracting from the quality of their marital relationships. If the therapist's assessment of the total situation is that the marriage is being harmed by a continuing affair, he or she should inform the EMS client of the reasons for this belief. In these instances, however, the choice about continuing the EMS relationship or not still rests with the client.

Dealing with Ambivalent Feelings

Often, EMS clients reveal high levels of ambivalence about their feelings toward both the marital partner and the EMS partner. In treating these feelings, therapists should proceed in a similar manner as for any other ambivalent feelings. They should explore the feelings to discover both their conscious and unconscious meanings, assist the client in facing these, and then support movements toward a resolution of the ambivalent emotions. EMS clients who choose to terminate their outside relationship and to keep all aspects of that relationship confidential between themselves and their therapists appear to have as good a chance of revitalizing their marital relationship as do clients with other types of marital problems, all other factors being equal. Some of these clients may carry a significant amount of guilt for long periods of time, but many report that this is a small price to pay for sustaining and improving their marital relationships.

TREATMENT OF THE
NONPARTICIPATING SPOUSE

Concurrently, therapists should be treating, again in both individual and conjoint sessions, the partner who is unaware of the EMS activities of the spouse. These sessions will be conducted in much the same fashion as sessions for those whose marital conflict issues consisted solely of non–EMS complaints. The individual meetings will concentrate on the nonparticipating spouse's feelings, behaviors, and motivations in respect to his or her marriage. Conjoint sessions should be utilized to concentrate upon current issues of importance to both marital partners.

When Both Partners Know

Marital therapy proceeds somewhat differently when both partners know about the EMS activities before therapy commences. In these situations, partners who are not in the EMS relationships themselves will ordinarily use their individual sessions with therapists to ventilate their hurt and angry feelings, to explore all their feelings about the EMS and about their partners, and to work on the ambivalence they frequently feel with regard to themselves and to their partners. The knowledge that one's marital partner has been sexually involved with someone else frequently challenges husbands' and wives' own feelings of sexual adequacy and self-respect. Both men and women often blame themselves for their partners' EMS.

Responses of Nonparticipating Partner

It is the exceptionally rare husband and wife who have never argued over some aspect of their sexual relationship. These arguments often become magnified in clients' minds when their marital partners engage in EMS. A person's sexual feelings toward the EMS-involved marital partner may vary from total rejection and repulsion to highly eroticized responses. The latter may be characterized by frantic sexual activities in the attempt to "prove" that married sex can be equal to or superior to sex with the EMS partner. Sexually rejecting partners often unwittingly push their mates further out of the marital bed toward the EMS person. Even when they become aware in therapy that this is what they are doing, they are often unable or unwilling to stop. Sexually rejecting one's marital partner has been a common form of marital fighting and may continue to be used in spite of the negative input it has in terms of the total marital system. Overt feelings of sexual repulsion toward partners who engage in EMS are difficult to resolve and may remain for long periods of time—months or years, or even permanently.

Marital partners who call themselves "innocent" in these EMS relationship cases—that is, the ones who are not involved in EMS activities—tend to emphasize the affair during therapy almost to the exclusion of all other aspects of the total marital relationship. While these clients need ample opportunity to resolve their feelings about the EMS, they also need to be directed by their marital therapists to examine other aspects of the marriage.

Effect of Others Who Know

In cases in which the partner's EMS affair becomes publicly known, a nonparticipating spouse frequently receives considerable sympathy and support from children, family, and friends. The one engaging in EMS, on the other hand, may be treated as a traitor and an outcast. The support of other, consoling network members may contribute to the difficulty the nonparticipating partner has in examining his or her own overall role in the marital difficulties. Frequently this person expects the marital therapist to "naturally" condemn the EMS partner; some even terminate therapy when the therapist will not become an ally in "punishing that no-good so and so."

People who are engaged in an EMS relationship benefit greatly from opportunities to discuss the relationship and their feelings in a neutral, confidential atmosphere with their therapist. Because they ordinarily meet with much opposition and criticism from family, friends, and co-workers, the experience of therapeutic neutrality and acceptance of them as troubled persons is a welcome relief to these clients, in addition to providing them with an opportunity to resolve their problems.

CONJOINT SESSIONS

Resolution of Strong Feelings
of Conflict

Conjoint therapy sessions, when the EMS relationship is known to both partners, are necessary but tend to be extraordinarily tense. Few other marital conflicts generate such strong feelings of bitterness, rage, hurt, defensiveness, and rejection as EMS relationships do. Thus, conjoint sessions are often characterized by such activities as blaming, threatening, evasiveness, and pleading. The therapist's task is not to stop the flow of these intense feelings but to share them, to reduce their intensity, to channel them into potentially constructive directions, and to assist the couple in resolving this highly emotionally charged issue. If the conjoint sessions become so tense that they appear to be adding to the couples' dilemmas rather than reducing the tensions, the therapist may choose to terminate a specific conjoint session and to devote additional time to individual sessions with each partner. However, sooner or later, each couple is going to have to come to some resolution of their feelings of conflict—regardless of whether they reach the decision in the therapist's office or in their home—and the therapist should aid them in this process.

Therapist Plays Active Role

The therapist in conjoint sessions serves as a catalyst to assist the couple in communicating their troubled feelings and in arriving at some decisions about them—or, at the other extreme, as a benevolent authority figure who prevents both persons from doing excessive damage to themselves or to their partner during the sessions. Again, this vividly demonstrates the fact that marital therapists, like all family therapists, must be *active*. They must be prepared to move in, to take charge, to challenge, to confront, to support—to do whatever is necessary at a given moment to assist the process of conflict resolution and to maintain the integrity and emotional well-being of each of the marital partners. In order to perform this latter task, the therapist must often play a role in clearly supporting individual marital health over marital stability or personal convenience.

Some rejected marital partners, in EMS situations as well as in other types of marital conflict, become so depressed that emergency psychiatric care becomes a necessity for them. As a temporary suicide precaution, the "rejecting" partner may have to be encouraged to remain with the depressed partner until emergency psychiatric treatment is obtained. These extreme situations are not as common in marital therapy, however, as are the painful—but not life-threatening—situations in which the resolution of the EMS triangle requires someone to be rejected—either the spouse or the EMS partner.

TREATMENT OF THE "OTHER PERSON"

Another issue that arises for the marital therapist treating EMS cases is the question of what should be his or her role in respect to the "outsider"—the person with whom one of the marital partners is conducting a relationship. In all probability, that person too could benefit from therapy. He or she may be married, and hence engaging in EMS him- or herself. Even if he or she is single, such a person faces difficult and conflicting pressures and emotions.

Apparently this issue is somewhat academic because very few therapists ever concurrently or conjointly treat the "other" person while also treating the husband and wife as "primary" clients. Perhaps therapists find their own countertransference feelings so complex if they also treat the "other person" that they simply abstain from broadening the treatment units to include these individuals. Systems-oriented therapists should realize, however, that these "other persons" are playing significant roles in the marital systems—usually highly disruptive ones.

Many "rejected" marital partners refuse to have anything at all to do with the spouse's EMS partner—including dealing with that person in the context of therapy sessions. Yet it is not unusual for husbands or wives to telephone their "competition" or even to confront them in person—often in an abusive or threatening manner—but still reject "their" therapist's seeing "those persons."

Because therapists should have a sense of obligation to all persons affected by the problems of couples they treat, they may act responsibly in such situations by assisting in the referral of the "other person" to a separate therapist who can conduct treatment in a manner that will result in an optimal resolution for most of the persons involved.

OTHER TREATMENT CONSIDERATIONS

When One Partner Moves Out

In a significant number of cases, the mate who is having an EMS relationship moves out of the marital home, either in an attempt to relieve stress or as an indication of dwindling interest in continuing the marriage. As long as both the husband

and the wife finds them helpful, conjoint sessions should continue at these times. As is true in any situations involving separation and potential divorce, there are many complex issues that such couples must resolve between themselves, especially if they have children. Therapy will assist the couples in resolving these issues, in dealing with their feelings about EMS and about the separation, and in helping them plan for their respective individual futures. As soon as one of the marital partners has made a decision to terminate the marriage, however, therapy should be increasingly directed to resolving lingering feelings toward soon-to-be ex-mates and toward planning for each person's future. Conjoint sessions are usually terminated at this point and individual sessions become the treatment method of choice from then on. Marital partners having EMS relationships usually derive considerable support and affection from their EMS partners and terminate their therapy sooner than mates who have been "left behind."

Outcome Determined by Couple, Not Therapist

The treatment process described in this book is based upon psychodynamic and systems principles and understandings. These indicate that in order for a marriage to succeed, it is imperative for *both* partners to want it to be continued. In addition, it is vital for *both* of the partners to accept—at all levels of consciousness—the conditions under which their marital relationship will be conducted. It is the task of the marital therapist to determine whether or not these desires are present and these mutually acceptable conditions exist. It is not up to the therapist to determine whether or not these desires and conditions *should* be present for specific couples. Reality dictates that, in treating EMS cases, the therapist should pay careful attention to the interactions of the multiplicity of factors in these complex issues, how these factors are impinging upon the individuals in the marital units, and what developments must occur to make possible resolution of the contradictory needs. If the therapist follows the recommendations and treatment procedures described here, he or she will not judge personal efficacy as a therapist by the number of individuals who terminate their EMS activities, the number of couples who decide to stay married, or the number of couples who divorce. All of these outcomes may result because of—or sometimes in spite of—marital therapy, but the outcomes will be determined by the clients themselves—not the therapist.

Divorce Initiated by Nonparticipating Spouse

Therapists may anticipate that a significant proportion of EMS cases will be concluded by divorce actions. These actions are usually initiated by the marital partner who did not engage in the EMS activities. He or she may initiate divorce proceedings because his or her spouse has refused to terminate the affair, because he or she finds that love for the partner has been replaced by apathy or hate, or because the EMS activities have served to bring to a head other long-standing and unresolvable issues that have weakened the marriage.

EMS Ended, Marriage Survives

Another sizable group of EMS therapy cases will terminate because the EMS relationship ends, with the surviving marriage reaching various levels of reconciliation, caring, and renewed trust. A decision by the husband and the wife to continue the marriage may represent a new and higher level of commitment and caring—the EMS affair and the marital therapy having both contributed to this—or it may represent a reluctant acceptance of the status quo. Complicating factors, such as children, finances, health problems, and so forth all contribute to these compromises between ideal resolutions and reality.

Both EMS and Marriage Maintained

Finally, therapists should anticipate a minority of case outcomes wherein decisions are made to continue the EMS activities and also to maintain the marriage. These may represent secret affair situations or may be marriages in which the affairs are known but other considerations lead both the husband and the wife to continue the marriage under far less than ideal circumstances for everyone involved.

TERMINATION OF THERAPY

Termination of therapy in EMS-involved cases should not be determined by the status of the marriage or of the EMS relationship but rather by whether or not each marital partner has reached an optimum level of adjustment to his or her total life situation. This frequently results in one of the pair remaining in therapy longer than the spouse. Decisions to terminate therapy ideally are mutual decisions reached between the couple and the therapist. In reality, however, many individuals in EMS-involved cases—as is true in other types of marital therapy—will terminate earlier than the therapist recommends. It is incumbent upon therapists in these instances to continue individual therapy with the spouse who desires it until maximum treatment results for that individual have been obtained.

CASE EXAMPLE:
RALPH AND MOLLY CANDLES

Background

To illustrate the issues and process of marital therapy when one of the partners is involved in an extramarital sexual relationship, we turn to the case of Ralph and Molly Candles. They were an attractive, upwardly mobile couple in their thirties. When therapy started, they had been married for fifteen years and had two sons, aged 2 and 5. They lived in a beautiful suburban home surrounded by trees, vast green lawns, and all the possessions typically owned by middle-class families, including a high-powered performance car for Ralph and a station wagon for Molly, the kids, and the family's long-haired dog.

Ralph and Molly both were college graduates. Molly had worked outside the home until shortly before the birth of the first child. Ralph was a consulting engineer and maintained an office in the nearby city as well as in one room of their home. When the sessions began, it seemed apparent that Ralph worshiped money. He spoke scathingly of his own father because the latter had never made much money. Ralph's mother, a nurse, had always worked at her profession, even when Ralph and his two younger sisters and his younger brother were still in school. His mother had completed her professional training when her children were small and Ralph occasionally hinted to Molly that she might consider furthering herself by taking college courses rather than devoting so much time to their children, teaching Sunday School, and serving as treasurer of the local League of Women Voters.

Molly had three siblings, an older sister and two younger brothers. Her mother had never held a job outside her home after marriage and was described as a wonderful and devoted wife and mother. Molly's father, an accountant, had been an accepting but somewhat remote person in her life. The Candles met in college, and their early years of courtship and marriage were described by both Molly and Ralph as uneventful and happy times.

Ralph and Molly Candles had been referred for marital therapy by one of Ralph's engineering customers. While they were closing a contract over a few beers, Ralph had cautiously shared some of the dilemmas he was feeling. The customer and his wife had been in therapy with the author in the past and their marriage had improved greatly.

Session 1—Initial Evaluation

Individual interview: Ralph.   In his private individual first interview with the therapist, before he and his wife were seen conjointly, Ralph poured out a story of dissatisfaction, of ambivalent feelings toward Molly, and of an extramarital sexual relationship that had lasted for three years. He stated that he had had his first EMS relationship when he and Molly had been married for two years. Since then and the present EMS, he had been involved seven times; five of the liaisons had been of short duration and two others had lasted for a year. He said he had enjoyed "fantastic sex" with most of his EMS partners, but described a deep level of passionate and loving care for his current EMS partner. He was not sure he had ever really loved Molly, he said, but he had always "liked and respected" her.

Ralph complained of Molly's lack of interest in intercourse earlier in the marriage and of her inhibitions, contrasting these with the wild exploits he engaged in extramaritally. His current EMS relationship was with a woman named Martha who was eight years younger than Ralph and Molly. Martha had broken off from Ralph several times because she sensed he would never divorce his wife and hence she saw no future in her relationship with him. He had always been successful in getting her to take him back.

Ralph seemed amused as he described the irony of his situation. His wife now wanted intercourse with him more than ever before in their whole marriage—but he often refused her because he felt guilty. He successfully hid this from Molly by claiming to be tired. At the same time, he was spending large amounts of time and money pursuing the often reluctant Martha. He guessed that maybe he enjoyed "forbidden fruit."

Ralph's ambivalence was strong. He was proud of his wife, his children, their home, and his career. Leaving Molly would cost him a very high price—both literally and figuratively. He reported that at that time in his life he wasn't sure he wanted to be married to anyone. He envied his unmarried and divorced buddies who could date whomever they wished.

Individual interview: Molly.   In her individual first interview, Molly concentrated on her fears, on Ralph's growing emotional and sexual rejections of her, and on her strong hopes to save the marriage. She said she had been surprised when Ralph had announced that he had made an appointment for them to see a marital therapist, but she was also relieved, because she had sensed an increasing distance between them, particularly in the sexual aspects of their marriage. Ralph, she said, had occasionally refused to have intercourse with her, saying he was "too tired." Molly interpreted this as somehow reflecting on her own sexuality and had made numerous efforts to rekindle her husband's interest in sex. She purchased a waterbed, and had a huge mirror installed on the bedroom ceiling. It was she who currently initiated sex, in contrast to her passivity in the earlier years of the marriage. She said that she had signed them up for a marriage encounter weekend the year before, but Ralph spent most of his time there talking about whether or not he really loved her. Molly expressed strong love for Ralph, was appreciative of their high standard of living, but was very frightened about their future together.

Conjoint interview.   During the first conjoint session, which immediately followed the separate sessions with Ralph and Molly, the couple were very tense. While both had spoken freely during their individual time with the therapist, each was most cautious about sharing much with their partner present. The therapist encouraged them to tell what was most troubling them about their relationship. Molly cried some and said that she was worried that Ralph didn't seem to love her any more. Ralph agreed that he had been distant and sometimes rejecting. He said that he believed that he was more unhappy with the marriage than Molly was and hoped that therapy would help them resolve their discomforts. Neither mentioned a word about EMS activities or worries during the joint session and the therapist respected these omissions.

Therapist's observations.   This couple was seen as quite typical of many marital therapy cases in which extramarital sex is an issue. The husband was highly intelligent, aggressive, and successful in his profession, and had strong needs for intercourse and for recognition from his wife. The wife, also very bright, appeared to be devoted to their children, their home, and her husband—in that order. The demands of being first a "career person" and later a mother and homemaker had taxed her energy and lowered her need for intercourse, sharing, and intimacy with her husband. The husband had reacted to the frustration of his needs by seeking outlets in several EMS relationships while still maintaining a modest level of commitment and involvement with his wife. She suspected that he may have occasionally been sexually unfaithful but blamed these possibilities on her own "sexual inadequacies" and on their youthful marriage, which she believed had "prevented Ralph from sowing his wild oats." He had hinted to her that he would like to engage in EMS but she had dealt with her anxiety by repressing such thoughts and then later attempting to seduce him.

The prognosis for the outcome of marital therapy was difficult to make. The couple was verbal, intelligent, and both appeared motivated to improve the quality of their lives. Molly desperately wanted to keep and improve the marriage, however, while Ralph was profoundly torn between his marital satisfactions, his EMS relationship, and a wish to be single again. The therapist offered to see Martha, Ralph's EMS partner, both to evaluate her feelings about her relationship with Ralph and also because it appeared that she was also quite ambivalent about the relationship. This offer was rejected by Martha, even though Ralph, when discussing this in his individual sessions, said he had repeatedly encouraged her to do this. She became aware that Ralph and Molly had entered therapy and again tried to break off with him, pleading with him to "get his head straightened out" and then let her know where she stood with him. Ralph refused to heed her requests, however, and continued to phone and visit her whenever possible.

Therapy began along the model recommended here—weekly appointments which consisted of 45 to 60 minutes of conjoint interviewing followed by 30 minutes of individual time with each partner. During ongoing treatment, couples are seen conjointly first and then the individual sessions follow. The conjoint sessions almost invariably bring out pertinent issues that lend themselves to further examination with the individual partners in their confidential sessions.

Session 2

Conjoint interview. This was a tense session. Ralph discussed his ambivalence about staying married or divorcing. Molly recognized his feelings but clearly stated her hopes and intentions of keeping the marriage together. Both discussed his past dissatisfaction with the frequency of intercourse, and Ralph acknowledged to his wife that he had no current complaints on the issue. Each person spoke freely, although Ralph tended to dominate. The therapist intervened numerous times to elicit Molly's feelings and perceptions and actively encouraged her to share more of these with Ralph.

Individual interview: Ralph. In Ralph's individual interview, he tended to focus on Molly versus Martha. He had seen Martha the week before and was worried about her possibly moving out of her apartment and going back to live with her sister, thus reducing her freedom to see him. Currently, he said, he "tolerated" Molly. He stated that whenever he consented to have intercourse with her, he thought about Martha.

Individual interview: Molly.   Molly revealed that Ralph's talk about divorce was frightening her. The session focused primarily on these fears plus things she was doing to try to convince Ralph that their marriage could be a positive experience for him.

During the individual sessions, the therapist's goal was to offer support, to focus on each client's ambivalence, and to increase their insight into their own feel ings and personality dynamics.

Session 3

Conjoint interview.   Most of this session was on Ralph and Molly's sexual adjustment. Both perceived that Molly had become much more open and assertive about sex. Ralph explained to her that he hesitated because he did not want her to misunderstand that "having sex equals a sure sign of love." Both recognized that Ralph had felt rejected and unloved earlier in the marriage because of Molly's lesser sex interests. They mentioned that Ralph had been away on business for a few days following their first therapy session, and that when he returned they had had an enjoyable weekend, without the kids, in the city.

Individual interview: Ralph.   In this interview, Ralph concentrated on his visit to Martha and described how pained he was over her refusal to commit herself to continuing to see him as long as he was so unclear about his marriage. While he was on his business trip, Ralph had frequented several bars and disco bars by himself, reveling in his freedom. His ambivalence about staying married, as opposed to divorcing, was troubling him greatly. (His basic narcissistic drives were in strong conflict with superego feelings of obligation to his family.) He had thought more about separating temporarily, he said, but this was discouraged by the therapist, with the observation that physical separations complicate issues by serving as public notice to friends and relatives about a couple's problems. If a husband and wife are working on resolving marital problems, interfering outsiders may easily inhibit this process.

Individual interview: Molly.   Molly had become keenly aware of Ralph's ambivalence toward her and toward their marriage. She said she had been fearful about pressing him for a decision—or a declaration of love—since she preferred not to hear anything that might be more negative. With the therapist's encouragement, Molly was beginning to ventilate some of her anger at Ralph for his continual aloofness with her, but Molly was too fearful of rejection to express this anger directly to Ralph.

Session 4

Conjoint interview.   During this part of the fourth session, the therapist sought to get an update on Molly's and Ralph's feelings and to try to help each see how their respective attitudes about their sexual relationship had provided some of the background for Ralph's current doubt about the marriage.

Individual interview: Ralph. The therapist continued with Ralph, during the individual session, to help him with his ambivalence about Molly, Martha, and marriage in general.

Individual interview: Molly. During Molly's individual session, the therapist was supportive and, at the same time, he focused on her increasing anger at her husband. The therapist believed that if this anger was not handled directly, there was danger that Molly's depressed feelings would increase.

Session 5

Conjoint interview. The couple discussed a major renovation of the family room in their house with which they were currently involved. Molly said that she found herself crying more and more often, and that Ralph offered little support to her during these times.

Individual interview: Molly. (Note: Couples are ordinarily allowed to choose who has the first individual session. This usually results in a system whereby the spouses alternate. The therapist may select one person over the other if he or she believes that that particular partner is under special stress, or if an unequal amount of time may be needed with that person, or for similar reasons.) During this interview, Molly admitted that she was feeling increasingly depressed. The therapist focused on what limitations Molly might accept in her marriage (if Ralph's feelings did not change) and how Molly would handle the future if the couple decided on divorce.

Individual interview: Ralph. Ralph's ambivalence focused primarily on his positive feelings for both Molly and Martha. Tears flowed when he aired his frustrations over not being able to continue his relationships with both of the women. He had come close to "confessing" to Molly about his EMS relationship with Martha when they were talking late one night in bed. The therapist supported his decision to refrain from sharing this issue until Ralph had resolved his conflict and made a decision about the future of his marriage.

Therapist's observations. At this time, the marital therapy process was typical of most EMS-involved relationships. Molly was feeling rejected, did not know about Ralph's EMS, and focused primarily upon saving the marriage. The therapist, aware of all the issues, was attempting to be supportive about Molly's feelings and, at the same time, was beginning to help her face the possibility that the marriage might not be continued. Meanwhile, the therapist was concentrating on trying to help Ralph resolve his ambivalence about Molly versus Martha versus becoming single again. Knowing of Molly's increasing anger and realizing that continued feelings of rejection ordinarily lead to loss of love, the therapist was also confronting Ralph with the fact that Molly might make the decision about the marriage for him—in the negative—if Ralph could not resolve his dilemma soon. Thus the reality of the dynamics of human feelings dictated the gradual shift toward encouraging each partner to face a future he or she did not completely want.

Session 6

Conjoint interview. A major holiday had occurred, so this session was held two weeks rather than one week later. Things between Molly and Ralph were much less tense. Molly discussed her decreased fears of the possibility of Ralph leaving her, and her wish to "get more strokes" from him. Ralph stated that he understood her feelings but reiterated his intention not to mislead her into thinking all their problems were solved.

Individual interview: Molly. The decrease in tension was contributing to Molly's increased self-confidence in facing the future. Therapy focused intensely on her positive qualities and Molly utilized this very effectively.

Individual interview: Ralph. Ralph indicated that much of the decreased tension in their home was probably because he was losing interest in Martha. He discussed the low-status job she held and how this bothered him. He said he was finding other women attractive—including his wife—and Martha "wasn't everything." He was still highly ambivalent about marriage to Molly as opposed to being a "swinging bachelor."

Therapist's observations. At this stage of the process, it was evident that it was nearly impossible to predict the outcome of the marriage, as is true in most EMS cases. Clients continue to lead their daily lives; feelings may change; specific events may occur. The outcome relies to a great extent on these factors, as well as on the process of therapy itself. It is the therapist's responsibility to continue working with the couple on their feelings and the issues involved—but the pace and the direction of change remains the clients' ultimate responsibilities.

Session 7

Conjoint interview. At this point, things in the Candles home had been proceeding fairly calmly. Within a few minutes after the session commenced, however, Molly was verbalizing her increasing frustration with their "so-so" marriage. Ralph was "less scared" of divorce but wanted to debate other possibilities with his wife, such as "open marriage." Molly said that she refused to accept anything for them but traditional marital patterns.

Individual interview: Ralph. Ralph revealed that Martha had recently expressed love for him—the first time she had ever done that—and he was delighted. Yet he said that if Molly divorced him, he probably wouldn't marry Martha. The therapy focused on Ralph's essentially narcissistic personality and his tendency to take far more than he gave. He showed considerable insight into this idea and his feelings about it, but showed little interest in any major personality changes for himself.

Individual interview: Molly. Again Molly ventilated considerable anger that Ralph demanded so much "understanding" from her while he gave so little of himself. She still found it too threatening to express this anger directly to Ralph at this point, however, for she feared he would use it as a reason to leave her.

Sessions 8 and 9

Two more treatment sessions followed with Molly and Ralph without much change in their overall situation. Then Ralph telephoned the therapist to cancel all future appointments. He stated that he had terminated the relationship with Martha and had decided to stay with Molly. He said that he wasn't sure whether there would be other EMS relationships for him in the future, but he felt that, at least for the present, his marriage was where he wanted to be. He told the therapist that Molly was delighted with the increased attention he was giving her and shared in his decision to discontinue therapy.

SUMMARY

The Candles's case exhibited many typical EMS issues. The relationship was a "secret" to the wife, although it was evident that she suspected that some infidelities had occurred. The husband demonstrated many insecurities and much narcissism, attributes that do not seem to appear in EMS-related cases any more often than they do in other types of marital problems. The therapist respected the confidentiality of the partners and focused on "him, her, and them" as each session occurred. The other person (Martha) in the EMS triangle was offered an opportunity for therapy but rejected it. The outcome of the case suggests that the therapeutic focus on the husband's ambivalence helped him to resolve it—and, in this case, he reached a decision to end the EMS relationship and stay with his wife. The wife, severely threatened by her husband's emotional and sexual distance from her, decided early in therapy to try her best to improve their marriage, but during the stage of therapy when it seemed to be a distinct possibility, she was nevertheless prepared by the therapist for the possibility of divorce.

It should be apparent that other cases with similar dynamics may just as often have the opposite outcome. It is the couples who make these decisions—right or wrong, happy or unhappy—not the therapists. Therapists attempt to help the couples establish constructive communication patterns; to gain insights and understanding of the individual and marital dynamics involved; and to resolve their differences if possible. Extramarital "other persons" may continue to exert influences upon the marital system—and this cannot always be discussed in the therapy sessions because of the issue of secrecy. Yet the influences of these others cannot be ignored. These influences must be treated directly in private sessions with the EMS-involved spouse, and indirectly treated in the case of the nonparticipating spouse who is unaware of the EMS. The goal of the marital therapy remains the resolution of marital distress, in EMS cases as also in other types of marital problems, but the outcome of both the marriage and the EMS relationship is always the result of the whole complex process of life for all of the individuals involved. In contrast to other forms of family therapy in which therapists often require and obtain the active participation of *all* the significant persons involved in the system (not just the identified patients), marital therapy in EMS-involved cases often has to deal with the influence and interactions of significant others obliquely and indirectly. This poses special problems for therapy—such as heightened confidentiality and often discrepant goals on the part of the husband and the wife—but these problems can be overcome if the therapist maintains a stance that is firmly rooted in reality and free of preconceived outcomes for the affairs.

CHAPTER FOUR
MARITAL
SEXUAL PROBLEMS

BACKGROUND

Conflicts about sex occur in virtually every marriage at some time or another. Many of these conflicts are based on behavioral issues—what to do and when—while others stem from differing values and attitudes about sexuality in general. Our society continues in its abysmal failure to provide youth with "pro-sex" positive sex education. Additionally, boys and girls are indoctrinated so differently about sex that adult conflicts between marital partners over sex are virtually guaranteed. Finally, certain undeniable biological differences between men and women, including menstrual cycles and the fact that males do not become pregnant, add further stresses.

In our society sex—usually meaning intercourse—continues to become more fused with love and affection in the lives and emotions of wives than it does for husbands. Yet in another dimension of human feelings, the *symbolic* meaning of sex, husbands are often just as vulnerable as their wives are. Men are taught to be sexually aggressive—but they resent having to carry this role throughout marriage. They complain loudly and often about wives who "never" initiate intercourse. Wives, on the other hand, accuse their husbands of making incessant sexual demands so that they feel valued only as sex objects, not as human beings. Many couples face opposite problems—sex-starved wives married to passive males with low libidinal urges. Some couples resort to the use of statistics in attempts to resolve their arguments. They come to therapists' offices armed with the latest "sex research" figures from popular magazines in the effort to prove *their* side of these issues. Debates over such things as how often couples should have sexual intercourse thus may become the basis of marital warfare. Each partner wants to "make love" *when* and *where* he or she chooses—and yet each one is directly dependent upon the marital partner to somehow be in the same frame of mind and body.

Vastly differing sex education and consequent attitude formation for males and females also shows up dramatically in the problems that surround methods and techniques of sexual intercourse. Young males are encouraged to experiment, to be innovative, to try out new ways to "do it." Young women, on the other hand, are more likely to receive the message that any technique or method other than the male-above, penis-in-vagina method is somehow perverted and obscene. Even though these generalizations do not hold for all couples, they are sadly representative of the sex-role stereotyping that goes on as part of the sexual growth and development process of young Americans. Men and women bring into their sex lives their unconscious values about sex as well as their conscious values, just as they do about household roles, finances, and all other aspects of marital interaction.

Earlier in the development of the profession of marital therapy, a great deal of attention was focused upon "premarital counseling," a term that was frequently a euphemism for sex education for couples about to be married and presumed to be sexually innocent. The contemporary marital therapist has no such delusions. By the time the 1980s arrived it seemed clear that the virgins were distinctly in the minority—perhaps even an endangered species! It has become increasingly rare for the marital therapist to be routinely consulted, premaritally, for information about sexual intercourse. Those clients who do appear for premarital therapeutic help on sexual issues bring problems very similar to those of already-married couples. This is not, however, to say that the conscious need to deal with problems about sex has decreased in recent times—quite the contrary. As sex has come out of the back alleys and out of the gutters, as it has moved from being "a woman's duty and a man's right," it has become an increasingly important part of human relationships. The net result is that good sexual adjustment in today's marriages is regarded as a reasonable and normal expectation for all couples—and failure to achieve and maintain a good marital sexual relationship continues to constitute a major source of complaints about marriage.

A major reason for conflicts about marital sexual adjustment is the fact that sexual interaction represents one of the most powerful forms of human communication. Couples don't talk of "copulating"—they say, "Let's make love." Actually, truly "making love" by having intercourse constitutes a minority of the times in which married couples engage in coitus. The majority of acts of sexual intercourse take place primarily because sex is pleasurable, because at least one of the partners is erotically stimulated, because they are bored, or because one or both of them is acting out neurotic insecurities. Yet we continue—through the mass media, through religious teaching, and through parental admonition—to make married couples think that every single act of intercourse must be loving, deeply passionate, and culminate in fantastic orgasm(s) for both partners. How unrealistic! Today couples still marry, on the average, in their early twenties. Given current life expectancies they may expect to be married for over fifty years, assuming they do not divorce. Taking the average frequencies of intercourse that have been reported by researchers, we may postulate that over the life of their marriage a given couple will engage in intercourse 4,200 times. If each act involving penile penetration lasts for 10 minutes (again the average supplied by researchers), this married couple will be locked together in alleged sexual ecstacy for a total of 42,000 minutes or 700 hours or over 29 twenty-four-hour days or about one whole month over their married lifetime! To expect that all of these 4,200 events—this almost one whole month—will always be loving, exciting, ecstatic, and passionate defies common sense. The marital therapist needs to keep this in mind lest he or she perpetuate the traditional nonsense about ideal reasons and motivations for engaging in intercourse.

Both consciously and unconsciously, sexual intercourse communicates messages that may be sent in a positive manner but received quite differently. Each partner's sexual value system determines how he or she may interpret the specific act and this, in turn, is influenced by the total context of the marital relationship of that moment. Many words describe these shared messages and all of them represent a continuum of possible meanings on a positive-negative scale. The meaning of an act of sexual intercourse varies from love to hate, acceptance to rejection, good to bad, clean to dirty, fun to duty, excitement to dullness, godly to evil, recreation to procreation—the list of possible positive or negative meanings is endless. Yet, in order for both the husband and the wife to feel good about the specific act of intercourse in which they are engaging, they *both* must perceive what they are doing from a positive viewpoint. All too often, this fails to occur.

COMMON COMPLAINTS
ABOUT SEX

Men and women have different bodies, different fatigue factors, and different sexual socialization experiences. Consequently, therapists hear certain sexual complaints from one sex more than from the other. A list of "typical" husbands' complaints might run like this: "We don't do it often enough"; "She won't experiment with the time, place, or way we do it"; "She rejects oral-genital sex"; "She holds grudges and expects me to beg her for 'some' "; "She's cold and inhibited"; "She talks, thinks, and acts like a prude"; and, in more recent times, "She expects me to hump her all night so she can have a whole bunch of orgasms." Wives have their own list of "typical" sexual complaints: for example, "That's all he ever thinks about!"; "He's a pervert to think I could enjoy doing *those* things"; "He's dull and unimaginative"; "How can he yell at me and then expect me to go to bed with him?"; "He 'comes' too fast and doesn't care about *my* pleasure"; "He smells (beer, sweat) and hurts me (beard, heavier body)"; "Why can't he be responsible for birth control?"; "He's crude and both talks and acts dirty." While these complaints are neither exhaustive or always linked to one sex or the other, they do represent common issues that therapists hear about repeatedly.

CONDITIONS FOR POSITIVE
INTERCOURSE

In order for couples to have a sexually satisfying relationship, at least seven basic conditions must be met.

1. *Adequate Time.* Although sometimes couples may enjoy a "quickie," they ordinarily require a reasonable length of time for intercourse. Given family demands, different working schedules, and all the interferences of modern life, it is often difficult for couples to have this.

2. *Reasonable Privacy.* While couples who must live in poverty conditions or in primitive societies may be used to having intercourse in close proximity to their children, extended family members, or neighbors, Americans in general are rarely able to relax sexually without both visual and auditory privacy. Couples with young children may need locks on their doors and nonsqueaking beds to achieve this.

3. *Freedom from Unwanted Pregnancies.* Worry about the wife becoming pregnant is less of an issue today with the accessibility of modern contraceptives, but ignorance, conservative religious teachings, and sometimes health problems that contraindicate chemical contraceptives may lead the fear of pregnancy to interfere with both partners' ability to relax and enjoy sexual intercourse.

4. *Acceptance of One's Own Sexuality.* Both the husband and the wife must accept themselves as male and as female. Conflicts over individual sexual orientation or sexuality must be corrected in order for a man or woman to deal comfortably with his or her own sexuality.

5. *A Free Conscience.* If either partner feels that sexual behavior is evil or bad, this will seriously hamper his or her freedom to act and to feel good sexually. Marriage, it should be noted, does not automatically erase years of premarital teaching about sex as a sinful act.

6. *Sensitivity to the Partner's Feelings and the Maturity to Respect Them.* Both men and women need to know, to respect, and to be able to act in accordance with their partner's feelings. Both must have the personal maturity necessary to allow them occasionally to be able to postpone their own pleasure in order to maintain their partner's caring for them. They must also be able to accept their partner's different level of interest in sexual practices at times.

7. *Practice.* Performing sexual intercourse is a learned art, not an instinctive behavior. Not only must each individual partner develop his or her own skill through practice, the couple must also develop and maintain their collective skill as a "team."

Couples for whom any one of these seven basic conditions are consistently lacking may not reasonably be expected to establish and maintain a good sexual relationship.

ASSESSING MARITAL
AND SEXUAL INTERACTION

The sexual adjustment. Marital therapists should routinely inquire about each couple's sexual adjustment as part of the total assessment of the marriage. While some couples request help for "troubles with sex" when they really have a relationship problem, other couples—especially more inhibited and conservative ones—may hesitate to talk about this vital aspect of marriage unless they are questioned directly about it. A part of marital therapy may well include some basic sex education. Often therapeutic help with negative sexual attitudes is an absolute must in the marital therapy program.

Cause and effect. Another significant aspect of the initial assessment procedures covering marital and sexual maladjustments is the diagnostic question: Which is cause and which is effect? Has sexual maladjustment caused marital conflict, or is sexual maladjustment the result of the marital conflict? The fact is it may be either, or both. Marital and sexual conflict are often so intertwined that determining which caused which, or by how much, may be an irrelevant issue. However, treatment strategy ordinarily dictates that relationship issues need to be addressed and resolved before sexual issues can be treated successfully. Angry or distrustful spouses cannot be expected to be happy sex mates. If the answers to the therapist's questions indicate that most of the seven basic conditions needed for successful intercourse are met, and yet sexual complaints continue, the therapist may reasonably conclude that the major focus of therapy should therefore be concentrated on the nonsexual aspects of the relationship. Because of the emotional symbolism attached to sexuality, it is very common for individuals to unconsciously displace other tensions into the sexual area. Treatment in these cases obviously should focus on the basic conflicts, not on the sexual symptoms.

MAJOR CONCEPTS
OF SEX THERAPY

Before we discuss the treatment of the three basic aspects of marital sexuality issues, it will be useful to take a brief look at some of the major concepts of modern sex therapy.

While these concepts have been chosen and developed primarily to help people experiencing sexual dysfunctions, they should be of immense interest and value to marital therapists because of their proven relevance in treating many types of relationship conflicts as well. Listed here, in no special order of importance, are some of these major concepts:

1. Sex is a natural function. In healthy partners, male and female sexual response cycles occur as a result of normal erotic stimulation just as naturally as heavy breathing follows vigorous exercise.

2. Every human being has his or her own unique S.V.S.—sexual value system. If a person does not act in accord with his or her sexual value system, conflict, guilt, and other such negative consequences will occur.

3. Sexual intercourse involves a mutual activity between two persons—hence there is no such thing as an "uninvolved" sexual partner who can blame his or her spouse for all the couple's sexual troubles.

4. First events carry special meanings to each person, so that such things as first orgasms, first acts of intercourse, etc. are especially significant events in the life of individuals and couples.

5. Sex is a medium of exchange between persons. Partners must *give* pleasure in order to *get* pleasure themselves.

6. Authorititative "command" concepts (musts, shoulds, oughts) have no place in sexual activity. For instance, an attitude of "I must have an orgasm or I'll be unhappy" places excessive pressure on sexual performance and sexual functioning cannot be forced or ordered. An attitude of openness, neutrality, and vulnerability is necessary in order to completely "surrender" oneself to one's partner sexually.

7. Feelings are facts. For example, a man may despair that his wife feels that his sexual language is crude—but her feeling is a fact. He must therefore talk "appropriately" if he is going to be able to sexually communicate with her on a positive basis.

8. Intercourse does not occur in a psychosocial vacuum. What goes on outside the bedroom has a direct bearing on what goes on sexually within the bedroom.

9. Each sexual partner needs to speak for him- or herself, not for the partner. People should learn to use "I" statements to achieve this and avoid "mind-reading," second-guessing, or blaming their partners. Instead of saying "You weren't turning me on" persons can be taught to reframe the message by saying, "I wasn't feeling turned on by you . . . " thus acknowledging their feeling but not blaming the partner.

10. Good communications are of vital importance to the maintenance of any relationship. They are especially critical in communicating attitudes, feelings, and wishes about sexuality.

11. Good marital sexual intercourse is most likely to occur if it is engaged in regularly over the years. The adage of "use it or lose it"—referring to a person's ability to respond sexually—holds truth.

These twelve concepts are helpful for the therapist to keep in mind when couples discuss conflicts over sex. If the couple can be encouraged to adopt or accept these principles, many—if not all—of their sexual complaints can be expected to be resolved.

TREATMENT OF MARITAL SEXUAL ISSUES—ATTITUDES AND VALUES

Let us now turn to the specific treatments of sexual issues in marriage that are expected of contemporary therapists. Broadly speaking, therapy concerns fall into three separate and yet often intertwined aspects of human sexuality: (1) attitudes and values about sexuality, (2) sexual behaviors, and (3) sexual dysfunctions. First we shall address issues concerning sexual attitudes and values.

Congruence of Sexual Value Systems

For a couple to achieve and maintain satisfactory marital sexual adjustment, their individual sexual value systems must be reasonably congruent. Ideally, any major differences between the two people would be discovered during courtship and resolved at that time. However, a significant proportion of couples either fail to discover their sexual attitude differences early or, even if the differences are noticed, they rationalize or repress the problems that are likely to be caused. For example, consider the simplest and most common form of sexual foreplay—ordinary kissing and hugging. Suppose a couple, in the course of their dating, discover that she has a far greater desire to kiss and hug than he does. What will they do about this? There are several options: (a) he can encourage her to try to be comfortable with less kissing; (b) she can encourage him to try to engage in and enjoy kissing more; (c) they can break up and find more "compatible" partners; or (d) both can suppress their preferences and hope that the problem will disappear magically after marriage. It is the results of choice (d) that therapists are most likely to have to deal with. Choosing to do nothing, in a sense, and entering marriage with the matter unresolved—neither person really comfortable with the other's level of kissing enjoyment—means that it is probably only a matter of time before frustrations and hurt feelings about these differences will emerge. The same phenomenon may occur with all types of sexual attitudes and behaviors, from the simple kissing foreplay discussed here to such things as techniques and frequency of intercourse, attitudes about nudity and sexual language, and even issues about whether or not to have children.

Therapist supports healthy sexual values.   Earlier writings about the ethics and philosophy of therapy emphasized the importance of strict neutrality on the part of the therapist in respect to patients' values. Therapists were urged to complete their own psychoanalysis so they could gain total insight into their own needs and values, and also presumably so they could "cure" their neurotic needs to impose their personal values on their patients. However, the situation today differs. Contemporary marital therapists rarely undergo psychoanalysis and, even if they choose to do so, they are likely to reject the "idealized" concept of total neutrality in all areas of marital interaction, including marital sexual interaction. When the therapist is confronted with a couple who have disparate and conflicting sexual values, he or she first needs to assess the relative health, maturity, and strength of each partner's sexual attitudes and expectations. Is one—or both—sexually naive, repressed, or neurotically blocked from accepting him- or herself as a mature sexual being? If this is the conclusion reached by the therapist, he or she should recommend that at least one of the treatment goals should be to help the less sexually healthy partner with his or her sexual problems. This has to be presented in a most tactful way so that neither partner will think of the other as "sick" or "abnormal." Here the marital therapist may make use of one of the twelve concepts we discussed earlier: that there is no such thing as one partner being *uninvolved* with the other's sexual functioning. Hence the "well" spouse needs to accept that his or her attitudes and behaviors probably have a direct bearing on the partner's attitudes and behaviors. Treatment of both partners should therefore focus on understanding the sexual differences, the etiology of their development, re-education in respect to positive sexual attitudes, and effective communication between the partners so that they may work together to resolve the conflicts.

Replacing the negative with the positive. Treatment of negative attitudes and values about sexuality has historically been considered a most difficult process. Many inhibitions are the results of long years of hearing sex condemned as filthy and evil—or at least as something so laden with negative associations that young people come to assume that "nice people don't do that." These negative attitudes are taught at home; reinforced by our religious, educational, and legal systems; and become part of many young adults' conscious and unconscious value systems. The marital therapist's task in dealing with negative sexual values is first to establish a relationship of trust with the couple so that they can permit themselves to be open to new, "pro-sex" attitudes. They must believe that the therapist accepts them *as they are* but also wants to help them in the task of replacing their old, negative attitudes with new, accepting feelings about sex. The therapist does this by modeling positive sexuality in speech and attitudes, by sharing, by educating, by encouraging change, and by a positive use of therapeutic authority.

It is here that one of the numerous advantages of treating both marital partners emerges. Frequently one partner may already possess a more positive sexual value system than the other does. In these instances the therapist recognizes the differences and then proceeds to verbally reinforce the more positive partner's attitudes and to support the negative partner's efforts to become more open and accepting. Caution must be observed not to label the fearful partner with such pejorative terms as "bad," "resistive," "inhibited," "frigid," and similar terms. Because human sexuality is such a powerful force, once a partner is able to move into a more accepting attitude about a sexual matter, his or her attitude almost immediately becomes self-reinforcing. For example, if a hesitant person acts on the therapist's and the partner's encouragement and tries a sexual behavior that he or she had previously found repulsive—and discovers that it is enjoyable and rewarding to both the person and the partner—his or her attitude about the activity ordinarily becomes more accepting and positive. This, in turn, makes the person willing to repeat the activity and learning or attitude reformation is positively reinforced. The partner's attitude and cooperation during these learning tasks are crucial, however, and must be both sensitive and caring—not demanding or critical.

Therapists schooled in the more traditional psychoanalytical orientation frequently have great resistance to believing that sexual attitudes can be changed in short-term, conjoint marital therapy. One can only respect their resistance—while also encouraging them to try these more contemporary treatment methods.

TREATMENT OF MARITAL SEXUAL ISSUES— SEXUAL BEHAVIORS

Sexual "Normality"

Modern marital therapists are expected to be knowledgeable about most aspects of human sexual behaviors. Troubled marital partners often look to their therapist to judge questions of sexual normality for them. For example, a wife may want to try cunnilingus, but her husband may believe this activity is perverted. Therapists need to be very cautious about labeling any specific sexual behaviors as perverted or abnormal. How, for instance, is normality to be defined? Statistically? Legally? Religiously? Historically? Socially? Phylogenetically? Culturally? Is a given act defined as "normal" if 50 percent of a given population regularly engages in it? If there are no criminal statutes that clearly prohibit it? If the (clients') (therapist's) religion does not preach against it? If the practice has survived down through the ages? If it causes no harm to society? If it is practiced by other forms of animal life? Or if one's "cultural" reference group (social, educational, income, ethnic, nationality group, etc.) somehow treats it as normal?

The etiology of complaints of abnormality. Obviously, there are many potential sources to label any specific sexual behavior as normal or abnormal. The therapist's position, when called upon to rate a specific behavior as normal (and hence to be practiced) or abnormal (and hence not be practiced) should be, first of all, to assess the marital and sexual interaction, which we discussed earlier in this chapter. Is the behavior (or the lack of it) *causing* the marital conflict—or is it a *result* of the marital conflict? What are the attitudes and feelings of each of the marital partners about the practice? Are the issues of severe inhibition, fear, guilt, displacement, and similar emotions expressed about the practice itself only a symptom of something more pathological? If any of these issues are involved, treatment should focus on them first. Treating symptoms alone is like prescribing aspirin for the headaches brought on by a brain tumor. The symptom may be somewhat relieved but will recur until the real cause is successfully treated. Therefore complaints about sexual behaviors need to be treated according to the precise etiology behind the problem.

Therapeutic resolution of differences about normality. If the sexual complaint involves behavior that is considered by only one of the partners to be abnormal, the therapist may be required to make a judgment about that behavior. Such things as incest, rape, and practices that could cause physical harm to one or both participants are readily judged in accord with contemporary mental health standards. In these instances the marital therapist focuses the treatment on the elimination of these harmful behaviors and attempts to help both the partners with the mixed feelings each one may have about him- or herself as well as about the partner because of these practices. The therapist's role becomes much more ambiguous when conflict ensues as a result of complaints that do not involve harmful sexual behavior but which one partner may perceive as or refer to as "abnormal" or "wrong." For example, a wife may label her husband's interest in frequent sexual intercourse as "abnormal." But how frequent is too frequent? By whose definitions? The wife's? The husband's? The therapist's? The Kinsey or Playboy reports? In these instances the therapist must again move first to assess the fundamental, underlying issues. These involve numerous possibilities—different libidinal drives, different sexual value systems, different fatigue factors, dominance or power struggles, and so forth.

Next, the marital therapy proceeds by helping each partner first develop insight into his or her own individual psychosexual dynamics and feelings, then into those of the partner. Finally, he or she helps the couple to negotiate a compromise. Often the resolution of their differences takes the form of a *quid pro quo* between the husband and wife. If the husband wants more frequent intercourse, he is encouraged to understand his wife's feelings and values about his wishes and to express himself—through both words and deeds—in a manner that would more likely bring about a receptive attitude on her part or a diminution of his own requests. At the same time the wife is encouraged to understand her husband's feelings, to constructively communicate her own feelings to him, and then to explore ways in which her own sexual interests might be brought into harmony with her husband's or in which she might help him to accept a lower frequency of intercourse. In this situation either they both win or they both lose. If they both "win," each person will feel better—toward both self and partner. If either one of them "loses," both will feel angry and unloved. The therapist's goal is not to help the couple accept having intercourse a specific number of times per week, but rather to help them talk, act, feel, and negotiate in a positive manner that enhances the marital relationship, both sexually and emotionally.

The Young Parent Syndrome

Fatigue.   One of the most common types of sexual behavioral conflict occurs around what we choose to label the "Young Parent Syndrome" (YPS). A large percentage of the couples coming to marital therapists fall into this category. Typically, these couples are in their twenties and thirties, have one or two young children (or more), and are striving to be excellent parents, marital partners, and career persons. They work long and hard, lead very busy lives, and are often considered model couples by their friends and relatives. However, one of the greatest enemies of sexual interest is fatigue. This may be either physically or emotionally induced. Women, especially in these years of young parenthood, appear to be more sexually vulnerable to fatigue than young husbands are. Complicating the situation is the frequent practice of the wife foregoing her own career advancement to stay home with the kids—a move she often unconsciously, or maybe even consciously, resents. The husband, working hard to get promoted and to be a "good" husband and father by making lots of money, often expects his wife to be just as "sexy" as he feels and to "reward" him sexually for his efforts. Young men are rarely educated about the fact that being a mother is one of the most demanding roles of modern life. When the physical and emotional demands of caring for the children and the household are added to the wife's frustrations over being "just a housewife" or of carrying the dual career role of being a full-time mother, homemaker, and outside-the-home career person herself, it is no wonder that many perfectly healthy married women find their energy and their interest in sex waning by the time they finally get to bed at night. Their young husbands, less negatively affected by fatigue, are dismayed, hurt, and angry at their wives' apparent coldness or indifference to "making love." The wives, in turn, resent their husbands' demands and complaints, feel even less romantic than they did before the argument commenced about "doing it," and thus a vicious, self-perpetuating cycle of frustration, anger, and alienation is often set into motion.

Therapeutic Resolution
of Complaints about Behaviors

Treatment of couples affected by the Young Parent Syndrome cases may be rapid and effective—if they seek help before love and self-respect have been dangerously eroded. These couples often respond well to conjoint therapy sessions in which the focus alternates between one person's, then the other person's needs, feelings, wishes, and caring. Long-term improvement requires that both partners achieve a better understanding and acceptance of the fact that parenthood is a most demanding role, that sexual complaints can easily become divisive elements in an otherwise satisfactory marriage, and that all human relationships—including marital ones—require constant, repetitive "nourishment" and care in order to continue on a satisfactory basis.

While the main issue chosen for illustration here has been that of conflict over the frequency of intercourse, treatment of almost all types of sexual behavior complaints between marital partners is similar. The basic issues are determined early; the partners are conjointly engaged in understanding both their own and their spouse's dynamics; communication and sensitivity between the partners are increased; and the husband and wife are encouraged to seek to formulate goals and develop attitudes and behaviors that diminish or eliminate the sexual complaints and, at the same time, increase each partner's satisfaction, self-respect, and caring for the other.

TREATMENT OF MARITAL
SEXUAL ISSUES—SEXUAL
DYSFUNCTIONS

Sexual dysfunctions refer to problems that couples experience with male ejaculation and potency; female orgasmic responses and vaginismus; and sexual aversions on the part of either or both. These symptoms commonly occur together in couples. The wife of a man who has premature ejaculation problems often loses her capacity to have orgasms. Husbands of wives suffering from severe sexual aversion, to take another common example, often develop secondary impotence.

Who should treat? The question has been debated as to whether couples suffering from sexual dysfunctions should be treated by marital therapists or referred to specialists in sexual therapy. The answer appears to lie less in the specific title therapists possess and more in what their actual training has been. Marital therapists who have also been trained in modern methods of sex therapy should proceed with treating these sexual dysfunctions within the context of the total marital relationship. The writings of Helen Singer Kaplan have proven to be especially helpful to dynamically oriented therapists who are qualified to simultaneously treat both marital and sexual dysfunctions (Kaplan 1974, 1979).

Marital therapists who have not received special training in treating the sexual dysfunctions should recognize their own limitations and refer the troubled couples to competent sex therapists. In these situations it may be feasible for the marital therapists to treat the marital relationship problems while their professional colleagues treat the specific sexual dysfunctions. In these latter instances, the work of William Masters and Virginia Johnson (1971), as well as of later writers such as Ard (1974) and the LoPiccilos (1978) are valuable guides to treatment of sexual dysfunctions. A third type of treatment plan calls for the marital therapist to treat the marriage relationship until the couple has adequately resolved their marital differences and then make a referral for sex therapy. Time, money, and psychological stresses may all dictate when this third model should be utilized.

We shall not attempt here to examine therapy techniques for sexual dysfunctions because it is our conviction that they require special techniques and skills that are best handled in texts such as those referred to above. Contemporary treatments for sexual dysfunctions constitute one of the more dramatic and positive advancements in the field of psychotherapy in recent times. In the past, treatment for such problems was at best only partially or occasionally effective. One result was that many otherwise healthy marriages were eventually destroyed when the sexual dysfunctions continued to be a problem. Today almost all types of sex dysfunction can be rapidly and effectively treated, and marital therapists should feel ethically bound to be certain their clients receive the full benefits of these improvements.

CASE EXAMPLE:
MARILYN AND JOE SWENSON

Background

The case of Marilyn and Joe Swenson illustrates how sexual complaints are frequently presenting issues but are often symptomatic of other issues. Marilyn and Joe were in their late twenties, had been married four years, and had a 1-year-old daughter. Joe called for the initial appointment. He was very anxious, and described the situation as "desperate." The Swensons arrived at the therapist's office in separate cars, symbolizing how angry they were feeling with each other. Because Joe had called for the appointment, the therapist suggested he begin the individual, confidential intake evaluation sessions by talking to Marilyn first. (Often the person making the call for the initial appointment is attempting to manipulate the situation. Seeing the other partner first frustrates this strategy and minimizes any sense of therapeutic favoritism or bias on the part of the more "reluctant" client. While this therapeutic maneuver is not always utilized, it has often proven helpful in establishing quick rapport with particularly reluctant, anxious, or fearful partners. Such a person is instantly reassured about confidentiality, quickly begins to experience the therapist's interest in him or her as a person, and rarely fails to react positively to this procedure.)

Session 1—Initial Evaluation

Individual interview: Marilyn. Marilyn looked her stated age, was neatly dressed, composed, and anxious to talk. She said she had requested therapy many months before but Joe had refused. Recently he had suggested that they see a therapist and she agreed, but left the responsibility of finding the therapist to him. Joe obtained the therapist's name from a colleague in the municipal building where he was employed as a city planner. Marilyn wasn't sure just how therapy could help, but said she was willing to explore it.

Marilyn rapidly poured out her story. Raised in a very strict Protestant home, she had done little dating as a teenager. She was the oldest of four children, and was her "Daddy's favorite little girl." Although her parents never spoke to her about sex when she was growing up, she sensed that it might be "OK" in marriage but "hell, fire, and eternal damnation" was her fate if she indulged in it premaritally, according to the religious teachings she had received.

Marilyn said she had been married soon after high school to a childhood classmate. That marriage lasted three years, ending when her first husband "ran off with another woman." She described highly ambivalent feelings about her first intercourse with her first husband. Both of them were scared, she was very tense, and for the first week of marriage penile penetration did not occur because of her tenseness and her husband's premature ejaculations. Slowly, however, the young couple relaxed, and by the beginning of their second year of marriage Marilyn was occasionally able to have an orgasm. Her husband rarely complained about their sex life and so she was very shocked when he left town with another woman, leaving behind a note for her. The note expressed his frustration with their sexual relationship, hinted that he had found sexual bliss with his new partner, and wished Marilyn well in the future.

Some months after her divorce became final she met Joe. According to Marilyn, their courtship was "one long sexual orgy" because she was determined that she wasn't going to make the "same mistake" twice. The first two years of marriage went "fine." Marilyn worked as a typist in a real estate office, had been promoted to office manager, and was happy at work and at home. Sometimes she resented the fact that Joe expected her to do all the housework and felt his own mother had "spoiled him rotten." However, she considered the marriage to be highly satisfactory.

Then came their daughter. Both wanted the child and were delighted. Marilyn took a leave of absence from work for six months, returning to work when their daughter was three months old. A very competent older woman in the neighborhood provided excellent child-care services and Marilyn was happy to return to her position as office manager. She usually did not get home from work until after 6 P.M. Meantime, she said, Joe always arrived home at 4:30, relaxed with a beer and read the paper, and never helped prepare the evening meal. She described him as an excellent father who was loving and helpful with the baby—but housework wasn't for him. She called him lazy and selfish. He expected her to put him in the number 1 spot, the baby in the number 2 spot, and her job last.

She said that Joe's big complaint was not enough sex—"That's all he wants." When he didn't get it, she said, he "pouted like a little boy, ranted and raved," and called her a "two-time loser." Marilyn said she couldn't be "superwife" and reported that she was tired and angry a lot. Recently she had moved out of the bedroom and had been sleeping on the living room couch. She was worried that she was going to stop caring for Joe if nothing changed. She saw no solution to their situation and said both of them were probably "too stubborn" to give in.

Individual interview: Joe.   Joe was seen next. He was informally but neatly dressed and, in response to the therapist's recognition, readily admitted to being very anxious and worried about his marriage. He was somewhat defensive about having refused to go for marital therapy when Marilyn first requested it, but emphasized that now he wanted help, perhaps even more than his wife did. While neither of the Swensons had had any previous therapy, Joe had a good concept of what it might entail. He hoped the therapist could help them talk to each other, respect each other, and that their sexual relationship could be improved.

Joe complained bitterly that his wife never initiated intercourse, that she put him off because she was too tired, and that currently they were not even having intercourse because she was sleeping on the living room couch. Not only had his wife displaced herself from being his bed partner, she had also developed a "screwed-up set of priorities," Joe felt. Her job came first, then the baby, and Joe was last.

Joe poured out his complaints without any mention of his and Marilyn's different schedules or his refusal to help around home with anything except some child care. He said that they were both stubborn, but he expressed resentment that he always had to be the one to give in when they argued. He firmly believed that Marilyn's long-term goal was to get him to do all the housework and child care, leaving herself more free to concentrate on her job. For his part, he said he "probably talked too much" and maybe he should expect less of her.

Conjoint interview.   When the Swensons were seen conjointly at the end of their individual sessions, the focus was on their mutual feelings and whether or not they thought the therapist could help them. Both were highly resistant to considering the other's feelings and glared at each other with hostile looks. The only thing they agreed on, when asked if they wished to discuss briefly what was troubling them, was that they "didn't communicate well." The therapist expressed a willingness to treat them but recommended that they return home and discuss treatment before they made a decision about going ahead. Conjoint treatment alone was recommended because there were no secrets, dyad interaction was going to be the main focus, and, from a practical standpoint, their finances would have made combined individual and conjoint sessions too expensive for them.

Therapist's observations.   The Swensons appeared to both be bright, articulate, and healthy persons. When angered, Marilyn's primary defense was to stop talking, cry, and retreat from her husband. Joe, on the other hand, verbally lashed out when he was angry and had long since mastered the art of hitting his wife where she was vulnerable—her "failure" in her first marriage, her sexual "coldness," and her "choosing her career over housework." Joe's mother had modeled for him the role of a traditional, homebound wife and mother who appeared to do everything for "her menfolk." While saying he respected his wife's career work, it was obvious that he resented it and the extra "burdens" it potentially put on him. He was deeply attracted to her sexually, found her a fine partner "when she was in the mood—which was rarely," and claimed to have enormous respect for her as a person.

While Marilyn was usually orgasmic when she was "in the mood," she verbalized several statements which suggested that the rigid, moralistic, antisexual teachings of her childhood continued to bother her and lead her to worry frequently about her femininity. Her husband's attacks on her sexuality served to reinforce her own preconscious doubts about herself.

While the Swensons were very hostile to each other during the sessions, the therapist's impression was that the treatment outlook for the marriage was fairly positive. The couple's severe conflicts were of relatively short duration and in their private sessions both had taken some responsibility for their problems and had also expressed hopes that the marriage would continue.

Session 2

A few days after the initial consultations, Joe called, said he and Marilyn had been talking quite a bit, and wanted to begin therapy. At the beginning of session 2 the tension level between them was very high. Both of them spent the early part trying to convince the therapist that their own roles in the marriage were "right" and that the partner was "wrong." The therapist was not caught in the triangulation attempts and handled the situation by agreeing that they had some profoundly different concepts of male–female roles.

The therapist recommended that Joe and Marilyn attempt to focus, for a starter, on some area in which they thought they might succeed. Joe immediately brought up communication. In his work as city planner he had attended several workshops given by outside consultants who had strongly encouraged total communication between persons in all their relationships. The therapist challenged Joe on this, because it sounded as if Joe were using his "Human Relationships" workshop ideas to rationalize his need to unload all his frustration and anger on Marilyn with little or no regard for what it did to her. The therapist encouraged the couple to consider the concept of selective communication, whereby they shared all their significant feelings but withheld those that were not germane to the issues or those that their partner might not be able to handle at that particular moment in time. Marilyn strongly agreed with this concept and Joe agreed to try. Shifting the discussion toward positive efforts to communicate gave Marilyn the courage to share some of her positive feelings about Joe, particularly his strong wishes for a good family life. Softened by his wife's taking the positive initiative, Joe reciprocated by saying how much he admired the way Marilyn related to people. With the tension considerably reduced between them, it was not surprising when Marilyn spontaneously offered to start sleeping with Joe again. Again he responded quickly to her initiative and, for his contribution, offered to prepare the evening meal on weekday evenings.

Therapist's observations.   This apparently rapid movement from strong anger to beginning reconciliation and compromise occurs quite frequently in marital therapy with couples for whom the severe symptoms have not existed for a long time and where both still have a major psychological and caring interest in the marriage. Here the therapist is often performing the role of a catalyst, one who provides a neutral setting and a framework that permits and accelerates the healing process. It is also significant that sex was hardly mentioned in the second session; both Marilyn and Joe were guided by the therapist to the more fundamental issues troubling them.

Session 3

By the next week both Swensons reported that they were much happier. Their sexual "problems" had all but disappeared, although both recognized that maybe the improvement was only temporary. Their overall adjustment had improved dramatically immediately after the second session—but then quickly regressed over another issue, one of separate identities and control. They had started a major discussion of their finances, and Joe felt they should destroy all of their credit cards. Marilyn refused to do this and he was furious. Neither one would consider the other's feelings.

The therapist encouraged Marilyn and Joe to consider an opposite approach, one in which they both tried to emphasize total giving to the partner (one must give in order to receive). In the ordinary process of relationships, such selfless giving tends to bring reciprocal rewards. Joe said he was willing to try this but Marilyn hesitated. Discussion revealed that she feared Joe would exploit her. Her worry was directly tied to what she called his sexual exploitation of her. As long as she gave him lots of sex, she said, he was happy—but he didn't give *her* anything special. Joe listened intently as Marilyn brought out her feelings and worries. He appeared to vacillate between wanting to deny what she was saying and, on the other hand, beginning to genuinely listen to her deeply felt feelings. Sensing this latter feeling on Joe's part, the therapist quickly moved in to support and encourage this beginning move on Joe's part to consider his wife on a more equal basis.

Therapist's observations.   Again in this session we see how marital therapists must be active, not passive. They must be prepared to champion efforts by either or both partners that appear to be constructive. Strict therapeutic neutrality is abandoned in favor of supporting positive principles of human interaction.

Session 4

The Swensons started this session by saying that things had gone well during the past week. They had both tried the therapist's idea of selfless giving and each was delighted with the results. However, while driving to the therapist's office, regression had occurred. Joe had said the marital therapy hadn't been necessary after all. If he had just given in to Marilyn, as he had originally charged, everything would have been smooth—except that he would have hated himself.

Marilyn reacted typically. She cried, refused to talk, and said it was "hopeless." The therapist pointed out their rapid improvement, their regression, and explained that the process of giving up control and risking oneself with one's partner rarely proceeds entirely smoothly. Somewhat reassured by this, the Swensons moved ahead to once again discuss their sexual frequency differences. Marilyn verbalized her recognition that intercourse meant so much to Joe—and to herself—but she also attempted to get him to understand and accept that she could not immediately believe that he really cared about her, in contrast to merely needing her body. With much support from the therapist, she clearly explained to her husband what fatigue did to her sexual feelings and, perhaps even more importantly, how she needed to experience equality with him in order to feel sexual toward him. Here the therapist strongly supported Joe's efforts to be patient, to actually hear his wife's feelings, and to begin to emotionally accept the fact that Marilyn was not his mother, that she would not act sexual with him as a "duty," and that he could actually feel better toward himself, as well as toward Marilyn, when he was able to treat her differently in many spheres of their life.

Session 5

During this session the Swensons again said that they had experienced improvement and then regression during the week. Joe had been angry at Marilyn because she did not appear to be very sympathetic about his complaints concerning the newly elected mayor, who Joe believed was making his work as a city planner almost a waste of time. The therapist used the session primarily to help Joe tell Marilyn how hurt he had been by her seeming indifference to him—and to do it in a way that was responsible (many "I" statements) and nonattacking. Marilyn responded very sympathetically to Joe's job frustrations and also apologized to him for not having "heard" him at home. Hearing this, Joe apologized to her for not having taken the responsibility to get his feelings known. (What was happening here was that the Swensons were both taking more responsibility for their interactions and for not having handled the situation as maturely and as constructively as they might have. Both seemed more comfortable about taking responsibility for their feelings.) In the remainder of the session, both Marilyn and Joe made themselves more vulnerable to the other by sharing many of their hopes, fears, and plans for doing things that made the other feel more valued.

Session 6

This was the last session for the Swensons. They brought up the subject of ending therapy almost as soon as they were seated in the therapist's office. They were both feeling very good about themselves and about each other. Joe poked fun at himself for having complained so loudly about being "sexually deprived" by Marilyn. He felt he had learned many things from her and from the therapist that "totally" changed his ideas about sex. He still valued it strongly, but said he saw it now as part of their total relationship. He said he valued Marilyn's feelings for him even more than he did her sexual responsiveness.

Marilyn was also in a reflective mood. She shared the fears she had had initially that she would lose all her feelings for her husband if he continued to be so sexually demanding but so insensitive to her need for more help around home, and for more equality in their relationship. Both of them felt that while problems would undoubtedly arise again in the future, they had developed methods of communicating, of negotiating, and of compromising that would enable them to handle these. They also knew they could return to the therapist in the future if they felt the need for more help.

SUMMARY

The Swenson case demonstrates how a couple's arguments over sexual frequency are often part of a power struggle—a struggle for control, for having one's omnipotence needs satisfied, and for maintaining one's self-respect and integrity. The Swensons came from families that were very different in the way they indoctrinated their children concerning sexual relations and sex roles. At the time of termination of therapy Marilyn and Joe were not "cured" as persons or as a couple. They had, however, achieved a better level of marital and sexual interaction, a level with which they were satisfied. While there was considerable risk of regression for them due to the relatively short period of their improvement, their wishes to end the treatment were respected. Marital therapy ordinarily is short-term treatment. Its goals are more apt to involve more effective functioning than the achievement of total insight and personality reorganization. Thus the Swenson case might be rated as both typical and successful in its outcome.

CHAPTER FIVE
MARITAL COMMUNICATION PROBLEMS

BACKGROUND: THE ROLE OF COMMUNICATIONS IN MARITAL INTERACTION

Clear, positive, congruent communications between a husband and a wife are a necessary ingredient for the establishment and maintenance of a successful marriage. Human beings have many expectations of marriage. They expect to receive and experience love, caring, respect, concern, validation, and a host of other feelings and emotions with their partners. In order for this to occur, the need for these essential components must be communicated from one person to the other and acknowledged by the receiver. Marital therapists should be aware that every single one of these communication transactions involves (a) a sender, (b) a receiver, and (c) a message.

Happily married couples, as compared to those with a troubled relationship, talk to each other more, demonstrate more understanding and sensitivity to the partner's needs and feelings, communicate more readily and openly, and more often back up their verbal messages with congruent nonverbal ones. In order to carry out his or her share of the marital relationship, each partner must know the other's feelings, wishes, and needs. Even though traditional romantic myth suggests that every bride and groom is somehow magically and permanently endowed with a sixth sense that enables both partners to instantly and always understand the other, without the partner so much as having to utter a word, marital therapists should know better.

The Communication Loop

Marital communicative interaction may be illustrated by the following diagram:

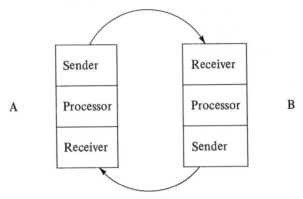

Person A has a message for person B. A sends this message to B. B receives the message, "processes" it, and reciprocates by sending a message back to A, completing the transaction. In Chapter Two this communication process was compared to messages being sent between two walkie-talkie radios. The mind, emotions, and physical sending and receiving apparatus of human beings, however, are far more complicated than are any electronic devices. To illustrate, human beings' "transmitters," "receivers," and "processors" have both conscious and unconscious portions. What person A consciously believes she told her partner or heard her partner say may, in fact, be diametrically opposed to what the unconscious (latent, "real") message actually was. This may come about because of interferences with the way A sent the message (e.g., voice too soft, ambiguous wording), interferences with the actual transmission (e.g., crying baby, telephone ringing), interferences with B's receptive mechanism (e.g., preoccupation with another matter, belief that A is always "jabbering" and hence not worthy of attentive listening). Or there may be no interference whatsoever—B may receive the message accurately, but he may have unconsciously distorted the message—for example, as a result of his earlier experiences with A or with other (females) (wives). Then, on the "feedback" portion of this loop system, similar interferences may occur in B's sending abilities, with transmission interferences between B and A, and with A's receptors and psychic apparatus. In fact, when one ponders the multiplicity of potential problems and interferences with even the simplest form of marital message (such as "Hi, how have you been today?"), one can see that a complicated message (such as "Maybe I'll like you better if you guess what I'd like to do this evening") can easily lead to disaster—or at least to misunderstanding. Yet marital partners must know how their mates feel if they can respond to them in a manner that is congruent with their own *and* their partner's feelings, wishes, and needs. Marriage always involves reciprocity. How, what, and how often A communicates feelings to B play a vital role in how B will experience A; this, in turn, is a determinant of how B will reciprocate and feel toward A. Love of one's mate does little good for the relationship if this love is not shared between the partners in ways that each can clearly see, hear, understand, feel, and respond to positively.

The importance of message contents.   At the same time, therapists sometimes naively appear to believe that satisfactory methods of communication solve all relationship problems. Nothing could be further from the truth. If a husband clearly and openly communicates "I hate your guts" to his wife, he may be an excellent communicator but he is also helping to destroy the wife's feelings for him and simultaneously to assist in ending the marriage. The role of communication in marriage, therefore, lies not only in the establishment and continuation of clear patterns and methods of communication, but also in the *content* of what is communicated. The content must be, on balance, primarily positive—for both the sender and the receiver. It must affirm, support, validate, and enhance the partner's self-esteem. It must do so initially in the marriage and it must continue to do so over the entire lifetime of the relationship.

As each partner's needs change over time, so also must the communications between the couple. Early in marriage partners seek repetitive protestations of love, of sexual longing, and of deep intimacy. As the partners mature and become more comfortable with themselves, with each other, and with the relationship, the messages often shift toward expressions of caring, of friendship, and of the joy of sharing. Always, however, married individuals must depend upon their ability to communicate these messages to their partners in order for the relationship to be sustained. Feelings kept to oneself and not shared with the partner are, in some respects, wasted feelings. Even if they are loving ones, the partner cannot guess them and feed back his or her own caring. If they are angry feelings, the partner cannot understand them if they are not shared and hence cannot take potential steps to rectify the anger-producing situation.

Verbal and nonverbal messages.   Human beings communicate both verbally and nonverbally. There must be congruence between these two major types of communication or the receiver will be confused by possible double meanings. Witness the wife who shouts, at the end of a long argument about finances, "Go ahead and buy that lousy sports car—I couldn't care less!" Where are her eyes directed? What is her body position? What does her facial expression suggest? Her words appear to say to her husband "Go ahead and buy the car you want; I don't mind"—but her nonverbal cues probably reinforce her tone of voice and convey her anger and disapproval. If he buys the car, he loses because she will be even more angry. If he doesn't buy the car, he can't complain because his wife verbally "agreed" to the purchase. This phenomenon has often been called the double-bind situation. Poor communication methods, especially those that contain elements of inconsistency, can be very harmful to a married couple.

FOUNDATIONS
OF COMMUNICATION STYLES
AND PATTERNS

The Influence of Parents
and Social Systems

The foundations of every individual's communication patterns and abilities are laid down in their formative childhood years. Parents have a very important role in determining how verbal or nonverbal their children will be in their communications. Children raised by taciturn, stoic, New England Yankee-type parents of the Calvin Coolidge genre may verbalize much less than children born to excitable, highly verbal parents. As children grow, numerous other social systems influence their communication patterns; those of race, ethnic origin, religion, socioeconomic class, educational milieu, and gender all are especially influential. Persons who marry other individuals from their own social groupings are more likely to experience fewer barriers to clear communications in their relationship than are those who marry someone from a distinctly dissimilar background. In the United States, however, there is considerable intergroup marriage. Every one of these "mixed" marriages must surmount the differences that often exist in the partners' differential use of both verbal and nonverbal communications.

Gender stereotyping. All couples in heterosexual marriages must overcome at least one socially influenced communication barrier—that imposed by one's gender. The stereotype so often portrayed in nursery rhymes, literature, drama, and other areas of the mass media is that females are more verbal than males. Not only are females expected to be more verbal in general, they are also reputed to be more verbal than males are about emotions such as love, caring, and tenderness. In her courtship days a woman may tolerate the man's reluctance to talk about "soft things" such as love and tenderness, but when they are married she expects him to gradually accommodate to her need to hear his spoken words of affection. Men, on the other hand, are stereotypically raised to be tough, demanding, and reticent about voicing "weak" feelings—such as caring ones. These conflicting gender-linked differences in communication styles between husbands and wives thus become frequent sources of disappointment and conflict in marriage.

Sometimes the gender-linked discrepancies are further exacerbated by such things as personality characteristics and employment roles. Marital therapists employed in geographical areas in which there are large concentrations of scientists, such as in the aerospace industry, frequently see the "cold, rational, calculating" male engineer married to the "tender, warm, needy, emotional" wife. The husband fails to talk to his wife enough, and with sufficient sensitivity, to please her; the wife infuriates her husband with her "incessant chatter" and her seemingly constant need to be told that she is loved, sexy, a great wife, and so forth. He tries to communicate his love by working hard, making a good income, being faithful to her, and expressing himself in other ways that he perceives to be characteristic of a "red-blooded American male." She often receives these messages as confirmation of his inattentiveness, of his placing his job before their marriage, and of his being too sexually demanding. It is difficult to know how well these stereotyped conflicts represent the majority of marriages, but one thing is clear—marital therapists hear a lot about them.

C.V.S.—COMMUNICATION VALUE SYSTEMS

An important element in effective marital communication is the issue of congruence in C.V.S.—Communication Value Systems. Earlier it was pointed out that every human being has his or her own unique S.V.S.—Sexual Value System—and that it must function in relative harmony with that of the partner in order for the couple to have a good sexual relationship. The same holds true for Communication Value Systems. Just as Sexual Value Systems have to be "adequately" balanced, so too do the couple's Communication Value Systems. Couple A love to talk for hours to each other; while couple B, on the other hand, only rarely desire to carry on long conversations and verbalized sharing. Both couples can be considered well-matched, happily married pairs. But if Mr. A had married Mrs. B or visa versa, chances are that numerous complaints would have rapidly surfaced: "my spouse never talks to me"; or "how do you shut up a motor mouth!" Numerous studies indicate that there is a positive correlation of similarity in a couple's values and marital success—and this includes similarities in communication value systems. Repeatedly, couples tell their marital therapist things like, "we probably represent the old adage that opposites attract," thus explaining how Mr. Talker happened to marry Ms. Quiet. The therapist could realistically reply that opposites may indeed attract—but that they often "wear" very poorly. Differing communication systems and styles typically result in marital conflicts. Treatment of troubled couples must be addressed to helping them gain insight into their different styles, into the messages being conveyed, and finally, into either some self-initiated changes or some accommodations to the partner, or a combination of the two healing processes.

MARITAL SHORTHAND

Description and strengths. "Marital shorthand" is a term developed by Clark Vincent to illustrate the communications process (both verbal and nonverbal) that usually develops between marital partners after long exposure to each other. It is a result of the gradual learning process which permits two people to share complex messages between themselves with a minimum of verbal and/or nonverbal messages (Vincent 1973). For example, suppose Mr. and Mrs. Maydoit usually have intercourse only after they go to bed in the evening. If Mrs. Maydoit winks at Mr.

Maydoit as she heads for the bedroom at 10:55 P.M. and says, "Feel like coming to bed with me now?" she is probably saying "I'd like to have sex with you tonight." Without the wink, the message could be "I'm tired, I don't feel like going to bed alone. I would like your company there—but don't expect any sex tonight." If the husband understands the subtle difference the wink has introjected into the statement, he is proficient at marital shorthand.

Marital shorthand may also enable couples to "fence" with each other without openly admitting what they are doing. For example, after Mrs. Maydoit delivers her message and her wink, Mr. Maydoit may leap into action and follow her to the bedroom. Or, delighted with her message but wishing to savor the pleasure of her interest in him, he may reply "OK—I'll be there as soon as I finish this story I'm reading," meaning, "Let me enjoy how nice it is to have you want me by getting you to give me another message like that—but I don't want to really admit to this enjoyment so I'll feign some mild indifference." If Mrs. Maydoit is adept at marital shorthand she will understand that her husband's seeming indifference is not that at all but is a little game that he likes to play with her; thus she will coax him again to join her. If, on the other hand, she is not a good shorthand reader, she may very well feel rejected or, at the very least, assume he is not interested in sex that evening. Marital shorthand thus may function to assist couples in their communication processes and to minimize the need for extensive verbal interchanges.

Potential dangers.   At least two dangers exist with marital shorthand, however. One danger is that some partners may enjoy sending or receiving long, complex messages and resent the fact that their partners always seem to communicate in "shorthand" and say very little. This is exemplified by mismatched communication styles in a couple. The "talker" complains that the "shorthand" type is a virtual noncommunicator while the "shorthand" person complains that the talkative partner is an insufferable chatterbox. Another danger is that the opportunity for misunderstanding between the partners is high if one of them suddenly abandons the usual "rules" governing the marital shorthand process and attempts to convey a totally different message than the partner interprets them to mean. For example, in the second example given above, when Mr. Maydoit says he will join his wife as soon as he finished the story he was reading, he may have meant precisely that—and appeared in the bedroom an hour later to find a frustrated and angry wife. It is evident that Mrs. Maydoit could have averted this unfortunate occurrence by issuing another message to "check out" or insure that her husband received her first message accurately. However, people often resent having to send their messages repeatedly. Had Mr. Maydoit admonished his wife for not sending him a second message when he failed to quickly follow her to bed, she might have declared "You knew damned well what I meant—do I have to beg you?" Here we have a miscommunication, frustration developing followed by anger, and a common—but unnecessary—marital spat occurring over failures to communicate clearly and adequately.

SOCIAL ROLES AND
COMMUNICATION PATTERNS

In every marriage both husband and wife simultaneously occupy a number of roles. The wife, for example, is a person, a female, career person, wife, mother, lover, the household financial wizard, a cook, and so on. The husband also occupies multiple roles. Conflict may develop, however, when either party slips out of the role he or she is in at the moment and takes on, or appears to take on, the communication style of a different role. When the husband throws his socks on the floor as he undresses and the wife rebukes him, he may reply, "Quit talking to me as if I were your son. I'm your husband, not your son!" Perhaps his behavior is childish and inconsiderate, or perhaps his wife really spoke to him in a too-maternal fashion; but the problem comes because he expects his wife to address him in his roles as individual, male, adult, husband—not as a child. When a husband is employed in an authority role, such as a policeman, a military officer, or vice president of sales, he may fail to drop his authority role when he is dealing with his wife, thus creating great resentment in her. Obviously, identical situations exist when a female company president similarly reverts to her managerial role when she is at home interacting with her husband. People set up expectations of communication patterns for the different roles they and their partners occupy. Failure to communicate appropriately for these roles can be a common cause of marital conflict.

ASSESSING COMMUNICATION
PROBLEMS

One of the most common reasons clients cite for consulting a marital therapist is that they have "communication problems." It is important that the therapist assess what this complaint means to each of the partners and he or she also understand its etiology. Broadly speaking, communication problems may occur because adequate communications were never established in the marriage; they were established but later broke down; or because there were outside influences that interfered with them.

Failure to Establish Good
Communication Patterns

The failure to ever establish good communication patterns may arise from the inability of the husband or of the wife to communicate with *anyone*—not just the marital partner (an individual problem); or it may derive from the husband's and wife's basic failure to communicate with each other (a relationship problem). Persons who bring widely divergent communication value systems into their marriage may have great difficulty in ever establishing good communications with each other.

Distortions of sent and received messages. Individuals handicapped by excessive insecurities and low self-esteem, for example, often feel, both consciously and unconsciously, unworthy of having their feelings and messages heard by significant others. They have difficulty understanding messages from other persons accurately and, in addition, they often are not aware of the true nature of their own feelings. Thus the poor communication cycle is completed when they send discrepant, confusing, and inappropriate messages to others.

On the receiving end, a person with low self-esteem may be incapable of accurately perceiving others' messages; a combination of unconscious defenses, training, and total life experiences may lead such an individual to distort incoming messages with absolutely no insight into what he or she is doing. Frequently, an ineffective or dysfunctional communicator is so burdened by past events in his or her life that he or she experiences great difficulty in believing that present messages can be positive, accepting, and caring. The marital partner of such a person is not the only one to experience difficulty and frustration in coping with the person; other family members such as parents, children, and siblings are similarly affected. This person perceives others and their messages in a distorted way.

In planning treatment for couples who have never established good communication patterns, the therapist should reserve a portion of treatment time for work that is individually focused on the person(s) with the difficulty. The therapist will probably not be able to help the couple improve their marital relationship until both persons have overcome individual communication problems. One question the therapist should take into consideration in the assessment process is, "Would this person have trouble communicating no matter who they married?" If the answer is yes, either individual therapy with the person is indicated or a type of conjoint therapy should be offered that is directed toward supporting growth and increased capacity for the partners to communicate, first as *individuals* and later as marital partners.

Breakdown of Constructive
Communication Patterns

The second major area of communication problems in marriage stems from a couple's failure to maintain good communication patterns as the months and years pass by. Cynics have suggested adding another line to marriage vows: "I take you for better, I take you for worse, and I take you for granted." This latter element of one partner taking the other for granted often reflects a communications breakdown.

Boredom. Probably one of the greatest enemies of successful marriage is monotony. As time passes couples may use marital shorthand excessively. There are no more secrets. Exciting new developments occur only rarely. Boredom sets in, with accompanying apathy, depression, and dullness. Such partners may stop communicating except about essential matters. In other marriages, communication patterns may break down as a result of one or both partners simply losing their capacity or their willingness to communicate clearly and functionally.

Repetitive faulty communication.   Another major cause of communication breakdowns stems from repeated experiences with faulty communication patterns. One of the most common of these destructive patterns is the process of "mind-reading"—one persons thinks he or she knows what is in the other's mind without checking it out with that person. This is often vividly portrayed in the therapist's office when one spouse habitually speaks for the other one. When one partner is more verbal and more domineering than the other, the couple is especially vulnerable to this syndrome.

Therapist's goals usually include helping husbands and wives develop a better understanding of the partner's feelings, thoughts, and needs. Mind-reading, however, involves *faulty* understanding of the partner, unwillingness to consider the partner's wishes and needs, or, most destructively, deliberate distortions of the partner's thoughts, needs, and intentions. Partners whose minds are being "read" by their mates usually bitterly resent this violation of their integrity. They may fight back with statements such as, "Don't you dare tell me how *I* feel"; or, over time, they may passively submit to the process with a resigned attitude of "What's the use of telling my partner—he or she knows it all anyway." Mind-readers are often prone to global and total accusations like "She *always* . . . " and "He never. . . . " Such statements need to be carefully assessed and ultimately challenged by the therapist.

Perhaps less dramatic than mind-reading but equally damaging is the failure of people to act on the partner's communications constructively. In these cases the communications themselves are accurately sent and received but there is repeated failure by the receiver to do anything about the message. In due time the sender gradually stops sending, since nothing of consequence is accomplished. This problem is similar to the passive acceptance described above except that in this case the sender knows his or her message is sent, received, and understood—but that is the end of the transaction. The receiver fails to "process" the message and complete the final portion of the interaction by responding appropriately to the sender's wish or feeling. Again, partners describe attitudes of resignation: "I've told him or her a million times about this . . . and nothing ever happens, so I just quit even trying to tell him or her."

Breakdown of Communication
Because of Outside Interference

Finally, assessment should examine whether marital communication has broken down due to interferences external to the couple themselves. The pressures exerted by children, time, careers, illness, household schedules, and the like can be included as causes of such interferences. Many of these interferences are normal occurrences in marriage, but they must be successfully coped with or they can cause marital communications to break down.

Children.   Children are a graphic example of this type of hazard. Certainly the majority of American couples desire children and place parenthood high on their lists of priorities. However, there is virtually no preparation given to young parents to help them realize that children can easily come between the parents in numerous ways. Young mothers, indoctrinated since their own first year of life with the expectation that they will deeply involve themselves with their children's lives, devote enormous amounts of time, energy, and attention to their infants. This is ordinarily time, energy, and attention that had hitherto been largely available to their husbands. It is not surprising that a husband often reacts negatively to this, since his own preparation for parenthood is likely to have been similarly lacking in some of the less glamorous facts of life about parenthood. Often, communications from the children appear to rate a higher priority in the wife's mind than communications from the husband. An example of this occurs when a couple's lovemaking is interrupted by a crying baby. Immediately the wife's sexual and maternal training leads her to become distracted; she suffers a loss of sexual interest, communicating what the husband feels is a "you and sex come after the baby" message. Sexually frustrated, the husband may attempt to persuade his wife that the baby's cries mean nothing and that their lovemaking should continue—or he may erupt with anger and impatience. The couple's original communication of making love—that of caring, intimacy, and libidinal need—has been negatively interfered with by the intrusion of their baby's cries. By themselves, incidents such as this hardly present a threat to a stable marriage. Their cumulative effect, however, can be devastating. Such intrusions into husband-wife communications constitute common and expectable hazards to marital happiness and stability in all marriages, but are especially devastating to marriages that are already experiencing problems in other facets of the relationship besides the area of communication.

SELECTIVE COMMUNICATION

The "Let It All Hang Out" Ethic

Earlier in the book, note was made of the fact that many modern couples have become intellectually aware of the need for good communication in human relationships. It was also noted that many couples—and many therapists—have misconstrued this message to mean that "more" always means "best." Popular belief has become that *all* of one's thoughts, feelings, and needs *must* be expressed to one's partner or somehow the individual is being "untrue" to him- or herself by neurotically repressing "real" (hence presumably valid) feelings and, at the same time, is letting the partner down by failing to be "honest."

This type of a belief system, frequently referred to as the "let it all hang out" ethic, appears to be little more than an intellectual excuse for impulsive, immature, narcissistic gratification of one's Id impulses. It utterly fails to consider the potential consequences of one's verbalizations on another person. It has repeatedly been emphasized here that marriage involves a reciprocal, interdependent relationship between two persons. Because of the reciprocal nature of this relationship, each person bears a level of responsibility for the partner's feelings toward him or her.

Hence, both partners must bear some responsibility for *what* they communicate as well as how they share it. One of the goals of socializing young children is to help them acquire the ability and the willingness to consider what impact their "messages" have on others. The "let it all hang out" ethic encourages adults to regress to the earliest stages of childhood, back before the Ego and the Superego had developed sufficiently to enable children to assume much responsibility for their own actions and decisions.

When, How, and What
to Communicate Selectively

What is needed in adult marital relationships is the communication of all significant feelings and needs to one's partner, but in a *selective fashion.* The sender must "select" *when* to communicate, *how* to communicate, and *what* to communicate. This requires, first of all, that the timing of the message must be considered. If the receiver is already under severe stress, he or she may become overburdened by difficult or threatening communications. Similarly, if he or she is already distracted by other concerns (worries, excitement), he or she may be incapable of "hearing" the messages. The *method* of conveying the message also needs to be selective. This may involve tone of voice, choice of words, use of appropriate nonverbal signals, and so forth. The method used often determines whether a message will be perceived as an attack or as a genuine statement of the sender's feelings. For instance, the use of "I" statements often prevents a feeling on the part of the receiver that he or she has been attacked, and thus mitigates the creation of instant defensiveness. Compare "You don't give a damn about my feelings" with "I feel as if you are totally uninterested in my feelings." The first statement attacks and uses inflammatory words. The second lets the receiver know that the sender is taking responsibility for the message and is communicating a troubled feeling rather than delivering an accusation. This permits the receiver far greater latitude in considering the issue ("He is telling me that he thinks I don't consider his feelings . . . "). And, because it is nonaccusatory, the possibility is increased that the receiver will be able or willing to do something constructive about the situation instead of having to expend all of his or her energy on defending him- or herself from the sender's attack (". . . so I'd better make sure I give him more attention and listen more carefully to him").

How much to tell. Perhaps the most controversial issue in selective communication concerns *what* to communicate. We have stressed that marriage requires clear, open communications and that it is important for each marital partner to accurately perceive how the other one feels about him or her. Speaking of selectively choosing *what* to communicate may therefore appear to be a contradiction in terms of the necessity of accurate understanding of one's partner. There are numerous times in the history of many (most?) marital relationships, however, when the withholding of certain facts or feelings may prove, in the long run, to be beneficial to the relationship. Clearly one of these instances involves extramarital affairs or sometimes even the thought of extramarital affairs. Does honesty with one's partner demand that *every* feeling, impulse, and fantasy be shared? Every time a husband or wife has a fantasy about having sex with another person, should this result in a disclosure to the partner? Will this disclosure please the partner? Worry him or her? Cause anger? Be offensive? What is the sender's purpose in providing such disclosures? The sharing of information? The relief of guilt? The deliberate imposition of hurt? It appears difficult to defend all of these disclosures, especially when they add nothing positive to the relationship and may, in fact, damage it. On the other hand, if extramarital sexual fantasies occupy the majority of a person's time, or if a partner becomes obsessively absorbed with thoughts of a person outside the marriage—or if we are not discussing fantasies at all but are dealing with a *real* extramarital affair—then the issue of selecting *what* to communicate takes on a very different dimension. Even if an affair is being conducted by one of the partners, however, the issue of *when*—if *ever*—this information should be shared for the sake of the marital relationship is highly debatable, as was discussed in Chapter Three.

THERAPEUTIC CONSIDERATIONS

The Therapist as Catalyst and Mediator

In treating marital couples who are experiencing communication problems, there are many roles or functions that the therapist may perform. A common role for the therapist is that of catalyst and mediator. As a catalyst, the therapist helps the process of communication to be resumed or carried on. The therapist's office conveys an atmosphere of neutrality and this may be all that is required for the resumption of communications. The therapist in the mediation role guarantees that each person will have his or her message heard and considered. This may require considerable activity on the therapist's part, including the forceful use of his or her authority role when one partner refuses to even consider the other one's message. It may also involve having the therapist introduce new thoughts or considerations into the messages being shared, especially if this appears to be needed to lower the level of attacks. The therapist, principally through verbalization, encourages rapport, the lowering and elimination of barriers such as name-calling, the dropping of pretenses and phoniness. He or she encourages each partner to listen to the other before responding.

Sometimes couples feel that therapists are truly magicians. "Dr. Humphrey suddenly had us really *talking* to each other, something we've never been able to do on our own." At least part of the credit for this "magic" must go to the fact that therapists usually do not enter into the lives of their marital clients until one—and it is hoped, both—partners make an effort to understand themselves, the issues, and the partner better. This is what sets the stage for better communications; the skill of the therapist has helped the partners help themselves.

The Therapist as Positive Model

In addition to the verbalizations of the therapist, one must also consider that person's role as a model to couples of good, clear, effective, open communication. This part of the therapy process goes on continuously on both the clients' conscious and unconscious levels of awareness. People who cannot communicate clearly themselves certainly will make ineffective marital therapists. Through the unconscious process of identification, clients who feel positively toward their therapists try to emulate and copy him or her in many areas, including that of communication patterns. When they experience the therapist as an excellent listener, they have a real, immediate, and positive reaction themselves and hence can gain insight into why their partners desire this experience.

During conjoint interviewing, the therapist can model openness with both of the partners. This often leads one of them to say to the other, "Why can't you listen to me the way the therapist does?" This may be a question, or it may be an accusation. The therapist can exploit its positive potential by helping both partners examine why they "can't" act like the therapist does and increase their understanding of what each one needs in order to share with the other. Or, if the therapist detects that the remark is an accusation, the "sender" can be helped to achieve insight into how, through manner and choice of words, he or she may be defeating the very thing he or she claims to want.

The Therapist's Role as Educator/Coach

An additional role for the therapist in dealing with communication problems is that of educator and "coach." Readings may be assigned on the subject if the therapist knows of some that are highly relevant to the couple's problems. More commonly, the therapist educates and provides the couple with insights about themselves, about the complicated process of communication, and about what is going on between them that is interfering with effective communication. The therapist then, within the reality of the interview (particularly the conjoint interview), "coaches" the couple in implementing their newly acquired knowledge. The therapist lends support and encourages the couple to take part in constructive acts of communication, and he or she discourages negative types of communication. Learning proceeds most rapidly and is most effectively retained when it occurs in a real-life situation—and the therapy session presents a continuous flow of such opportunities. Therapists who have been labeled as "communications therapists" spend most of their time with clients working on helping them to learn and acquire these new abilities to communicate (Satir 1964).

The importance of feedback. Perhaps one of the *most* vital aspects in teaching about the communication process concerns feedback—the verbal and nonverbal messages that "receivers" are taught to send to ensure that the transaction has been completed plus, quite often, to "check out" some aspect of the sender's message that lacked clarity. As recommended in Chapter Two, the author sometimes utilizes the technique of "pseudo-stupidity" with clients in order to enhance the process of checking out messages.* The therapist "acts" stupid or uncomprehending when he or she receives confusing messages and deliberately makes the sender repeat the messages until they come across with utmost clarity. This technique serves both to increase the clarity of the communication and emphasize the content of the message. Regardless of the techniques or specific therapeutic mechanisms being emphasized, the goal of marital treatment of communication problems is always the same—to help couples establish or to re-establish and then to maintain adequate mechanisms of communication between themselves.

INTERVIEWING TECHNIQUES
AND SPECIALIZED EQUIPMENT

Conjoint, Group, and Individual
Therapy Sessions

Treatment approaches to communication problems in marriage may utilize all types of interviewing modalities, but conjoint and group therapy are felt to be particularly helpful. Both methods permit the therapist to model, to "check out," and to work with the couple together "in vivo" as communication problems actually arise. Group marital therapy, particularly if it is conjoint group therapy (also known as marital couple group therapy), has the added advantage, as discussed in Chapter One, of giving a couple multiple models of communication to emulate, observe, and learn from.

Use of an opposite-sex co-therapist.   Many therapists performing group marital therapy utilize a co-therapist who is ordinarily a member of the opposite sex, thus enhancing even further the opportunities for both marital partners to observe constructive and congruent communication patterns between men and women.

The use of individual sessions, on an alternative basis with the conjoint or group approaches, should not be overlooked. If an individual client is highly resistant to change in conjoint or group sessions, seeing him or her in a private, confidential session may prove to be both diagnostically revealing and therapeutically rewarding. Undisclosed secrets or major sources of psychological blocking often can be worked with more productively in the privacy and the protected atmosphere of an individual session. In addition, the individual session often permits the therapist to confront the client in a fashion that is contraindicated in conjoint or group sessions. Examples of this might be when the therapist sees progress hampered be-

---

*While the origin of this term is obscure, the author believes it was originated by Hilda S. Goodwin, DSW, formerly on the staff of Marriage Council of Philadelphia and now a private practitioner in West Chester, Pennsylvania.

cause of apparent faulty communications which the therapist knows, from earlier individual sessions, to be due to high levels of ambivalence (such as may occur when secret extramarital sexual affairs are involved). Another example is when the therapist believes it would be inappropriate to confront a client in front of his or her spouse because the relationship between the marital partners, at that particular point in time, would be damaged rather than helped by the confrontation.

Use of Electronic Recording Devices

Electronic recording devices are considered by some therapists to be especially helpful in dealing with communication problems in marriage. Both audio- and videotaping are often employed in these cases. Videotaping is far more expensive than is audiotaping, but it has the additional advantage of enabling the therapist to work on the couple's nonverbal as well as their verbal communications.

Characteristically, an entire session, or at least a portion of one, is taped. The therapist reviews the tape before the next therapy session and makes notes of sections that highlight specific communications issues. The tape is played back to the couple at their next session so they can obtain first-hand, objective evidence of their own communication patterns—both positive and negative.

Many therapists believe that the use of videotaping is of special value in reducing projection, in teaching more effective communication skills, and in diagnosing dysfunctional patterns. There are numerous variations of precisely when, where, and how audio- and videotaping are used. Training programs in family therapy have made extensive use of this medium and most of these techniques can be directly adapted with the smaller, two-person marital dyad.

CASE EXAMPLE:
GUS AND PAM FRANKEL

Background

Gus and Pam Frankel illustrate many of the issues encountered in performing marital therapy with couples having communication troubles. The Frankels came to therapy for problems in numerous areas of their relationship, but in this narrative we shall concentrate primarily on issues that repeatedly involved their dysfunctional communications. It is uncommon to see couples whose *only* problem is that of communications and the Frankels were no exception to this. They were referred to the therapist by Gus's former therapist, a psychiatrist who only performed individual psychotherapy. He had treated Gus two years earlier for phobias, the most disabling of which had been a fear of flying. This had seriously interfered with his work as a computer programmer because his company had expected him to travel extensively. Treatment had been successful through the individual therapy and, in addition, changes in his work assignment no longer required him to travel very often. When Gus called his former therapist for help with his and Pam's marital difficulties, they were referred to the author.

Session 1—Initial Evaluation

Individual interview: Pam. Pam, age 26, was a slender, attractive young woman who was currently completing her master's degree in Anthropology. She was unsure about the marriage and listed the major problem as "poor communications." She described Gus as an "intelligent, reserved, noncommunicative, dependable, honest, nice guy" who was nonresponsive to her needs and rarely talked to her. He liked to read and listen to music; she liked to socialize with friends. She loved to dance and play tennis; he was essentially nonathletic. She had recently become very attracted to a fellow graduate student, but stated it was not "an affair."

Pam felt she meant little to her husband. They had been married for six years and he had told her he loved her "not more than eight times." She also complained that he was not very physically demonstrative. There were no problems with sexual performance, but their rate of intercourse was low. Whenever she tried to talk to him about her feelings, he showed resentment. Recently when she had told him she was considering a divorce, Gus appeared shocked and offered strong statements of love for her. He felt she was reacting to her lack of career plans after she received her Master's degree and that their marriage was "OK."

Pam said she was lonely and sick of subjugating her interests to those of her husband. In essence, she felt cut off from him and believed it was probably best for her own sake to get out of the marriage.

Individual interview: Gus. Gus, age 31, was a neat-appearing individual whose pot belly gave away his dislike of exercise. Marital therapy, he said, had been his wife's idea and he had been shocked when she suggested it. He had thought their marriage was better than those of many of their "screwed-up" friends and so when Pam expressed doubt about whether she loved him anymore, he was surprised. He realized he wasn't the "lovey-dovey" type. He loved sex but "didn't go much" for hugging and kissing.

Gus then discussed his individual therapy experience, describing how helpful it had been, but also suggesting that the fact that he valued great self-control was partially a defense against becoming phobic again. He also acknowledged that there was a major personality and cultural heritage difference between himself and Pam.

He described himself as hard-working, loyal, compromising, and very patient in light of his wife's tendency to flit off in different directions in regard to her studies and her hobbies. He said it wasn't easy for him to verbalize his emotions. "If something is obvious, why talk about it?" Gus claimed he had "no emotions"— a statement that was immediately challenged by the therapist. Gus was aware that Pam was "very friendly" with a male graduate student at the university where she studied. He said it was not "an affair" so it was of little consequence to him. Gus reaffirmed his love for Pam but also indicated he would not "sell his soul" to keep her. He would try to meet her emotional needs "halfway," but he wasn't going to abandon his own control and "scientific personality."

Conjoint interview. Immediately after their individual sessions, the Frankels were interviewed in a conjoint session to complete the assessment process and to share the therapist's recommendations. In this session Gus talked openly about his wish to keep the marriage, while Pam voiced her uncertainties. There was fairly good verbal interaction between them, with Gus being the more controlled one and Pam obviously tense and distressed. The therapist affirmed their concerns with the couple (as they had expressed them in the conjoint session but without revealing any confidences from the individual sessions) and pointed out that, for starting tasks, Gus had every right to try to convince Pam that he could be an "ideal husband" for her—while she had every right, as an individual, to reach a decision as to whether she wanted to stay married to Gus or not. They decided they would like to start marital therapy and utilize a treatment format that would combine the individual and conjoint approaches with the therapist.

Therapist's observations.   Gus appeared to be a "cerebral," highly overcontrolled male with a great fear of emotional expression and with much repressed anger. Pam was an extremely insecure person who had initially been attracted to Gus for his "strength" but who now experienced him as cold, distant, and controlling. Her relationship with another man had increased her dissatisfaction with her husband's inadequate emotional nurturing of her needs and had tremendously increased her ambivalence about leaving the marriage in spite of its many creature comforts. Pam appeared to be gaining in her own self-confidence and self-respect, hence lowering her neurotic need for Gus's dominance. Thus marital therapy would commence with some common issues and themes—a marriage, of the "strong, silent male" and the "dependent, expressive female," which was now being shaken to its very foundations. The wife appeared to have changed sufficiently to no longer value her noncommunicative mate and, in fact, was feeling increasingly angry and dissatisfied with him.

Session 2

Conjoint interview.   The therapist found it difficult to penetrate both Pam's and Gus's intellectualized approach to discussing their feelings and their relationship. Pam had "left" her husband for one night the previous week but had agreed to return home, after he pleaded with her to do so. She had demanded that henceforth, until she "got her head straightened out," Gus would have to sleep on the living room sofa. With the therapist's encouragement, she shared most of her unhappiness with Gus, as well as her uncertainties about the marriage. The therapist concentrated on helping her communicate these feelings to Gus and then "double-checked" to ensure that Gus had accurately received the messages.

Individual interview: Gus.   Gus reiterated both his wish to keep the marriage and his fears of Pam exploiting him if he changed. Therapy focused on his nonverbal style and Gus attributed this to his strict, European-type upbringing during which no one in his family allegedly showed any emotions to each other.

Individual interview: Pam.   Pam concentrated on her loneliness and how her student friend had been more distant with her after she told him marital therapy had commenced. She expressed much fear of unknowns in her future. The therapist concentrated upon strengthening her self-confidence gains by emphasizing the fact that she appeared to have progressed so far in her efforts that total regression to her earlier dependency state on Gus seemed highly unlikely.

Session 3

Conjoint interview.   The Frankels utilized the conjoint interview constructively to interact extensively about their current feelings and actions. Gus said that every day he "learned more" about Pam's needs, but Pam remained cautious about her husband's "newly found" sensitivity to her.

Individual interview: Gus.   Gus said that earlier he had the idea that Pam wanted him to always act in a "macho" style. He had prided himself on his self-control but realized now that his wife primarily wanted and needed sensitivity from him. The sessions, he said, were clarifying for him the fact that he had been blocking out her communications on this because of his own intrapsychic patterns.

Individual interview: Pam.   Pam concentrated on her ambivalence about staying married to Gus. In part, she feared she would regress as an individual if she didn't divorce him.

Therapist's observations.   In these interviews the therapist was continuously working to increase Gus's awareness and sensitivity to his wife's needs while recognizing his own long-felt needs to hide his feelings from others. Pam, in the meantime, was being helped to increase the clarity of her communications with her husband and to try to resolve her ambivalence about staying married to him.

Session 4

Little new emerged in this fourth session. Gus had "opened up" more and Pam clearly sensed his needs for her.

Session 5

Conjoint interview.   Pam was having many mixed feelings about her sister, who was moving away. In the process, the sister had been pushing Pam to be closer to her, raising many intimacy issues for her. She had recently injured her arm and Gus was being extremely helpful to her. Gus was "praised" for this but felt uncomfortable about being "a nice guy." He was talking more, but Pam wasn't sure how "authentic" he was.

Individual interview: Pam.   A transference issue arose when Pam aired her feeling that she wasn't sure the therapist always "heard" her. This was discussed at some length, with the therapist pointing out that Pam was accusing him of acting the same way she believed her husband did. This revealed her lifelong feelings of insecurity and inadequacy and that she deeply feared rejection by any person important to her.

Individual interview: Gus. Gus was not in a mood for introspection during this session and spent most of his allotted time griping about the persons at the company where he worked and how he had to use his (superior) mind to outwit them.

Session 6

Conjoint interview. The week before, while driving home from the therapist's office, a discussion between Pam and Gus about their respective feelings had led to her inviting him back into their bed. Both shared happy feelings about this symbolic act while the session also concentrated on what Pam could do to enable Gus to keep sharing more of his feelings toward her.

Individual interview: Gus. This session concentrated on Gus's earlier expressions of how he valued his "stoic" nature. The therapist strongly supported Gus's new efforts to share his feelings with Pam.

Individual interview: Pam. Pam vacillated between her ambivalence about "taking Gus back"—expressing resentment at Gus's European mother who has so negatively influenced her son as he grew up—and her own lack of clarity about what she wanted to have as a life career.

Therapist's observations. In these sessions the therapist provided support for all the changes in the Frankels' communications, especially in what Gus was doing. Pam continued to use the therapy sessions to discuss the more positive interactions with her husband and also her own self-doubts.

Sessions 7 and 8

Little in the way of significant changes or events occurred during these weeks. The couple's outward appearance was calm and relatively contented.

Session 9

Conjoint interview. During this session Gus went into a detailed explanation of a group he belonged to that discussed complex economic theories. This led to Pam and Gus looking at the latter's proclivity for intellectualizing in many spheres of his life and the complications that this presented in their marital relationship.

Individual interview: Gus. Gus had made much progress toward internalizing some of the changes discussed in therapy. He now saw himself as having been "pretty screwed up" before. He appeared quite sensitive to his wife's emotional needs and much more comfortable about trying to meet them.

Individual interview: Pam. The therapist concentrated with Pam about how she could "educate" her husband about her needs. Over the years so many people had rebuffed her that she had developed much anger at Gus—feeling he was just one more "rebuffer." Pam said that she felt her husband "owed it to her" to be nice to her and now resented having to "teach" him about herself after several years of marriage. The therapist remained supportive but firm about what she had to do if she wanted Gus to be more sensitive.

Therapist's observations.   This session provides a good example of the reciprocal interdependence that exists between a husband and wife. It also illustrates how, in the marital system, one partner can—and *usually must*—play an active role in helping make his or her partner comprehend personal wishes and needs more effectively. Often clients react negatively to this responsibility and must be helped to see that it is a positive opportunity for them to increase the quality of the relationship and that, in the end, both of them may benefit from the efforts they make.

Sessions 10 through 16

Little change occurred for the couple during this time. The sessions were reduced to an alternate-week frequency. Conjoint sessions often focused on the Frankels' mutual efforts and activities. Individual sessions with Gus concentrated on maintaining his more open communications with Pam and his occasional frustration with her sometimes less-than-enthusiastic responses. Pam's sessions, meantime, concentrated on her continuing uncertainties about both her marriage, her career goals, and sharing her wishes with Gus.

Session 17

Conjoint interview.   A fairly dramatic change had recently occurred for the Frankels. Pam had been preoccupied with some of her friends and with searching for a job now that she had received her Master's degree. Gus had become upset over some things at work and had felt rebuffed when he tried to talk to his wife about his feelings. The next day both of them realized how they had each cut the other off and a long, involved, sharing and caring discussion followed. Since then, they reported, they had felt profoundly more positive toward each other.

Individual interview: Pam.   Pam continued to share her increased positive feelings toward Gus. She now realized, from the therapist's interpretations, that she had been staying in the marriage partially because of the security it provided her when she was feeling so adrift and insecure, and partially because of her husband's positive points. Increasingly she found that she could—and did—believe that he really cared about her.

Individual interview: Gus.   Gus concentrated on his troubles at work and on the pleasure he derived from his wife's concern about him. He appeared to be strengthening and affirming his increased ability to share both his positive and his negative thoughts with her.

Sessions 18 through 22

The remaining five sessions with the Frankels were concerned with consolidating their gains. As the weeks went by and both of them became more comfortable and trusting about the improvements in their marriage, both also dropped much of their earlier defensiveness. After the twenty-second session, Pam and Gus terminated therapy, having improved their relationship greatly and deciding to stay together.

SUMMARY

Marital therapy proceeded with the Frankels for a somewhat longer period of time than usually occurs with troubled couples. However, it was clear from the onset that their "communication" problems were not their only difficulties. Both of them had many insecurities, most of them stemming from unresolved childhood issues. While treatment focused on these intrapsychic issues periodically, especially during the individual sessions, the main thrust of the marital therapy was upon increasing communications between them. When this occurred, it released Gus from much of the tyrannical grasp of his past and enabled him to go much further toward meeting his wife's needs. For her part, Pam received acceptance of her right to stay in—or not stay in—her marriage, and this relieved much tension for her. She then gained insight into the reciprocal nature of all communications systems and was able to assume more responsibility for her own role in their communications failures, as well as for other problems she was experiencing.

While the final outcome for the Frankels was their highly positive and happy decision to maintain their much-improved marriage, the reader should be cautioned that in many cases of this nature the clients do not seek professional marital therapy until the communications between them have been irreparably damaged. In these latter instances, trust and caring often cannot be regained and the termination of the marriage is a common outcome. Communications are vital to human relationships but, by themselves, they are adequate neither to keep a marriage functioning successfully nor to repair a severely strained one.

CHAPTER SIX
MARITAL
LIFE-CYCLE
PROBLEMS

BACKGROUND

The marriage relationship between a husband and wife is profoundly influenced by many forces that act upon them both as individuals and as a couple. Exactly *when* and *how* these forces affect them is determined by what "stage" of their marital life cycle the couple is in. Theorists have divided the marital life cycle into a variety of stages. Here we shall consider it as occurring in eight stages. These are: (1) early marriage, (2) parenthood and early childhood, (3) middle childhood, (4) adolescence, (5) launching, (6) middle age, (7) preretirement, and (8) retirement and old age. These stages are not necessarily discrete and often they overlap. For instance, a couple may have both a preschool child and an adolescent in the family. Some couples do not appear to "fit" these stages because they have no children. In many ways, however, their marital relationship changes and alters over time in a manner quite similar to that of couples with children.

In Chapter Two we emphasized that the initial assessment session with every couple should include obtaining information about the clients' ages, occupations, children, and extended family members. This information becomes particularly relevant as we examine how marriages are influenced by each stage in the marital life cycle.

EARLY MARRIAGE

Loosening Family Bonds

At the first stage of the marital life cycle, the young husband and wife should be deepening their commitment to each other, and drastically loosening their ties to their families of origin. Those who show evidence of clinging to their parents or siblings at the expense of their marriage relationship need to be encouraged by the marital therapist to separate from these earlier bonds or at least to alter them in a fashion that does not seriously intrude into the new marriage. Danger signals here include frequent and extensive visiting to the parental homes (or by the parents), excessive phoning to or from parents, seeking advice from parents rather than joining forces with the new mate to accomplish tasks, and sometimes even living with parents. The latter situation may reflect a temporary financial necessity (although one may legitimately question the success potential of any couple who marry with so few assets that they cannot set up their own housekeeping arrangements) or even a transitional issue (between college and graduate school, temporarily after a job relocation, and the like). However, if the therapist believes living with parents reflects a continuing emotional dependence, he or she should confront the couple with the implications of what they are doing. This will frequently elicit an "I told you so" response from the mate who is living with his or her in-laws, revealing a suppressed dissatisfaction with the partner's continuing dependency. Some ethnic and cultural groups maintain closer ties to the family of origin than others and the therapist must be sure to understand and respect this.

Altering Previous Social Networks

In addition to the need to become increasingly independent of both families of origin, couples often need to alter their previous social networks. A common complaint of young wives involves the new husband who is still extremely closely tied to his "old buddies." Many women tolerate these "buddies" during dating and into early marriage, but gradually tire of their intrusion into the couple's privacy. Here the therapist supports those factors which encourage positive growth for the marital relationship, and may choose to actively side with the more mature partner in discussions on these matters.

Unrealistic Expectations

Performing marital therapy with couples in the early marriage stage frequently reveals the common role of ignorance, overromanticizing, and/or unrealistic expectations about marriage and human personalities during the courtship and mate selection stages of a person's life. If the therapist asks a partner who has been married for less than three years if he or she noticed the presenting problems with the mate *before* the marriage, the answer (and therapeutic response) is likely to be one of the following:

1. "No, *I didn't know her well enough.* I was off in the military (or at college or at work in a distant state), and we had relatively little time to spend together during courtship." This response reveals the client's ignorance of the "true nature" of the person he was marrying. Therapy in this case may be directed toward helping the husband and wife adjust to the realities of their choices.
2. "I realized he was this way, *but I loved him* and felt that was all that mattered." This demonstrates the "love conquers all" theory that still prevails in the American courtship system with its strong emphasis upon romanticism.

Therapists need to help these persons understand the true nature of mature love—love in which the partner is valued for what he or she really is, not for what romantic fantasies suggest he or she may be. The client's dynamic here is the use of suppression. Clients need to have this interpreted to them, and therapeutic efforts should be directed at providing each partner with a more mature understanding and acceptance of the realities of the other, and of the role of mature love in a committed relationship.

3. "I knew she was this way before I married her but *I felt I could change her.*" Typically, this response was given by a young husband whose wife was late for almost all of their dates during courtship because she had to leave her apartment in perfect order—all dishes washed, dried, and back in the cupboard; ashtrays emptied; magazines returned to their place in the bookshelves, etc. Rather than recognizing that she was a "crazy clean" person whose defense against anxiety forced her to handle her life this way, the young husband naively assumed he could get her to "relax" and drop her compulsive defense mechanisms just because he wanted her to do so. The idea that people can somehow magically get their partners to change for them so that they become "ideal" partners is another prevailing myth in our mate selection system.

All three of these typical early-marriage problems point out that marital therapy at this stage often involves a combination of education, interpretation, confrontation, and support of realistic changes accompanied by emotional acceptance of that which cannot reasonably be expected to change.

Power, Intimacy, Inclusion-Exclusion

Berman and Lief (1975) have written of three major marital dimensions which have an impact upon all couples throughout their marital life cycle and which must be coped with almost immediately by the "early marrieds": these are power, intimacy, and inclusion-exclusion. *Power* relates to issues of who is in charge. Who is dominant and who is submissive? Who leads—and in which areas of the relationship—and who follows? *Intimacy* becomes an issue as the marriage partners attempt to work out, both emotionally and physically, how close or how distant they wish to be with each other. The *inclusion-exclusion* dimension, according to Berman and Lief, refers to who will be included into the marital system (in-laws, extended families, "his" friends or "her" friends, etc.) and who will be excluded from it. One of the tasks of newly married couples is to work out a mutually acceptable consensus on these dimensions.

Neurotic complementarity in human relationships often enables strange couple combinations to be quite functional—at least for a limited period of time. It is not the role, or the right, of the marital therapist to impose his or her own ideas of how clients may choose to resolve these issues, but it is the therapist's duty to help clients attempt to reach agreements that will be positive in terms of each partner's intrapsychic and interpersonal needs.

Early Marriage: Hope and Danger

One advantage of marital therapy performed at this very first stage of the marital life cycle is that younger and "newer" couples appear to be more malleable and amenable to change than are couples who have been married longer. These young couples may have serious conflicts, but they often have not given up hope and still retain strong needs for each other. If the marriage has been supported by family and friends, the couple has strong support systems that may help them—in contrast to older couples who have to accomplish most things on their own. On the other hand, it must be recognized that these early married years are also dangerous years in terms of divorce probabilities. The peak time for seeking a divorce is between the second and fifth year of marriage and the peak period for separations that precede divorce actually occurs in the very first year of marriage (Bowman and Spanier 1978). We may speculate that many of these marriages were doomed to failure before they were even solemnized; this supposition strongly supports the concept of premarital therapy. However, for the reasons referred to earlier in this section, many of these very same couples would probably reject premarital therapy. They may have been intellectually aware of potential conflict areas during courtship, but they probably would have coped with their anxieties about these conflicts by repressing, suppressing, and/or rationalizing. When such couples present themselves to the marital therapist, they may be seeking either magical "cures" or professional confirmation of the improbability of marital success. Therapists should be quick to reveal their impotence in the magic-making department and realistic enough to eventually share their professional impression as to whether or not the marriage can be "saved."

PARENTHOOD AND EARLY CHILDHOOD

Pronatal Pressure

Designating the second stage of the marital life cycle in terms of the parenthood and early childhood stage illustrates the values and expectations American culture places upon the role of parenthood in marriage. So strong is this "pronatal" pressure (the pressure exerted on couples to feel that they *must* have children) that many couples who fail to have children but would like to often suffer severe marital stress as a result. In dealing with these "infertile" couples, the marital therapist who is not an obstetrician-gynecologist should obtain a medical report or make a referral to competent medical help if the husband and wife have not already done so. The therapist's task then becomes one of helping them cope with their feelings about the failure to become pregnant, to reduce or resolve blame if it is present (as it often is—both consciously and unconsciously), and to help the couple plan for one of the alternatives to their own "natural" biological parenthood—artificial insemination, embryo implantation, adoption, or a childfree life.

Decision not to have children. Modern contraception methods have done much to improve the sex life of married couples. At the same time, the high protection contraceptives offer against unwanted pregnancies has contributed to a new source of marital tension—the issue of whether or not to have children. An increasing number of young couples are postponing the first pregnancy until several years after the marriage. This often contributes to the question of whether they ever wish to have children. Deliberately chosen lifelong, childfree marriages are occurring with greater frequency. A vital issue in these marriages in which pregnancy is either postponed for several years or totally rejected is whether or not *both* the husband and the wife agree on the decision to postpone parenthood or to reject it entirely. If either partner disagrees with the other on this issue, marital tension automatically occurs. One spouse cannot be a parent without the other also assuming this role. In these cases the marital therapist ascertains the relative strength and meaning of each partner's wishes, assists them in the process of negotiating their differences, and then supports the reality of their decisions. Couples who choose to remain childfree may be referred to a community support group, such as the National Alliance for Optional Parenthood,* for assistance in coping with the societal pressures that invariably result from their decision. These pressures range from family disapproval to pity, scorn, and criticism by the many pronatal groups in our society.

Preparation for parenthood.   The majority of young couples marrying in the United States at this time, however, intend to have one or more children and to accomplish this goal within the first few years of marriage. Parenthood introduces a profound change in their lifestyle and in their marital relationship. The marital dyad suddenly becomes a triad. While an increasing number of couples participate in childbirth education classes to prepare for the birth experience, especially of their first child, few have any formal preparation whatsoever for the changes and responsibilities that come with parenthood. American families have become smaller in recent decades, and new parents only rarely have served as surrogate parents for their own younger siblings.

Another pressure on the marriage at this time results from separate and often conflicting ideologies with which young men and young women are indoctrinated as they grow up. Nursery rhymes, toys, books, and family members continue, for the most part, to prepare females for their future roles as mothers. Males receive little or no support for their future roles as fathers and may, in fact, be socialized in ways that directly contradict a fathering role. One classical example of this rests with the pressure for young men to obtain a good skill or education, to work hard, to earn as much money as possible, and to "get ahead." These young men are often too busy and too tired to be of much help in caring for their infants, let alone to care for their wives' needs for affection. Common complaints of young parents involve pressures about time, money, physical fatigue, and the intrusion of the new child into the previously established intimacy level of the couple. An added contemporary problem at this stage of the marital life cycle concerns the question of the wife's career outside the home. Women increasingly consider motherhood as only one of several options open to them; they expect greater equality with their

---

*The National Alliance for Optional Parenthood, 2010 Massachusetts Ave. N.W., Washington, D.C. 20036.

husbands in many spheres of their relationship together. Thus it is not surprising that tensions often arise between the mates over child care, changed meal schedules, financial control, and a multitude of other household management issues that arise if the wife chooses almost anything except a stay-at-home, traditional role in the marriage.

Potential Therapeutic Problems

In performing marital therapy with couples in this early parenthood stage, therapists will often find their own values challenged about a variety of issues. Will young mothers feel that male therapists cannot possibly understand the anger, the ambivalence, and the fatigue that they often feel? Will female therapists' own countertransferences preclude their accepting young fathers' frustrations and anger at wives who will not play the traditional roles of cheerleader, alterego, mistress, and chambermaid? Therapists must be doubly certain about their own feelings on these issues and be prepared, if necessary, to refer some cases to others who can handle these countertransference issues more satisfactorily.

In addition to the usual therapeutic issues such as promoting communication and conflict resolution, therapy with couples who are young parents often requires considerable education—about themselves, their partners, their children, and the sacrifices that are ultimately necessary in order to keep a marital relationship going while under the considerable pressure of parenthood. Therapists need to resoundingly reject the myth that children somehow "save" marriages. The divorce statistics show quite the contrary. Therapy with young parents must always remain completely reality-oriented, supportive, and flexible in respect to goals and values. Frequently both the husband and the wife complain, "He or she does not understand me"—and they are correct. Therapy is aimed at improving knowledge of the partner's feelings, hopes, and sensitivities until genuine understanding does exist. Feeling that one is understood by a significant other is a rewarding and strengthening experience. Reaching this level of relationship may be all that some couples find necessary to be satisfied. For all couples, however, genuine understanding becomes a necessity in order to resolve marital conflicts.

MIDDLE CHILDHOOD

Surviving Marital Perils,
Facing Parenthood Traumas

By the time couples arrive at this stage, we may assume that the marriage relationship has considerable strength, because they are survivors of the most likely periods in which couples seek divorce. By the seventh year of marriage, over half of all divorces have occurred. During their children's middle years, couples who have stayed together have mastered most of the tests of early marriage, both of them have invested themselves heavily in their relationship and are bonded together, at least in part, by the presence of one or more children.

Children first, marriage last.   The parent role is quite demanding for both the husband and the wife. This is the time to join the PTA, become a Brownie or Cub Scout leader, and to emphasize family togetherness. At this time the children are increasingly being influenced by their peers, are actively intruding more and more into the "private space" and time of the parents, and are becoming financially more burdensome with their teeth braces, demands for sports equipment, and the like. "Good" parents, the media and other forces in society say, should sacrifice their own self-interests in favor of the children's needs. One result of these societal pressures is that husbands and wives often put their children and their careers in front of their priorities for their marital relationship—and to themselves as individuals. Extramarital affairs blossom as substitute partners provide the warmth, understanding, and sexual excitement that is disappearing from the marriages. "Good" marriages, on the other hand—those that marital therapists rarely meet professionally—are becoming stronger, more intimate, and settling down to well-established patterns.

Therapeutic Considerations

Couples in this middle childhood stage constitute a major group of the marital therapist's clientele. Their conflicts run the gamut of problems, from sex adjustment and extramarital affairs to child discipline and personality clashes. Many report that their problems have existed for years before they sought help. Angry feelings have often hardened, and loving feelings have either been suppressed or lost entirely. Couples talk about staying together "for the sake of the kids"—another myth that is directly contrary to the facts concerning children's mental health in conflicted but intact families versus separated but nonconflicted families.

Staying married or not.   Both during the initial assessment and then repeatedly throughout the course of therapy, the therapist will have to make judgments about the strength of the marriage, the motivations of each spouse, and what needs to change if the relationship is going to endure. Many of these couples are deeply ambivalent about divorcing versus staying married. They have invested heavily in the marriage—time, energy, devotion, children, dependence on the partner, and community recognition—and they fear losing these elements of satisfaction and meaning. At the same time, they may be equally fearful of continuing the marriage as it is, often feeling they would be better out of it; moreover, they may feel held down and "stifled" by their many responsibilities and by their partners. Women may be especially vulnerable to these ambivalent feelings. Their increasing economic independence from their husbands as the sole means of financial security, along with growing societal support systems, makes separation and divorce a far more viable option for women than has ever been true before. At the same time, it is clear that the role of the divorced woman, especially one with children, is an extremely demanding one in our society. Similarly, men may feel it would be easy to get a "replacement" for their wives—only to discover that their emotional ties to the wives and/or the children make separation extremely painful.

Working through ambivalence thus becomes one of the most common issues in performing marital therapy with clients in this particular stage. Here is where the practice of combining conjoint sessions with individual, confidential sessions with each partner is very helpful. During the conjoint sessions mutual issues are discussed—such as improved communications, ventilation of anger and hurt, the expression of individual needs, and negotiating about and evaluating each partner's efforts to resolve conflicts. Here the therapist is the catalyst, the one who provides a neutral and protected atmosphere in which to discuss painful feelings, and the one who actively supports all that is positive. At the same time, the individual sessions allow each marital partner to examine his or her feelings, wishes, and needs more candidly without the sometimes intimidating presence of the spouse. The therapist attempts to help the couple clarify *what* they want to do about the marriage and then *how* they can set about reaching their goal.

Family therapy an option.   By this time in the marital life cycle the issue of family therapy may arise. While the conflicts may appear to primarily exist between the husband and the wife, the growing children increasingly intrude into the marital system. Parents may push the children to take sides, children may actively intervene to drive a wedge between the parents, and the parents can no longer hide their quarrels from the children—if they ever could. Family therapy should be considered in these instances, with conjoint marital sessions interspersed as needed.

ADOLESCENCE

A Time of Low Marital Satisfaction

When couples reach the stage in their marital life cycle at which they have adolescent children, they are likely also to have arrived at their point of lowest marital satisfaction (Rollins and Feldman 1970). This fact has been revealed by studies as well as the unsolicited testimony of millions of parents—both in and out of therapy. Fathers and mothers commonly experience many concerns about the "normal" perils of their teenage children—drugs, sex, driver's licenses, cars, pimples, dating, identity crises, friends, clothes—the list often appears endless. These concerns of the adolescents cannot help but impinge upon the husband–wife relationship. Worries over the "kids" are then easily displaced onto the spouse, and frequently expressed in the form of irritation, criticism, and fault-finding. Parental arguments occur when wife and husband disagree with each other over the boundaries of inclusion-exclusion of the adolescents in the family vis à vis the young person's increasing movement out of the home. Arguments frequently erupt between same-sex members within the family unit—mothers fight with daughters and fathers fight with sons. The opposite-sex parent then intervenes and the issue becomes a marital conflict—not just a parent–child issue. As each parent struggles with his or her own feelings about the adolescents' demands for independence and freedom (or with the opposite, about the dependent, insecure adolescents who fail to emancipate themselves from the parental home) both convey their own worries, angers, and frustrations to the partner.

Therapeutic Considerations

Just as adolescence may be a stormy time for young people and their parents, so too is it apt to be a stormy time for marital therapy. These couples have "dug in." Their feelings and their attitudes have hardened. The adolescents themselves frequently actively intervene in the marital squabbles. Both the husband and the wife have much at stake in the marriage, and its threatened instability arouses fierce emotions. The issues in therapy may remain focused primarily on problems between the partners or they may involve the adolescents to such an extent that family therapy becomes mandatory. Many adolescents act out their parents' conflicts and get into trouble with outside authorities—school and police. In these latter instances, family therapy would appear to be the obvious treatment method of choice, but again the clinician is cautioned to make conjoint and individual sessions alternately available to the couple.

Marital ego investment is primary.   Some family systems purists will object to these alternate sessions, claiming the total family should always remain the exclusive treatment unit. It is the author's opinion that this narrow viewpoint fails to recognize the primacy of marital ego investment over parental ego investment. Parents know that the child or children will be out of their lives soon—at least in respect to most significant issues—and hence their egos should be invested more in the marital relationship than in the parental one. When parents fail to accept this, and consciously or unconsciously choose to favor their parental roles over their marital roles, they create enormous tensions between themselves and their mates. "She or he cares more about that damned kid of ours than she or he does about me" is the way this conflict is often expressed. The therapist should address these feelings directly in conjoint sessions without contaminating the session with the adolescent's presence. This is not to argue against family therapy in these cases, but rather to suggest that family treatment, by itself, is often insufficient to resolve marital struggles.

LAUNCHING

Marriages that have survived the adolescent stage appear to increase in satisfaction for the partners. This positive thought may serve as a motivation for couples with teenage children to "hang in there." During this stage, the children are launched into the world—out of the home and into jobs, college, and separate lives of their own. We may speculate that marital satisfaction increases at this point because of the opportunities for greater intimacy between the mates, because of the removal of the stresses the adolescents have placed on the marriage, and because the parents have completed most of their own psychological maturation processes and are now apt to be highly productive persons.

The Midlife Crisis

This stage may also be characterized by the beginnings of midlife crisis for husbands and wives as individuals. Wives who have forsaken their own development in favor of fulfilling their maternal roles now feel more free to return to school or to their "outside" careers. This often upsets the balance of power that had previously existed between the mates and can threaten the husband's role as the major breadwinner and head of the household. Husbands at this time are having to reconcile their dreams of personal glory with what they realistically have—and have not— achieved in life. Issues concerning job attainments, sexual adequacy, and "success" in general contribute to such problems as extramarital adventures, overindulgence in alcohol, and other forms of acting out one's fears of impending decline.

Redefinition of roles. Marital therapy during this stage needs to focus heavily upon the couple's tasks in redefining their roles in the marriage. The impending absence of children, often for the first time in two or more decades of marriage, requires the couple to develop new rhythms of daily living and may lead them into constructive attempts to rediscover each other. Many women begin to reach their peak of sexual response in this stage only to find that their partner's sexual drive has lessened. These wives often need the therapist's support in learning to accept themselves as being capable of sexual aggression and assertiveness with their husbands.

For some couples, the impending absence of children removes the old rationalizations that the marriage had to be maintained for the sake of the children. Now there remains primarily one major purpose for continuing the marriage—because both partners *want* to do so. This fact can be utilized by the therapist to emphasize each person's responsibilities and self-investment in the success or failure of the marriage. Once the children are launched, the marital pair may experience an improved financial position. Living expenses are decreased, joint personal incomes are up, and these fortuitous circumstances permit therapists to encourage couples to indulge themselves in activities that may never have been possible before. Nights out on the town and exciting vacations will not make an otherwise dull or devitalized marriage completely satisfactory, but they can enhance couples' efforts to put more *joie de vivre* into their relationships.

MIDDLE AGE

The middle age stage of the marital life cycle, like many of the earlier stages, portends both positive and negative implications for marriages. On the positive side, this stage represents the zenith for the couple's income, career developments, and position in the community. On the negative side, couples become more and more aware of the aging process; moreover, they often become burdened with caring for their own aging parents. Due to early childbearing, small family size, and increased longevity, this stage of the marital life cycle represents a relatively new period in marriage. Until the twentieth century, few American couples spent much time together in middle age because by the time the last child had left home, one marital partner was likely to be already dead or near death. Now an ever-increasing proportion of American couples can anticipate over a decade together, without any of their children still present at home, before death breaks up the marriage. Divorce for couples in this stage becomes an increasing rarity. By this time, marital partners' lives have become so intermeshed and interdependent that the idea of resolving marital conflict through divorce is chosen by only a very small percentage of couples.

Therapeutic Considerations

Marital therapy during the middle age stage tends to revolve around issues of personality clashes, irritating personal mannerisms, changing roles for husbands and wives, and combatting apathy, chronic disenchantment, and monotony. People tend to become set in their ways and increasingly resistant to change. Irritating personalities and behavior patterns become more and more difficult for partners to cope with after decades of marriage, and yet marital partners often refuse to try to change to increase their spouse's pleasure and contentment. Husbands and wives often vary as to how fast they "age"—or, contrariwise, how much they resist aging. Therefore the therapist may hear one partner complain, "He's already retreated to the rocking chair, and I'm ready to go dancing!" Illness of one or both partners becomes an increasing problem for this age group as they begin to cope with cardiovascular disorders, arthritis, diabetes, and other chronic and often disabling diseases associated with the aging process.

Focus of therapy.   Therapy with middle-aged couples focuses on the realities of the strengths and weaknesses of their marriages and on helping them to adjust to these realities. Personality changes are not fixed and do not automatically cease at age 40 or 50, but many persons in this group despair of change. These clients often benefit from being challenged by their therapists to take on new interests in their lives. Monotony is a deadly enemy of happiness—and it is very easy after several decades of marriage for a couple to lapse into slovenly and dull ways of interacting with each other. Marital therapists are not recreation or social directors, but they can encourage their clients to explore new ventures in these areas. To paraphrase an old slogan, "The couple that plays together stays together."

PRERETIREMENT

For couples in marital conflict, the preretirement stage often represents an exacerbation of issues that emerged during middle age but were not satisfactorily resolved then. By now, however, hope or intention of change on the part of one or both partners begins to rapidly decrease. In addition, health problems increase in both number and severity. Deaths in this age group, particularly among males, increase rapidly, bringing on increased fears of death as a new issue in marital therapy. Another problem that usually emerges during this stage, if it has not already done so, is that of preretirement planning. Couples become increasingly sensitive to potential retirement issues—financial benefits, medical coverage, living arrangements, and how they will spend their time after retirement. Husbands, in particular, often need to be encouraged by the therapist to begin preparing for their upcoming leisure time, since they ordinarily experience retirement as a greater time of crisis than wives do. Women's roles in American society ordinarily shift less drastically than men's when gainful employment ceases, but this difference will probably decrease in the future as women's roles outside the home increase.

On the positive side, the preretirement stage represents the culmination of many couples' life achievements. Improved nutrition and health care, among other things, have led to more couples reaching this stage in good health and with high expectations of leading rewarding lives in their senior years. They often look forward to travel, moving to a more desirable location, and spending more time in pursuit of neglected hobbies or other interests.

RETIREMENT AND OLD AGE

Retirement represents the last stage of the marital life cycle. It commences when at least one of the marital partners ceases employment outside of the home and lasts until one partner dies. Given current life expectancies, we may expect to see an ever-increasing number of married couples reach this stage. Many of them are couples who have been together for over half a century; others are the products of second and third marriages. All of them, however, share the concerns of the aging about health, death, finances, personal security, and being valued.

Relationship problems between partners in this final stage of the marital life cycle are rarely brought to the attention of the professional marital therapist. By now, issues that were never resolved are being tolerated with varying degrees of success. With the exception of therapists primarily employed in medicine, religious activities, and social work, few marital therapists treat many aged couples. Whether or not this will change in the future, as the number of couples in this age group increases, is difficult to predict.

Multigenerational family therapy.   Therapeutic work with couples in this final stage often is best handled by a multigenerational family therapy approach because issues tend to involve matters that concern the couples' middle-aged sons and daughters. Some of these older couples come for therapy because of the "usual" marital conflicts but, by and large, their concerns center around disagreements and worries surrounding health care, living arrangements, financial planning, and social isolation. Therapists who plan to specialize in marital therapy with the aged should add courses in Gerontology to their basic academic preparation. A small percentage of these retired couples seeking therapeutic help will be the "youthful" aged—those who possess excellent health and vitality and whose major conflicts center about disagreements about how to utilize their free time. Therapeutic concerns with these couples will be very similar to those couples in the launching, middle-aged, and preretirement groups.

CASE EXAMPLE:
EDITH AND PETE FISHER

Background

Ideally, we would present here a "typical" case from each of the eight stages of the marital life cycle, but space does not permit this. We have chosen, therefore, to present the case of Pete and Edith Fisher, a couple in the stage of parenthood and early childhood. Couples like the Fishers make up a large group of cases in any marital therapist's office and help to illustrate how the stage typically influences marital conflicts.

Session 1—Initial Evaluation

Pete made the initial contact with the therapist. He was employed as a counselor for the Department of Rehabilitation and had recently taken a promotion to another part of his agency. This required him to travel about two hours, morning and evening, from home to work. He had obtained the therapist's name from another member of the AAMFT.

Individual interview: Pete. Pete, age 33, appeared to be a presentable, neatly tailored man, very much in control of his emotions. He spoke readily about his marital conflicts and his concerns about both his marriage and his oldest son, George. Therapy, he said, was his idea. He reported that his wife rejected the idea of treatment, believing that their problems weren't serious enough; they couldn't afford therapy; and besides, any therapist would probably say the troubles were mostly her fault. In addition, she felt they wouldn't have any problems if the kids "weren't sick all the time" and if George, age 7, "wasn't so active." George had numerous allergies and infections, and was "always on the go," Pete said. Edith was also "hyper," in his view. He described himself as a calmer person, as was their 2-year-old daughter, Sara. The main problem, as Pete saw it, was that Edith couldn't handle the kids well and then took out her anger on him.

Pete and Edith both came from conservative Protestant backgrounds. They had met at college. Outside of the "sexual Puritanism" teaching they had both received at home and at school, Pete thought their upbringings had been pretty average. Their families all lived several hours' drive away and visits were rather infrequent. Pete said that as a child growing up, Edith had heard lots of quarrels between her parents, although the latter had never separated. Both Pete and Edith had received separate individual psychotherapy for three years before their marriage and for one year afterward. The treatment had been focused primarily upon their intrapsychic feelings. Pete thought the therapy had been helpful because he had been "very immature," but he reported that Edith now considered hers to have been a waste of time and money. Shortly after Sara was born, Pete consulted a marital therapist because of the marital tensions. Edith refused to go, for reasons similar to those she was currently voicing, and the therapist, Pete claimed, refused to see him again without Edith's participation. (Note: This "purist" approach to conjoint marital therapy is not common and the therapist's actual reasons for rejecting Pete as a client were never ascertained.)

Pete portrayed the marital interaction as one in which Edith gradually built up tensions, "raved and ranted" at him and the kids—especially George—and then the couple became both physically and psychologically distanced from each other. Edith was a "perfectionist" and neither he nor the kids were ever clean or orderly enough for her. He described his wife as engaging in a hateful vendetta against George, yelling at him a lot, "cutting him down," and telling him the cops would get him when he got older. Pete said his wife was tense, overweight, and deeply troubled by the tensions. Sometimes she cried for long periods of time and had talked of suicide. As a professional counselor himself, Pete recognized that she was under great tension. But he was angry, too. Their sex life was poor because when Edith was upset the last thing she wanted was sex. He thought she still cared for him but he, personally, was feeling "destroyed." Pete tended to be very passive and his typical response to his wife's complaining was to retreat. He "knew" this wasn't good, that it was probably a major factor in his dwindling affection for her—and yet he felt helpless about changing the situation.

Therapist's observations.   With these presenting problems, the therapist was cautious about what could be done for Pete—except, of course, supportive therapy and possibly divorce therapy—without the participation of Edith. As a responsible parent, Pete had no intention of abandoning his children and, in fact, feared for their mental health if their mother had to raise them alone. In addition, he still had many positive feelings for his wife and his hope was to "save" the marriage. Toward the end of the initial assessment session with Pete, therefore, the therapist concentrated primarily on how Pete might persuade Edith to come in—at least for one therapy session. Pete was very open to this and agreed to clearly share both his care for her and his concern *about them* as a possible way to involve her.

Session 2

Pete came alone for the next session because Edith persisted in her resistance to therapy. Pete reiterated many of the complaints and troubled feelings he had expressed in his initial session, saying it helped to "get it off his chest." Discussion of persons important to Edith brought out that she had a very positive relationship with one of her cousins who was a psychologist in a neighboring state. Pete decided to see if the psychologist could persuade Edith to enter marital therapy and the therapist supported his idea.

Session 3

Individual interview: Edith.   When the time came for the next appointment, the therapist was confronted with a very frightened, very angry Edith. The therapist immediately expressed his appreciation of her being there and recognized that she probably had some angry feelings about it. Edith, her dark eyes flashing, readily agreed with those feelings. (This is "inviting the negative"—in essence, saying its OK with you for the client to feel angry. This frees the client to air pent-up feelings and often leads to quick rapport. The therapist should let the client know that he or she has a "right" to personal feelings, that these feelings are very understandable, and that the therapist cares about the client's feelings and wants to be helpful.)

Contrary to her husband's portrayal of her as a highly resistant, difficult client, Edith rapidly proved to be an intelligent, highly verbal, deeply troubled woman who both needed and wanted help. Pete had issued her an ultimatum—go to marital therapy with him or he was going to leave her. That, she said, had made her furious—but it also alerted her to his strong concerns. Edith quickly shared her feelings about her "rotten temper" and "big mouth." She explained in some detail about the many illnesses the kids had had, how she worried about them, and how she wished she were a more patient mother. She was also quick to express her anger at Pete for not understanding her, for retreating from her barrages instead of standing up to her, and also of her fears that because he was a counselor, Pete and the therapist would "gang up" on her to make her look bad. She was reassured that the therapist considered himself "neutral" and that he was not there to judge either Edith or her husband as being bad or at fault.

Individual interview: Pete.　Pete was next seen very briefly. He told the therapist how much Edith had resisted coming to the appointment. He was very relieved to hear that she had related well to the therapist.

Conjoint interview (same evening).　Next, as is the standard procedure during the initial assessment phase of therapy, the Fishers were interviewed conjointly to discuss the issues and the therapist's recommendations. Both Pete and Edith spoke quite openly of their battles and the role child-rearing pressures played in their situation—particularly for Edith. Edith expressed her resentment at Pete for only being nice to her when he wanted sex and of ignoring her at other times. Pete explained how "turned off" he felt when she yelled at George and how he hoped, desperately, that she could learn to "handle her temper" differently. (Here both were engaging in typical initial behavior, venting their gripes about each other but not engaging in much introspection or reflection about their own parts in the process.) The therapist recognized the anger, worry, and tension Edith and Pete both felt. He acknowledged that they both wanted to be good parents; they worked hard, they expended much time and energy performing their roles, but that they were failing to protect themselves and their marital relationship in the process. Before the conjoint session ended, Edith said she was going to try harder to "quit hollering" and Pete expressed his intention of being more supportive of her. The couple left with plans to discuss marital therapy and to call the therapist back if they decided to go ahead. (It would have been easy to persuade them at that moment to schedule additional appointments, but allowing a couple time to consider this, without the pressure of the therapist's presence, insures a more solid commitment to therapy for "continuers" and prevents broken appointments by those whose decision is made in haste and who later decide not to commence treatment.)

Therapist's observations. These initial sessions had clearly revealed a major case of Y.P.S., Young Parent Syndrome, along with real questions about personality compatibility of the Fishers. Edith was seen as struggling with great hostility, currently heavily concentrated on her son and husband, and Pete demonstrated an uncanny ability to withdraw his support and acceptance from her just when she needed these the most. Without children, both of these issues would have been present but would probably not have contributed so heavily to the total pressures. In assessing a marital situation, the therapist must take into account the total numbers, types, and amounts of both satisfactions and dissatisfactions each partner is currently experiencing. Children provide both satisfactions and dissatisfactions; every spouse and every couple will react to these differently. For Edith, the children brought some satisfactions but many more tensions. For Pete, they brought more satisfactions but they also were causing, he felt, the deterioration of the marriage.

Session 4

Edith called back and said she and Pete wanted to enter therapy together. Conjoint therapy, probably exclusively, was recommended, and she said this was very acceptable to them. As the fourth session opened, Edith voiced much resentment at having to move to their present location because of her husband's career and discussed the current struggle they were having to sell their house and move again because of Pete's promotion. Pete had been disappointed in her persistent refusal to return to her nursing career, and felt it unfair of her to resent his job. It became clear that both felt very unloved and unsupported by each other. Pete, having been rather quiet about his own feelings up to this time, in spite of the therapist's attempts to "pull them out," now began sharing how desperate he felt. The therapist pointed out that both of them were currently so emotionally vulnerable that they were "ripe" to have an affair. It was pointed out that they either had to concentrate on meeting each other's needs more satisfactorily or one—or both—of them would feel they should get a divorce. (Clearly and firmly confronting clients with the realities of their situation, of measures that must be taken to constructively alter the situation, and of what *each* one of them may be capable of doing, often helps clients to organize their ego strengths better and to move ahead to resolve the issues.)

Session 5

This session was much like Session 4. Both were feeling alienated from each other but each one was too frightened, or too angry, or too "stubborn" to begin the necessary changes in their interactions. The therapist remained supportive but firm about the necessity of change while, at the same time, working to increase their insight into their personal and interpersonal dynamics and style.

Session 6

This session might have been labeled "Edith's evening." She began by discussing her feelings and needs and the therapist permitted the session to remain on this focus. (Many young parents know very little about the role of feelings and the pressures of parenthood, and need "education" about these matters. Husbands appear to be especially ignorant of young mothers' roles and pressures and, if motivated, can be much more thoughtful and helpful when they genuinely know and understand what their wives are going through.) Edith said she had hoped Pete would be less of a "traditional male" and help her more with the kids and the housework. Two-year-old Sara was in the "clinging" stage and Edith said she needed time off from Sara's incessant demands. Perhaps above all, she told Pete, she needed him to talk to her, to listen to her, and to recognize her presence—*not* to ignore her or use his (passive/aggressive) ways of controlling her. Pete acknowledged that there were many things he could do differently with Edith and that he wanted to do these things. Since the previous session he had experienced her as complaining less and said she was more fun to be around. Throughout the session the therapist acknowledged each one's feelings, made sure that each one "heard" the other, and vigorously supported the concept that they could effect many positive changes in their relationship if they were willing to work hard enough on it. This latter point was already clear because tension had begun to decrease for the Fishers, in large measure because of the inputs and changes both of them were introducing into the marital system.

Session 7

This session was very positive. Both had continued their attempts to understand their partner's feelings and each reacted favorably to this. Saturday night they had had an argument and Pete had later apologized for his (negative) part in it. Edith found this to be a welcome change from his usual "sulking" and silence. As is usually done at times like this, the therapist openly supported what they had done in order to reinforce these positive behaviors. The couple had "treated" themselves to the weekend special rates at a nearby comfortable motel resort and obviously had had an enjoyable time. Pete and Edith continued to share with each other how they felt—Edith's negative feelings about screaming, and Pete's anger and feelings of rejection when she attacked him. Edith also shared many of her frustrations about both the kids and their difficult behavior, but Pete seemed compassionate about her pressures—in marked contrast to his earlier attitude of condemnation.

It appeared that both Fishers were responding well to improved communications, more consideration, more giving to each other, and greater feelings of being valued by the partner. This demonstrates how rapidly the marital system can reinforce and perpetuate positive change when therapy proceeds effectively. The "self-fulfilling prophecy" can work positively as well as negatively, and marital interaction clearly demonstrates this fact.

Session 8

Regression had occurred for the Fishers. Edith's parents had visited over the weekend. George had misbehaved, Edith had screamed a lot, her parents had criticized her—and she'd ended up feeling like running away. Finally she told Pete that she and Sara were going to leave George (not Pete), since she couldn't stand him any more. They discussed how they had taken George to a child psychologist three years earlier and had been assured that he was "normal." Edith's compulsive perfectionism, however, was constantly challenged because her son failed to measure up to her expectancies. Pete now wondered what he could do to alleviate the situation. The therapist supported having Pete take over most responsibility for George (Edith appeared to be unable to function on an adult level with her son at the moment) and also emphasized Edith's particular need at that time for Pete's affection and support. Edith cried a lot during the session, but Pete did not make any supportive gestures toward her. (Some therapists might have instructed Pete to hug his wife at this time. However, how "real" and lasting this deliberate behavior is has been debated.)

Therapist's observations.   During this session the therapist had to make several important decisions. Did George require clinical assessment himself? Was multigenerational family therapy with Edith's parents, the Fishers, and the children indicated? Was Edith on the verge of acting upon her explosively angry feelings toward her son and harming him? In the end, the conclusion was that marital therapy should continue but with close attention being maintained on all three of these possibilities.

Session 9

Illustrating the proverbial calm after a storm, the Fishers reported that everything had improved. A routine visit to their pediatrician had reassured them that George's troubles were not pathological, and the physician had supported their being in marital therapy. The session focused on two major issues—George's behavior and how they were working together to handle it more constructively, and the marriage itself. Edith was feeling "distanced" from Pete and continued to push for more verbal interaction. Pete, for his part, was more contented with things as they were. The therapist pointed out each one was still a long way from genuinely accepting the partner *as he and she really were*—that this is a requirement for continued satisfaction in any long-term committed relationship. They both needed to continue to work on self-change and re-examination of how they needed and valued their partner if their improvement was to be sustained.

Sessions 10 and 11

Two more conjoint sessions followed for the Fishers. Another flare-up occurred over some of George's behavior, but both of them were able to act on their better communications, self-acceptance, and trust of the other and handled the situation in a way that resolved the issue fairly quickly. By this time the Fishers had completed their purchase of a new house, closer to Pete's work, and were planning to move there. They decided that extra moving expenses, time pressures, and greatly increased travel time to the therapist's office all combined to make it unfeasible for them to continue therapy. Much of the final session was spent, therefore, on reviewing the major issues between them, what had been accomplished, and what they would have to be sensitive to in the future if they were going to able to maintain the improvement in their marriage. Both realized that more therapy might be required in the future, but they decided to terminate for now owing both to their improvement and the increased obstacles to treatment.

SUMMARY

This case demonstrates how the particular phases of the marital life cycle may exert a major influence on a couple's problems. Each part of the cycle has unique pressures and must be dealt with accordingly by the therapist. The Fisher case also demonstrates that marital cases rarely remain "pure," in the sense that other treatment issues often arise, such as the potential or actual need for additional or alternate treatments. Each case has to be handled according to the therapist's skills, judgment, and philosophy concerning both what is needed and how it can best be provided. Readers will note that both Edith and Pete demonstrated some personality patterns that presumably might have benefited from more individual therapy. However, each one's own extensive individual earlier therapy had led them both to reject this idea from the beginning. Marital therapy, by its very nature, often aims to meet short-term, more limited goals than individual therapy historically attempts. This does not make marital therapy either better or worse—simply different.

CHAPTER SEVEN
CHANGING
MARITAL ROLES

BACKGROUND:
THE ACQUISITION
OF MARITAL ROLES

At birth, an infant is labeled as a male or a female—an action which immediately assigns that child's sex role. The infant might as well be labeled as a husband or a wife, a mother or a father, a homemaker or a breadwinner—for American society has also traditionally assigned a variety of marital and other such roles to individuals, and these assignments are based almost exclusively on gender. Many forces combine to influence growing children's acquisitions of these roles, presumably so that by the time young males and females are ready for marriage they will know what is expected of them in their marital roles. Some of these influential social forces include parents, siblings, extended-family members, nursery rhymes and games, literature, school systems, religious and political groups, and virtually all segments of the mass media. The following chart lists some of the marital roles that have been, at one time or another, traditionally assigned to persons in accordance with their sex.

SOME TRADITIONAL MARITAL ROLES

Males	Females
Husband	Wife
Father	Mother
Income earner	Homemaker
Sex aggressor	Sex recipient
Companion	Companion

Males	Females
Household mechanic	Social secretary
Child-care provider (limited)	Child-care provider (unlimited)
Sex educator (very limited)	Sex educator (limited)
Yard-care provider	House maid
Backyard cook	General cook and dishwasher
Purchaser of cars and appliances	Purchaser of groceries and household
Trash and garbage disposer	supplies
Athletic coach	Seamstress
Finance control and counselor	Guidance counselor

Children gradually assimilate these roles at both the conscious and unconscious level. One need only listen to preschoolers "playing house" to realize how effectively and how soon children incorporate and reinforce these assigned sex and marital roles. They often scold each other with admonitions such as "Girls can't do that" or "Boys shouldn't do that."

As children mature and finally enter the world of dating during adolescence, they begin to "try on" more adult roles with members of the opposite sex through the mechanism of dating. One of the potentially useful social functions of dating, at any age, is to determine how congruent the male's and the female's concepts are of these various marital sex roles. For example, dating should reveal whether or not the male is highly chauvinistic and whether or not the female accepts the complementary roles required of her in such a situation so that they may coexist and interact with each other harmoniously, or at least with minimum conflict. Dating may, for instance, involve a young woman demonstrating the stereotypical, narcissistic Daddy's Little Princess role, whereby the young man is "tested" to see if he is comfortable and willing to complement her by being everlastingly attentive, worshipful, and generous. In our society, dating serves a purpose in the mate selection process as young, soon-to-be-married individuals perform their separate sex roles with the particular human being with whom they may live as a marriage partner—potentially (though less and less likely) for the next fifty years. Presumably, those dates who seem to provide the best "fit" in respect to potential marital roles will be chosen as the winners in these "auditions," and the end result will be compatible marital pairs. Those whose "fit" is unacceptable will, following the same logic, be discarded and the search will be continued until a more congruent partner is discovered.

MARITAL-ROLE CONGRUENCE AND ROLE CONFLICT

Ignoring the Lack of Congruence

What is required for a marital couple to interact successfully is role congruence, the state that exists when both partners, at *all* levels of consciousness, agree on what they are each "supposed" to do in specific situations. Ideally, if the partners fail to have or to acquire this congruence during dating, they will experience sufficient conflict and unpleasantness to motivate them to break up and find more suitable partners who better fit each one's concepts of the male and female marital sex roles. Unfortunately, however, many couples fail to end their relationships even when they do experience conflict over their roles in dating. As was discussed earlier, they don't interact often and intensively enough to uncover their differences, or the differences emerge and conflict results but a temporary "solution" is achieved when the partners assume that "love conquers all," or when one of them secretly expects that he or she can change, reform, or make over the partner after marriage occurs. Hence, some couples are clearly targeted for serious conflict over their marital roles before the ink is even dry on their marriage licenses.

Acknowledging the Conflict

Early in married life many couples begin to realize that marital sex-role conflicts have developed but "love," hope, and a willingness to attempt to compromise often combine to help them negotiate and satisfactorily resolve their differences. As time progresses, however, and particularly when sudden, abrupt shifts in roles occur—such as when the first baby is born—couples often find themselves less and less satisfied with the way each feels about his or her own and the partner's roles. Sometimes this dissatisfaction becomes a conscious realization very slowly; other times it occurs more dramatically. One woman, who had been resisting the therapist's insight-oriented comments about her apparent dissatisfaction with her husband's demands on her, turned to her husband during a conjoint session and virtually screamed, "You know, Dr. Humphrey *is* right. I just realized that I'm fed up with your expecting me to be both mother and father to *our* kids. By God, I'm not going to put up with this arrangement any longer!" From that moment on, the marriage was different. It had to be. Having become consciously aware of her anger and her dissatisfaction, that woman could never again accept the role of submissive, compliant partner that her husband had expected her to fulfill and with which she had thought she was comfortable in her efforts to be a "good wife."

SUCCESSFUL MARITAL-ROLE ADJUSTMENT

Willingness to Adapt and Change Roles

Marital roles are not fixed in all dimensions. They ordinarily change over time as the partners move through their marital life cycle. In past decades, these roles tended to be democratically evolved and balanced early in the marriage. During the child-bearing and child-rearing years, however, the husband tended to dominate; then, during midlife, the couple moved back toward a mutual acceptance of each other's roles. Successful marital adjustment in current American society, however, tends to evolve not through traditional fixed roles but rather through the ability of both husband and wife to be able and willing to adapt and to change their roles—in both *direction* and *magnitude*—in a parallel and complementary fashion. At the same time, they must emotionally accept their partner's changes.

As we have previously noted, major changes in a marriage often require either reassignment or realignment of marital roles. The birth of a child, one of the partners changing his or her job, illness, a change in income—these and a multitude of other factors all involve "normal" expectations and requirements for change. Therapists must always take into consideration, when evaluating a couple for treatment, what each person's concept is of his or her own role and of that of the partner, whether or not both husband and wife agree on these roles, and where change is needed to reduce or remove conflict.

In colonial times, marital-role conflict was presumably less of a factor in marital strife because social change was slow and sex roles were relatively fixed by the State, by religious teachings, and by tradition. One may still see examples of traditional marital sex-role congruence by studying the marital and family life of the Old Order Amish and some of the conservative Mennonite sects. These groups, who follow the Christian Bible most literally, reportedly retain a smoothness of husband–wife interaction because of their fixed and socially supported devotion to Biblical injunctions about the roles of husband and wife. When there is any doubt about who should do what, the Bible serves as a clear guide on how to resolve the issue. Furthermore, family and group pressures combine to force the couple to adapt to these roles should they deviate. For example, the Amish still practice the ancient punishment of "shunning," of refusing to talk to an errant member of the sect. This social isolation, if the male elders so decide, can be applied to any adult member who fails to fulfill his or her expected marital roles and obligations. Such examples constitute a tiny minority of American marriages today, however. Marital therapists should, as a practical matter, study them more as a "pure form" of traditional marital roles than as a useful model for contemporary life.

THE TWENTIETH CENTURY AND MARITAL ROLES

Change: A Way of Life

The Amish have been one of the very few groups in North America to successfully resist the impact of the changing culture on marital roles. In the twentieth century, it is *change,* not permanence, that is a way of life. Technology has played a major role in making rapid, dynamic change inevitable. Electronics has created instant communications around the globe through the media of radio, television, and satellites. Pharmacology and chemistry have created medicines that have drastically altered death and illness rates, as well as having successfully controlled human fertility for the first time in the history of humankind. Physics has harnessed nuclear power—and also provided the awesome capacity to wipe out most of the populations of the earth in a few minutes' time. Engineering has created servomechanisms and hydraulic assist devices that have made the greater muscular strength of males irrelevant, permitting women to perform easily such previously "male" tasks as truck driving and construction work.

In addition to these technological changes, political, economic, and social changes have accelerated during this century. Women have gained the right to vote and to hold public office; households have shifted from being economic producing units to economic consuming units; and changes such as the Social Security Act have reduced the reliance of older or dependent individuals upon the family by helping to meet individuals' needs more through government programs. World Wars I and II and the Korean and Vietnam conflicts have destroyed any remaining illusions that citizens of one country can avoid interacting with persons from other nations on this earth. Organized religion, which through the ages has exerted a powerful force in maintaining traditional marital roles in the family, has lost much of its influence in this sphere: most Catholics use birth control, the divorce rate increases, and there is a decline in the rate of young men and women entering the religious life. Finally, we should note the impact of what has come to be called the modern Women's Movement. American women by the millions have marched, have left their homes to enter the work market, and have vigorously fought for equal status with men in all endeavors—from the political arena to that of the bedroom. Earlier, marital roles were forced upon women by the collective weight of Church, State, public opinion, and the male world, but today women can achieve levels of emancipation and equality that their grandmothers could only dream of.

The Push toward "Equality"

All of these dynamic changes have had a direct impact upon marital roles. Very few in our society can ignore or resist these changes; most Americans have been deeply affected by them. The question now is not: How many children will a couple have? It is: Will they have any children at all? The question now is not: Will the wife work outside the home? It is: How long will she work and under what circumstances? and Will the husband become the primary "homemaker" if his wife makes more money than he does? The question now is not: Will the husband desert his wife and kids if he is unhappy? It is: Will the wife do the hitherto "unthinkable" and leave her husband to care for the house and kids while she pursues a better life elsewhere? Males, for the first time in recorded history, are having to accept the fact that they are no longer the dominant force in their homes and hence are no longer the primary determinants of marital roles simply because of their gender. All these changes mean that the therapist, like the couples themselves, can no longer have a priori expectations about what the marital roles will be—or can be—for any particular couple until the marital partners themselves have worked this through.

INTRAROLE AND INTERROLE CONFLICTS

Confusion Abounds

Marital roles, like all social roles, are never "pure," nor are they any longer totally fixed and rigid. Ordinarily, healthy persons can make adjustments within themselves to accommodate to necessary changes *within* their roles (intrarole) as husbands, wives, men, women, and so on; they can also make adjustments to accommodate to changes *between* their various roles (interrole) (husbands–bread-winners, wives–breadwinners; men–lovers, women–mistresses, etc.). These alterations may become necessary because of changes in their feelings, in their life situations, or because of changes brought about by their partners. The rapid changes that have occurred in marital roles in the twentieth century, however, have left many married persons confused about what is expected of them—by themselves, by their partners, and by society as a whole.

Intrarole conflicts, for example, may occur when a husband feels confused about what is expected of him as a husband. Should he be "strong and masculine" or "sensitive and caring"? Should he work overtime to clinch a lucrative financial deal and make more money for his family—or quit work at his usual hour so he can go to an exercise club and jog for an hour because his physician says he needs to do this in order to maintain his health? Should he be a "good male model" and play baseball on Saturday mornings with his 5-year-old son, or is he supposed to be free to sleep late that morning and unwind from his week's pressures? And similar confusions exist for a wife. Is she entitled to show excitement because she's been given a big bonus at work for her outstanding performance, or should she "play it down" so her husband's ego won't be damaged? If a child is sick, is the wife supposed to stay home with him or should she further her career by appearing at work on time? Or isn't caring for sick children exclusively a mother's role any more? Men and women who are sure of their various roles and who are both consciously and unconsciously accepting of them have few struggles like these. But they may be the exceptions today.

Literally millions of husbands and wives suffer enormous amounts of conflict within themselves about what they "should" think or feel or do in their marital roles. Often these conflicts have arisen because of negative experiences within their families of origin as they grew up. Perhaps an even greater source of uncertainty today, though, are the cues that bombard persons from the mass media about the "oughts" of marital roles. One's own parents may no longer be suitable models to identify with because their more traditional roles are no longer functional for many younger persons. Thus marital and sex-role conflicts of many types represent a major source of problems for couples seeking marital therapy today.

IMPLICATIONS FOR MARITAL THERAPY

Understanding, Acceptance, Resolution

One of the major tasks for marital therapists treating couples with role-conflict problems is to help the clients understand what they are experiencing and then to help guide them toward a resolution of their confusion and conflict. In addition, the therapist will want to focus on attempting to help each partner understand, negotiate, and accept the changes that have occurred—or that need to occur—in the marital system when either partner experiences changes. Conjoint interviews greatly facilitate this process because they permit each spouse to hear how the other feels, to speak up for his or her own needs and feelings, and to instantly deal with and attempt to reconcile his or her own wishes with those of the partner. Here we are talking about emotional acceptance, not just intellectual acceptance, of these changes.

Therapists must be sensitive to the use of rationalization and of repression by clients when they unconsciously attempt to alleviate their anxiety over these important changes. Couples must be helped through interpretation to face their unconscious feelings and to determine whether experimenting with the changes and getting "strokes" from their partner provides sufficient ego satisfactions to bring about inner acceptance of the changes. Slips of the tongue, dreams, joking, and teasing are all clues that the change is still creating anxiety for one or both of the partners.

Therapeutic aids. In these role-change situations, some therapists refer clients to support groups to assist in this process of accommodation and change. Many communities have both men's and women's "consciousness raising" groups that can, if properly led, be most helpful. Bibliotherapy or reading relevant literature also helps many persons to understand the changes that are affecting them and to generalize their own unique experience to that of others similarly affected in our society. Group marital counseling is another treatment strategy that many therapists feel is particularly helpful—especially if there is reasonable homogeneity with other couples' problems on these issues.

Implications for the Therapist

In dealing with couples in marital conflict, therapists are often faced with people who possess values that are quite different from their own. This is frequently true in the area of marital-role conflict. The more divergent the clientele with which the therapist deals, the greater will be this value continuum. It is incumbent upon all therapists to stay abreast of current professional literature and theory in order to understand the role problems with which contemporary clients are struggling.

The age and the sex of a therapist, among other things, frequently results in treatment problems in this area. Younger therapists often possess personal concepts of male and female roles in marriage that are more contemporary—and hence more flexible—than are those of their older clients. Similarly, older therapists often view marital roles more traditionally than do their younger clients. Both male and female therapists may find their personal marital roles challenged by clients of either sex. Clients often expect their therapist to "side" with the client of the same sex, particularly if marital sex-roles problems are at issue. Obviously, this problem needs to be dealt with swiftly and effectively. The modern, nonsectarian therapist is expected to be *pro-human*—not pro-male or pro-female. Some clients may become so convinced of a therapist's sexist bias that they will terminate therapy over this issue (an appropriate step if the therapist truly is sexist). When such bias does not exist on the part of the therapist, however, it reveals the client's own symptoms and bias. In these instances the therapist may encourage each client to express his or her feelings and to see if they can risk themselves enough to actually "test out" the therapist's objectivity and remain in treatment. If a therapeutic impasse is reached, however, the wisest choice may be referral of the couple to a therapist of the opposite sex (assuming the complaining spouse's partner will also accept a change of this nature). Similar resolutions should be attempted with age-generated marital sex-role conflicts between clients and therapists.

In summary, the implications of marital sex-role conflicts for the marital therapist are many. They may challenge the therapist's own personal value systems and will certainly require constant re-education and re-examination of personal ideas of roles and values.

CASE EXAMPLE:
LINDA AND BOB PEAKS

Background

Illustrative of the role that changing marital sex roles may present to a couple is the case of Bob and Linda Peaks. They were self-referred, having learned of the therapist from one of Bob's dental patients. In accord with procedures presented in Chapter Two, the therapist obtained basic identifying data from Bob over the phone when he called for appointments. Sometimes persons go into some detail about their problems during these initial phone calls, but this is not encouraged as the telephone is not an ideal substitute for face-to-face interviewing when no therapeutic relationship has yet been established. Some therapists may feel anxious about sitting down with clients for the first session when they know so little about them. This ordinarily presents no special problems, however, and this anxiety usually ceases with experience. In the case of Bob and Linda, all the therapist knew (besides the basic identifying facts) was that they had both agreed to come for the assessment sessions. However, if great ambivalence or conflicting views about the need for marital therapy had been apparent over the phone, they would have been encouraged to discuss the issue of therapy further with each other before an actual appointment was set up. The result of handling initial requests in this manner has consistently been a broken first appointment rate of under 1 percent for over two decades of practice.

Session 1—Initial Evaluation

Individual interview: Linda.   Linda, age 28, was a short young woman, neat and attractive in appearance, who appeared determined to do something constructive about the marriage. She explained that neither she nor Bob had received any previous therapy, and that they both wanted marital therapy. She expressed relief that they were finally doing something about their situation.

In Linda's opinion, the marital problems were cyclical in nature. Things would go well and they would both be happy, she said; then they would drift apart and both end up feeling lonely, unloved, and taken for granted. A major issue was time—specifically, weekend time. Bob ordinarily worked Saturday mornings at his dental office. For the past year, Linda explained, she had also been working most weekends as the hostess for a fashionable restaurant near their home. She complained that Bob didn't spend enough time with her, either during the week or on weekends. For the first eight years of marriage, before their daughter, now age 2, had been born, she had worked as a research associate in a publishing firm. After the baby's birth, she stayed home full-time until she "almost went nuts." Then she found her present part-time job as a hostess.

Linda portrayed Bob as heavily immersed in his work and herself as the chief complainer in the household. Her own mother had been a "complaining bitch" and Linda did not want her own child to grow up in the same kind of loveless household she had experienced. Both of the Peaks came from another state and, with little time for travel, they had drifted away from any regular contacts with either family. What she wanted, Linda stated, was both more time with Bob and a better time when they were together. She described their sex relationship as "OK," but said that Bob often became angry when, after an evening of "ignoring her," she rebuffed his sexual overtures when they went to bed. They would "drift apart" for a few weeks; she would feel increasingly unloved; then she would become "hysterical." Then they would have a big fight, after which they would kiss and make up.

Bob had told her that he thought she was jealous of his work, his patients, and his investment in activities outside the home. She said he did not complain about her being away part of each weekend at her hostess job, but that she resented his taking time away from her on the Saturday afternoons or Sundays when she was home and he left to play tennis or jog with other husbands in the neighborhood. She still loved her husband, Linda believed, but she was worried that she was giving less and less to him while demanding more time and attention from him.

Individual interview: Bob.   Bob, also age 28, was considerably taller than his wife, lean and healthy-looking in appearance, and appeared quite calm and in control of his emotions. He was interested in marital therapy, he said, in preference to a marital separation that his wife had "occasionally" suggested. Bob immediately presented their problems as stemming from their different ideas about what marriage should be all about. He saw Linda as making many "unreasonable" demands on his time for attention, companionship, and affection. He, too, had begun equating Linda with the latter's complaining, demanding mother. "She's killing my love for her with her incessant demands, just like her mother did to her father," he said rather sadly. He portrayed himself as a struggling young dentist who was having to work exceedingly hard to build up his practice, to pay off large loans taken out for his many years in college and dental school, and to "properly support" Linda and their daughter. In effect, he was saying, his wife didn't appreciate him enough.

Filling the therapist in on their courtship and earlier marital adjustment, Bob revealed that the Peaks were in a pattern that had existed since the earliest days of their courtship. They would get along fine; then he would immerse himself more and more in his studies and later in his practice. Linda would begin to complain more and more about feeling unloved and neglected; and finally a major fight would erupt. Bob said their last such big fight had really scared him and he was very worried that they would end up divorced unless they could alter their patterns of interaction.

Conjoint interview. The conjoint assessment session brought out in greater detail the Peaks's divergent expectations of each partner's marital roles. Linda defended her absence from their home on the weekends because, she said, it provided Bob with a unique opportunity to interact exclusively with their daughter. "Besides," she said, "we don't do much when we are home together anyway." Bob, for his part, appeared stung by her attack on their "togetherness" time, but he also insisted on his "right" to spend some time by himself or with his buddies for his own needs. (Sometimes these demands for "separate" time are coverups for extramarital affairs, but neither of the Peaks was involved in these, although Linda expressed the feeling that she was "ripe" for one.) Both Linda and Bob agreed that their first priorities were to keep their marriage going and improve it—"if they could."

Therapist's observations. At the conclusion of this session the therapist recommended marital therapy with a treatment plan of weekly conjoint sessions. There appeared to be no secrets that either partner was holding; the couple were interested in, and clearly needed, better communication and better understanding of each other's needs. Moreover, there appeared to be a conscious, unified wish on the part of each to maintain and to improve the marriage. While much attention was placed by both of the Peaks on their negative interactions and personality differences, there also appeared to be a major question of role conflict. Both had their own idiosyncratic concepts of what their own and their partner's roles should be— in respect to marriage, work, sex, and meeting emotional needs—but these were not congruent and, in fact, were often in direct conflict. Therefore, when the Peaks called back a few days later to say that they had talked over therapy and had decided to go ahead, the therapist anticipated that role conflicts might well emerge as pivotal issues for this couple. While many more issues were present and were actually dealt with as they emerged in therapy, the concentration would obviously have to be on efforts to assist the couple with their role conflicts.

Session 2

The next session focused heavily on Bob and his feelings—both what they were and how he consistently repressed his angry feelings. (Individuals who repress their angry feelings tend to also repress their loving ones.) In discussing their role conflicts, it developed that the only household role that Linda refused to comply with was that of carrying out the garbage. While they joked over this fact, the therapist's questions elicited the fact that Bob was acting "typically" in denying his annoyance with her over the garbage incidents. This made it possible to shift the session from a discussion of straight role conflict to Bob's excessive control of his feelings. (While role conflicts are serious, they are often intermixed with personality characteristics that are also basic to the marital conflict going on.) By bringing out Linda's wishes to know more about Bob's feelings, the therapist helped Bob to hear his wife's needs in an emotionally neutral and supportive atmosphere. When she "screamed" about her needs when they were at home, in contrast, Bob immediately "turned off, tuned out," and, in fact, often left the house to go for a walk—leaving his wife angry, hurt, and feeling completely rejected. By concentrating on improving the couple's communication methods, the therapist was attempting to provide them not with the resolution of their conflict but with the basic tools to work on this process.

Sessions 3 and 4

The next two conjoint sessions followed at weekly intervals and were devoted primarily to increasing Bob and Linda's understanding of each other's needs—especially those concerned with time and work—and of negotiating their differences about these. Considerable good will and caring emerged between them and both appeared to be consistently attempting to *hear* their partner's feelings, to *share* their own feelings, and then, as often occurred, to compromise so that both experienced satisfaction with their decisions. Bob was thinking about running for election to the local school board and this served as a major focus of their discussions about their respective roles. The therapist utilized questioning to insure that both of the Peaks realized the time commitments that would be required as a result of the school board duties, and encouraged Bob and Linda—as a form of "homework"—to discuss their feelings about these between the therapy sessions.

Session 5

Two weeks separated the fourth and fifth sessions, and during this interval the Peaks had a major argument over time and "Bob's neglect" of Linda's emotional needs for him to pay more attention to her when they had time available. Instead of concentrating upon his wife's needs, he had gone off with his tennis buddies on several occasions—until she had "blown her stack." During this session Bob said he loved his wife a lot, and enjoyed sex with her—but admitted how difficult it was for him to verbalize his good feelings toward her. His pattern of gradually slipping from being an attentive husband to a seemingly disinterested one was also discussed. Bob was still not able to verbalize much anger at Linda and said that her wishes for more affection and attention were quite reasonable. Neither one of the Peaks concentrated very much on their hectic schedules or the fact that both were scheduling their "spare time" in a way that tended to prohibit much interaction with each other.

Interruption in Therapy

At this point the Peaks suddenly terminated their marital therapy by calling to cancel future appointments. They expressed their appreciation for the therapist's help, said they were communicating more effectively and understood each other better, and felt they were ready to get along on their own. The therapist accepted their statements but also expressed the willingness to see them again in the future if they thought it would be helpful. In actuality, the therapist believed that the ending was premature and that attention to basic role conflicts had hardly commenced.

However, the telephone is not ordinarily a satisfactory device to utilize in overcoming clients' resistances, and clients have the right to make their own decisions—even those the therapist may disagree with. Many clients end treatment long before they have adequately resolved their basic conflicts, only to re-enter therapy weeks, months, or sometimes even years later. Therefore, when faced with a premature ending of therapy, a therapist should accept the action as positively as possible and meantime let the clients know they may return later if they wish. This statement frees them of the guilt they often feel in "rejecting" the therapist and encourages them to return later on if they need to.

Return to Therapy

The following year the Peaks returned for an additional four sessions. At that time Linda was pregnant with their second child and many tensions had arisen. Essentially, these tensions were similar to the issues discussed earlier—Linda's anger and unmet emotional needs and Bob's sexual frustration and needs for more time by himself. At this time Linda was exploring some further education for herself. She was finding "just staying home" increasingly confining and unrewarding. While Linda did not articulate it, it appeared to the therapist that she was beginning to face up to some of the role conflicts (her need for more attention, Bob's need for separateness), in which she was playing a "typical female dependent" role and her husband was remaining fixed in his "I'm a good hard-working faithful husband so what else am I expected to provide" role. Linda was sensing that she was going to have to take some constructive steps to improve her own satisfactions in life instead of relying so heavily on her husband and children to provide these for her. Obviously, part of her (the more mature self) wanted this increased self-dependence but another part (the fearful, childish self) feared risking the predictable safety of the old roles. The therapist attempted to encourage her in this role shift and personal growth by emphasizing the adage that "when you protect yourself, you protect the relationship" and by being supportive of her efforts.

Therapists frequently see couples who are mired down in unsatisfactory and destructive relationships because they fear so intensely the uncertainties of change. In these instances the therapist should ordinarily support growth and change if there is even the slightest hope that a client may achieve a more mature and satisfactory life adjustment and marriage. Periodically therapists meet couples who claim that they both want to change but when one person makes a positive move, the partner sabotages any gains. Later, efforts by the partner to change are similarly frustrated by the first person. They both complain but what they are actually doing, at an unconscious level, is colluding with each other to present any significant changes in their neurotically balanced system. These alliances need to be directly challenged by therapists or they will go on endlessly. This represents not a moral or value-laden judgment by the therapist but rather the realistic recognition that the couple would not be seeking therapy and change if their old ways of interacting were mutually satisfying.

Linda was increasingly seeing herself as becoming more and more like her "bitchy" mother. Linda's father, like Bob, had been a dentist; her parents had fought continuously while she was growing up; and she repeatedly voiced her determination not to repeat her parents' problems. At the same time, the therapy sessions were confronting the Peaks with the probability that marital failure would occur unless a major shift occurred in their interactions. Bob was consistently supportive of his wife's need to get out of the house (not all husbands are) and he was also drawing a line as to how far *he* would go in accepting their marriage *as it was*. In retrospect, no great changes occurred during these four sessions. Both of the Peaks ventilated much frustration; both "tuned in" more attentively on the partner's feelings; and the marriage returned to a more satisfactory basis as the birth of their second child became imminent.

Second Interruption and Second Resumption of Therapy

While there are no particular reasons why marital therapy should be interrupted by the birth of a baby (and some couples even need extra therapeutic help then), many couples use this as a defense against "going deeper" into therapy and therefore terminate therapy at such a time. The Peaks did precisely that. They were next heard from two and one half years later when they returned for further help. Their complaints sounded like a broken record. Both had much invested in their children, their home, and their way of life—but both of them were feeling unloved, unappreciated, and questioning their commitment to each other.

Every human being needs a consistent supply of ego gratification in order to feel a continuing sense of accomplishment and reward. Men have traditionally achieved much of this from their jobs or careers, but women have had to rely primarily upon their marriages and family experiences for their gratifications. In the Peaks's marriage, Bob was the more satisfied; by now he had a fine practice, two beautiful children, a gorgeous home in Suburbia, and many friends. His relationship with his wife lacked excitement, and often she was irritable, but he looked at "the whole package" and felt he could tolerate the imperfections that existed. Linda, however, was not able to do this. Basically a bright and talented person, she often felt stymied and empty. Her role as the "traditional" wife and mother held many rewards, but not enough to keep her happy. As she became more unhappy, the whole marital and family system became disrupted and plunged into a negatively reinforcing, downward-spiraling mess. There was little question that Linda's intrapsychic scars and fears were consistently intruding into her consciousness and adversely affecting her feelings and her relationships. On several occasions the marital therapist offered her extra individual therapy time to work on these but she refused to do this. Increasingly, she dwelt on her unhappy childhood and her identification with her hostile, rejecting mother. Bob tried to accept her, to convey his caring for her, but she moved toward divorce.

After their fourth interview in this second series of treatment sessions, Linda reached the depths of despair and she and Bob talked openly, calmly, and realistically of divorce. Around this time, however, an event occurred which directly affected her role as wife, mother, and person. Having given up further education as a key to getting out of the house, she and a female friend had explored the possibility of opening up their own restaurant. While working as a hostess, Linda had acquired an extraordinary grasp of this type of business and the other woman had a background as an accomplished commercial cook. Even as she and Bob talked of divorce, they also talked of a new set of roles for themselves. Bob's practice was going very well and he anticipated that he could offer considerable financial backing if Linda and her friend started their own business.

Ordinarily, a time of acute marital crisis is an extremely inappropriate time for a couple to move ahead into a new commercial venture. For Linda and Bob, however, the opposite proved true. From its opening day, the restaurant was a major success. Linda devoted enormous amounts of time to it, forcing Bob to take on a much more active fathering role with the children than he had ever expected—but father and children all benefited. For her part, Linda almost immediately began to experience a new sense of value, of worth, and of self-acceptance. Concentrating on the needs of her business, she drastically reduced her preoccupation with how horrible her past had been. Although intercourse became even less frequent, Bob found her to be a more exciting person and partner. She, in turn, found herself happily surprised with her husband's acquisition of a new set of roles for himself— from buying the groceries and taking the kids to the pediatrician, to bragging about his wife's accomplishments. Her former hostility gave way to a new sense of caring for him—but with lessened needs to demand so much attention from him.

Eight sessions and several months after this turn of events began, the couple terminated therapy, with both of them far more satisfied with the marriage, and with Linda a happier person.

SUMMARY

What was the role of the therapist during all these sessions? In addition to working on communication, developing insight, and providing this couple with repeated opportunities to ventilate their hurts and angers, the therapist consistently supported Linda's movement into her new role as businessperson. He also supported the shifts that Bob had to make as a result of his wife's role changes. Psychodynamic purists may be quick to question whether Linda's intrapsychic troubles were really resolved or whether they were merely repressed further as she achieved the ego gratifications that went with her new role. Most therapists are skeptical of environmental shifts that seem to accomplish such rapid changes. However, in the modern world, women are increasingly enjoying the rewards that men have traditionally received because of their accomplishments in business, industry, and the professions. These rewards may very well have played a major role in the fact that fewer adult males have sought psychotherapy than was true for women. Certainly as Linda's personal sense of value and worth increased, she was able to contribute more positively to the marital system. Her husband responded to this appropriately, with greater respect and caring for her—a fact which in and of itself was of inestimable therapeutic value to her. Both of their roles changed, and in a way that was congruent with their individual needs. Role change, in the case of Linda and Bob Peaks, therefore brought about increased marital satisfaction and stability. By supporting this change, the marital therapist played a direct and positive role in their success.

CHAPTER EIGHT
DIVORCE, REMARITAL, AND GRIEF THERAPY

BACKGROUND

Every year over one million divorces are granted in the United States. In some cities and counties, the number of divorces granted each year equals the number of marriages contracted. The vast majority of those persons who divorce remarry within one to three years. Approximately one-half of all American children currently live in a one-parent household during some period of their childhood or adolescence. All of these facts combine to suggest that our system of marital monogamy should more properly be labeled a marital and family system based upon serial monogamy—one spouse at a time but with two or more marriages in the "average" person's lifetime. Inasmuch as only a minute fraction of divorces occur without some psychic pain and anguish, divorce and separation therapy often represent a major portion of a marital therapist's client load—especially if one considers the various stages in marital breakdown where divorce therapy may be indicated. These particular stages include reaching the decision to divorce, the time of physical separation, the legal divorce (or, as it is often legalistically referred to, the marital dissolution), the postdivorce period, and, finally, the remarriage or the adjustment to singlehood time. Therapists may treat clients throughout all of these stages or throughout just one or two of them. Individual clients' circumstances, needs, and motivations are the determining factors in arriving at how much therapy is utilized and when it will take place.

Marital therapists have historically carried the public reputation of being antidivorce, a fact that has led many individuals and couples to reject marital and/or divorce therapy as a necessary or constructive step to take. Some therapists, especially those in sectarian settings that oppose divorce on theological grounds, still maintain an antidivorce stance—both consciously and unconsciously. Therapists employed in sectarian settings where there are no theological barriers to divorce face an especially difficult public relations task. The public will often assume that such therapists are automatically antidivorce merely because they are working within religious settings. Hence, one of the first professional tasks that all modern nonjudgmental therapists face is to educate both public and professional referral sources about the services they can and will provide (see Public Relations, Chapter Nine). Before we look at these services, however, let us examime some of the current issues concerning divorce.

THE ETIOLOGY OF DIVORCE

The institution of marriage has never been experienced by all of its practitioners as a life of continuous connubial bliss. Marital conflict and/or dissatisfaction occurs within all marriages to some degree. Decisions to continue the marriage or to divorce are, for all practical purposes, made continuously by all married persons, although these decision processes frequently occur at unconscious levels. As long as the positives of staying married outweigh the negatives, marriages continue. As soon as one of the marital partners begins to more or less continuously experience the relationship as more negative than positive, however, the process of deterioration accelerates and the possibility that the marriage will terminate increases.

Rewards, Barriers, and Alternatives

While there are many theories concerning marital dissolution, marital therapists should find the Levinger and Moles (1979) concepts especially helpful. These researchers have written of (1) the *positive rewards* partners receive by staying in the marriage, (2) the *barriers* that exist to dissolving marriages, and (3) *alternative sources of satisfaction* that may be available in the case of marital disruptions. For example, many couples stay married not so much because they "love" each other but because they are reasonably comfortable with their mate; they like the emotional security of knowing they will have company when they are at home. Moreover, in American society, being married still involves many social rewards of acceptability and support. These same couples routinely face many barriers to divorce—widespread religious and social disapproval, a widely believed myth that children will always be psychologically harmed more by marital breakups than they will be by fighting parents staying together, and the fact that splitting up financial assets almost invariably leads to lower standards of living for all persons involved in a divorce. Finally, there is the question of what alternative sources of satisfaction couples can reasonably expect if they divorce—will there be more happiness "out there"? Will another Mr. or Ms. "Right" become available? Or are the available alternatives to continuing the marriage too bleak and frightening to make marital dissolution a possibility? Couples rarely sit down and compute their "scores" on these issues together, but mentally, they repeatedly engage in this "weighing" process.

Divorce—Here to Stay

The exact "causes" of the high incidence of marital dissolution in contemporary society continue to be argued. Certainly a shift has occurred away from the traditional value of marital permanence at any cost to a greater emphasis upon the health and happiness of the individuals within the marriage. The idea of marriage as a male-dominated economic support system has given way to a less one-sided arrangement in which both men and women bear responsibility for marital stability. Religious, social, and legal barriers to divorce have either decreased or vanished. At the same time that these changes have been occurring, new stresses on marriage have been developing. Work careers have emerged that take one or both spouses away from their homes for days or weeks at a time. "Swing" shifts in factories make consistent family routines difficult if not impossible. The advertising media work hard at trying to convince Americans that they can purchase anything they want—instantly and probably on credit—even in their marital relationships. Perhaps one of the greatest forces of change affecting the divorce rate encompasses those social and legal changes which have increasingly made women more nearly equal to men. No longer must women endure master–slave relationships with their husbands as, in Levinger and Mole's terms, the alternative sources of satisfaction reasonably available to unhappily married women are becoming more numerous and obtainable with each succeeding generation.

Regardless of the specific etiology, a high divorce rate in the United States appears to be here to stay. With today's newly married couples facing increased life expectancies that may mean fifty to sixty years of married life together before "death do them part," it can be reasonably expected that divorce therapy is here to stay and will continue to represent a significant portion of marital therapists' work.

THE PSYCHOLOGICAL PROCESS OF MARITAL DISSOLUTION

Divorce: When and How It Begins

Divorce may be said to begin at the time of the marriage ceremony. Numerous studies have shown that marital satisfaction is at its peak at the beginning of a marriage and soon thereafter begins to decline. A lessening of marital satisfaction does not necessarily cause divorce, but certainly therapists never see happily married couples divorcing. After the first stage of romantic disillusionment sets in, couples have to face the reality that marriage will not be all fun and games. Emotionally immature persons will have many problems accepting this fact and will experience accelerated disillusionment with their marriages. The normal pressures of everyday married life, from making a living to coping with kids, taxes, and illnesses, add further weight to the disenchantment process.

Marriage necessitates a very close and intimate relationship. Issues that may have been ignored, repressed, rationalized, or tolerated during dating and courtship begin to produce persistent and increasing irritations once they have to be faced and coped with on a daily basis. The young husband who quit going to sports events with his male friends so that he could please and be with his fiance during courtship may demand his "right" to resume his old habits—with or without his wife, and regardless of her feelings. As noted earlier, the arrival of children frequently serves to drive an additional emotional wedge between couples. Shared time, especially happily shared time, can become increasingly rare for a couple after parenthood commences. If couples postpone having children or decide to remain childfree, their careers may serve as equally demanding and emotionally isolating factors. As any marriage progresses, all couples face routine crises and conflicts. Couples who entered their marriages with good physical and mental health, stable financial basis, and a strong commitment to each other ordinarily develop a capacity to handle these many pressures and keep the marital relationship a rewarding and valued part of their lives. However, many couples—probably a majority of all young marrieds today—do not possess all of these positive attributes and skills. They become unhappy with themselves, their partners, and their lives in general. Their wishes to escape from their gloomy and unhappy situations gradually lead at least one of them to begin to seriously consider divorce as a "solution" to their unhappiness.

The process of deterioration. The majority of divorces occur before the seventh year of marriage with the highest rate occurring during the second and third years. This pattern suggests that the psychological process of marital dissolution moves at a relatively rapid pace. Obviously, however, every divorce therapy case contains unique aspects. Some couples describe a long period of marital contentment and then a rapid period of deterioration. This, for example, often occurs when an extramarital affair is revealed and suddenly intense conflict breaks loose. Other couples report that they have *always* felt emotionally estranged from their spouse and that conflict was simply endured until one partner reached the "breakup" point. Still other couples send "signals" to their partners for years that they are unhappy, but these signals may be ignored or, at best, placating efforts are made which reduce tensions only until the next fight occurs. Love and caring are like plants—they must be constantly fed, watered, cultivated, and nourished. If persistently neglected, they weaken and may die. Many couples seeking divorce therapy describe "the spouse who woke up too late" syndrome. Here, retrospective therapeutic investigation of the marital breakdown reveals a pattern wherein one of the partners has regularly and persistently communicated signs and messages to the other indicating frustration, feelings of being unloved and unappreciated, and a desire to change the situation. The other partner has ignored these messages or, at best, made only occasional efforts to deal with the problem. The pattern continues, sometimes for years, until the unhappy person reaches a point of total loss of interest in the marriage and wants a divorce. This divorce request often appears to the rejected spouse as "coming out of the blue." The previously complacent partner reacts with disbelief, quickly decides the situation is serious, and makes strenuous efforts to change. Whether or not therapy will help "save" such marriages depends upon a multitude of factors. One of the most crucial of these concerns the amount of motivation—if any—that the chronically unhappy partner has left to maintain the marriage. If that person has lost all interest, the marriage is probably doomed. Therapy in these instances will be oriented toward helping the couple dissolve the marriage with a minimum of further psychological damage to themselves and their children. If motivation to maintain the marriage remains, therapy will be focused on the more standard issues of improving communications, increasing self- and other knowledge, and helping the couple in the attempt to once again meet each other's needs and expectations.

THE STAGES OF DIVORCE

Bohannan (1970) identified six stages of divorce that are helpful for therapists to be cognizant of. First is the *emotional divorce*, the stage at which a husband and wife become psychologically distanced from each other. This may be reported by them as having been either unilaterally or bilaterally experienced. Second is the *legal divorce* stage of marital dissolution. Marriage is a legal institution and certain legalities must be accomplished if the parties are to end their legal obligations to each other and become free to remarry. Third is the *economic divorce*. This stage involves the process of disentangling the couple's financial assets. The longer they have been married and the more substantial and complex their financial holdings, the more difficult is this stage. It is at this point that expressions of anger and hurt often occur: sentiments like "I'll make the bastard pay for his or her freedom" represent a common theme at this stage. Fourth is what Bohannan terms the *co-parental divorce* stage. Persons can divorce their marital partners, but parental relationships continue for a lifetime. In this stage, custody, visitation rights, and other issues involving the children must be worked out. Fifth is the *community divorce* stage. The couple may divorce, but the community in which they live—made up of friends, neighbors, and ex-in-laws—have to evolve new ways of relating to each of the ex-partners. People who used to be "their friends" often become "his" friends or "her" friends—or even cease relating to either person. The sixth and final stage has been termed by Bohannan as "*psychic divorce.*" This represents the end of the divorce process and occurs when ex-wives or ex-husbands psychologically recover from their wounds and begin to relate to the world around them as single, distinctly separate and unique individuals again—not as the "wife or husband of so-and-so" but as Jane or John Doe—person, citizen, adult, and so forth. For many, this psychic healing process will not be completed until they remarry.

Therapeutic implications.   Obviously, divorcing couples do not move through these stages with predictable consistency or ease. They may become fixated at a given stage or stages, unable to cope with or resolve the particulars of that stage, or they may regress and engage in conflict in areas previously considered to have been resolved. Therapy should be directed at their feelings and the issues *of the moment*, in essence following the old therapeutic shibboleth of starting where one's clients are. Additionally, both the husband and the wife will not necessarily be reacting to the same stages at the same time. Often one partner, usually the one who first proposed the idea of divorce, will move rapidly toward completing the total separation and divorce process, while the mate may be still struggling with the earliest stages. One of the therapeutic implications for this imbalance is the desirability of combining individual and conjoint treatment sessions so that both individual and couple issues can be focused upon by the therapist.

THE ROLE OF AMBIVALENCE

One of the prominent characteristics of divorce therapy is the presence of high levels of ambivalence on the part of one or both of the partners. The origins of these ambivalent feelings stem primarily from "emotional divorce"-stage issues. When both partners clearly desire a divorce, the marital therapist is rarely consulted. However, when one or both partners have very mixed feelings about divorcing, there may be therapeutic impasses that are exceptionally slow to resolve. One of the major factors contributing to this ambivalence relates to what Weiss (1975) refers to as the persistence of *attachment* after the erosion of love. Couples may "rationally" agree that their love is gone—indeed, often a prospective new marital partner has already been picked out by one of them. However, as one client put it, "You just don't walk away from eight years of sharing your life with another person 365 days a year—especially if she is the mother of your children." Some clients have the fantasy that bigamy might be a theoretical answer to their dilemma. They feel they could maintain their positive feelings and their attachment to their legal partners but also take on new partners for more excitement, new experiences, and to put more joy into their lives. Both our legal system and other forms of social control make such "solutions" impractical—to say nothing of how the current partners would ordinarily feel about any such sharing arrangements.

Therapeutic implications.   Therapists need to focus on those ambivalent feelings of clients which stand in the way of the resolution of the problem. The pros and the cons of the conflicts must be discussed, reframed, and examined to help clients arrive at decisions about which of their feelings are strongest and most important for them. All this time, however, the divorce process continues and the other partner's feelings directly affect the ambivalent person's total life systems. Sometimes ambivalence may not be resolved so much as it simply ceases to exist. A person may have to shift his or her thoughts from "Do I want a divorce?" to contending with the reality of the total breakdown of the marriage because the partner no longer gives him or her any choice in the matter. It is when both husband and wife are ambivalent about obtaining a divorce that therapy may appear to drag on interminably.

THE IMPACT OF DIVORCE

Divorce: Severe Emotional Stress

With the rapid rise in divorce in recent times, one might assume that because so many people are doing it, divorce must have become a highly desirable and valued part of our social institutions. Many lay- and professional persons appear to treat divorce rather lightly. Some journalists and writers have described divorce as a growth experience, giving the impression that it should be experienced by everyone interested in expanding their human potential. Marital therapists should not succumb to any such delusions. Divorce remains one of the most severe emotional stresses that the average person will ever experience. It rates second only to death of loved ones in producing stress for the individuals experiencing it, and is an ego-threatening experience. Divorced persons suffer more psychiatric hospitalizations, more car accidents, more diseases and suicides—just to name a few such categories—than do married persons. Obviously, these conditions are not always caused *by* divorce. The fact remains, however, that divorce is almost always experienced *by at lease one of the marital partners* as rejection, a personal failure, and as a crisis. Therapists will find their clients expressing feelings of low self-esteem, worry, depression, tension, shock, irritability, fatigue, and—sooner or later—great anger. The intensity and the duration of these feelings will vary with each client's ego strength, where the person is in the divorce process, his or her supportive resources, and whether the person is the "rejector" or the "rejectee." Rejectors may experience many feelings of guilt and shame even though they feel they are taking steps that are ego-syntonic for their own life needs. Those being rejected will most likely feel the most severe depressions and the strongest angers. Hence it is essential for the therapist, upon receiving a referral for divorce therapy (or at the moment he or she realizes an ongoing marital therapy case is probably headed for divorce), to take several factors into consideration. How does *each* partner view the marriage? The possible divorce? Which one is the rejector? The rejectee? What unique therapeutic issues will arise for each person? These and more questions relate to who seeks the divorce "versus" who seeks to maintain the marriage. Therapy must be planned accordingly for both the husband and the wife.

LEGAL ISSUES

The majority of marital therapists are not lawyers and do not have special training in family law. Consequently, many issues arise during divorce therapy that require referrals to appropriate legal sources. All therapists should, however, have some general knowledge of the laws regulating marriage and divorce in their state or province. Until recently, the majority of marriage and divorce laws followed the fault or adversary system of legal dissolution of marriage. This ordinarily resulted in major perjury and hypocrisy issues arising during the legal divorce process. Today, many laws are based on the principle of the "irretrievable breakdown" of the mar-

146

riage under so-called "no-fault" statutes. On the surface it would appear that these changes would lower the amount of acrimony so often present in divorce proceedings. However, the issue may very well be that legal fights do not cause the acrimony but rather reflect the pre-existing anger that couples feel. The legal struggles over property distribution, as well as child custody, visitation, and support issues often represent displaced hostility. Clients who are unable to consciously accept their anger at their divorcing mates may unconsciously make major issues out of minor points, reflecting the displacement of their anger into different areas of their relationships—such as who gets to keep the furniture. In addition, these issues often become psychologically symbolic to divorcing couples. What will "others" think if mothers "let" their husbands have major—or even joint—custody of the children? Why should fathers be forced to move out of homes that are also theirs? When clients' feelings of self-esteem are on the line or their reputations are under attack, they may respond with unprecedented anger. Attorneys, by and large, are not schooled in psychodynamics and often become quite impatient with their divorce clients' mercurial feelings. (Some critics of the legal system have a contrary view and feel that many divorce lawyers understand feelings extremely well but play on these, one way or another, in order to help their individual clients obtain the most favorable settlements in their divorces.) Therapists respond to these issues in different ways. Some choose to remain separate from the legal issues but try, at the same time, to assist each partner with his or her feelings about what is transpiring in the legal negotiations. Other therapists take a different approach and attempt to cooperate with both the husband's attorney and the wife's by helping the lawyers understand the emotional dynamics that each partner is struggling with. Still others attempt to mediate the process, as described in the next section.

Divorce Mediation

In more recent times, a new movement has entered the divorce field—that of divorce mediation. In this process, a trained mediator works with both the husband and the wife in an effort to help them remain issue-oriented during the divorce proceedings. Often the spouses are required to agree to written rules on how the procedures will be carried out. A special attorney serves as a legal consultant to both the husband and the wife (Coogler 1978). This movement has been designed to minimize the adversary nature of most divorce proceedings in efforts to help all members of families obtain the best possible settlement. The results of this approach, however, are still uncertain. As yet, we do not know how well this movement will be accepted by the public, by the legal establishment, and by the marital therapy profession.

Courtroom Testimony

One legal concern of divorce therapists is the question of whether or not they should appear during court proceedings in favor of one of their clients or the other.

Obviously, when a therapist chooses to take the legal side of one of the partners, the other spouse will terminate his or her therapeutic relationship. Some therapists argue that court appearances by them, especially in matters involving child custody, are valid and appropriate professional activities. Others insist that the legal process should be an entirely separate process from the therapy because it could easily lead to a rejection of all marital therapy by large numbers of potential clients. If clients had to fear that whatever they said to their therapist in private and under promise of confidentiality might at a later date be entered as public testimony against them, they would understandably be unwise to trust in any therapist. Most marital therapists, technically speaking, do not enjoy the legal status of privileged communication. They do, however, subscribe to an ethical position of client confidentiality, a basic premise which underlies all marital and divorce therapy. Rarely have judges been willing to enforce subpoenas compelling therapists to testify against their will and so the matter, for all practical purposes, resides almost entirely in the particular position each therapist chooses to take.

Children of Divorcing Parents

A related legal issue concerns child custody, visitation, and support. A modern departure from the traditional awarding of the custody of all minor children to their mother has been the advocacy and use of joint custody. Many groups, especially divorced fathers' groups, have lobbied extensively to have the laws changed to both permit and show preference to having both parents retain custody of their minor children. Divorce has usually resulted in decreasing visits and prematurely terminated financial support from fathers who traditionally have only had visitation rights. Joint custody is being advocated as a means of giving fathers a more meaningful emotional investment in their children's future. An additional factor impinging upon child custody has been the large increase during recent decades of mothers of small children working outside the home. The old idea that the children should be placed with their mothers because mothers "didn't work" (outside the home) and could provide more consistent parenting for the children simply no longer holds for the majority of American parents.

All these legal and social changes need to be kept in mind by divorce therapists because they bear directly upon clients' feelings, their social and legal realities, and the kinds of decisions and plans they have to make as they contemplate divorce. Realistically, only a very small percentage of children are cared for by their divorced fathers. Hence, the implications for mothers contemplating divorce are far different than for fathers. These mothers' "alternatives"—life with minor children while they struggle with single parenthood—often serve as larger barriers to divorce for women than for men. Legal rights, civil rights, and women's rights are all major contemporary issues but divorce therapists, perhaps above all, owe it to their clients to be realistic. Supporting divorce actions for which clients may pay impossibly burdensome prices does not constitute proper and ethical professional practice.

THE POST-DIVORCE PERIOD—
SINGLEHOOD AND
REMARRIAGE

Psychic Divorce Necessary

Earlier it was noted that most divorced persons remarry. Their divorces do not represent so much a rejection of the institution of marriage as they do rejection of (or by) particular partners. Human beings are social creatures—they seek meaningful relationships with significant others. In order for divorced persons to successfully re-enter the world of dating, however, they ideally should reach stage 6 of Bohannan's typology, that of "psychic divorce." They must internalize the fact that they are now free and independent adults who are no longer under the restrictions of marriage when it comes to dating other persons. For many, this is a time of terror. They may not have been involved in the risky business of dating for years or even for decades. Marriage theoretically supplied them with a permanently available partner—now they have to risk the unfamiliar world of dating games. Women, socialized into passivity in dating (particularly if they are older), often find this time particularly stressful. Some recently divorced persons handle their anxiety by retreating from dating and utilizing massive denial of their needs for companionship. Others appear to overreact to their new freedoms and develop reputations as great party people and "bed-hoppers" as they rush from one new relationship to another. Marriage, in spite of all its pressures, contributes a great deal to every person's sense of personal identity. Divorce instantly dissolves this facet of selfhood and people may flounder. Some clients never reach these stages because they continue to deny the facts of their divorce and act as if they are just living out a bad dream that will soon magically end, with all returning to normal.

From the foregoing, it should be apparent that each newly divorced person must find peace with him- or herself, must go on living, and must cope with the world as well as possible. Therapy at this time tends to take on the characteristics of traditional individual therapy, except for those clients who are dealing with "un-finished business" involving problems related to their former mates, a process some believe is similar to the way young adults must resolve their unfinished business with their families of origin before they can move ahead into full, independent adult living.

Pressures on the Divorced

Remarriage is not for everyone, however. The older persons are at the time of their divorce, the less likely they are to remarry, especially if they are females. Historically, great preasure has been placed on divorced persons to remarry. Divorced men were considered lost, incompetent persons who needed a "good woman" to share their life. Divorced women, on the other hand, faced the stereotype of being promiscuous divorcees who were eager—and available—to get into bed with every married man in the neighborhood. Divorced women remain vulnerable to this malicious notion and often report that the first volunteers who show up after their divorces with offers to relieve them of their presumed sexual frustrations are the husbands of the divorcee's best women friends.

Singlehood

Today, however, increasing numbers of men and women are choosing a new lifestyle—one that involves deliberate post-divorce lifelong singlehood. These persons may or may not choose to live with a member of the opposite sex for the remaining periods of their lives, but they do choose to retain a fairly high level of independence by not remarrying. Again, marital therapists are cautioned to be aware of these changing lifestyles and to abstain from imposing their own needs and value systems on their clients.

Support Groups

A valuable assist for many post-divorce individuals are the support groups available to them. Some of these, such as Parents Without Partners, serve special populations, in this case single parents. Others serve all types of singles: the never-marrieds, the separated, the divorced, and the widowed, regardless of parenthood status. Sociologists have maintained that because there have been no role models for the divorced in our society, divorced persons could not know what to expect— or what was expected of them—in many different situations. Groups such as PWP and singles groups help people overcome many of these problems. They often provide instant comradeship, peer reference groups, role models, organized activities for both adults and children, and a source of minimum threat to persons venturing forth for the first times after separation and divorce. These organized groups vary greatly, however, in terms of clientele, activities, leaders, and appeal to different individuals. It is helpful to clients if therapists performing divorce therapy are aware of such available resources in their communities and can help evaluate them just as they would for medical, legal, and other lay and professional services clients may need.

REMARITAL PREMARITAL THERAPY

Clients may also seek therapeutic help for issues dealing with remarriage—a form of therapy sometimes labeled "remarital premarital therapy." For decades, divorce therapy has been recommended to help clients achieve insight into why their marriages ended in divorce on the theoretical assumption that insight might help them avoid "making the same mistakes" again. This concept has been widely accepted, and today many people are seeking remarital premarital therapy for this purpose. Others, however, seek out therapy before remarrying for the same reason that persons often come for therapy before first marriages—they are experiencing problems in their relationships, family opposition to their marriages, and the like.

At least two significant differences exist for remarital premarital therapy, however. First, large numbers of divorced persons carry intense feelings of failure—because they were divorced—and need to increase their sense of self-confidence before they risk themselves in marriage again. Second, remarriage commonly involves the issue of one's minor children, both his and hers. The presence of these children makes the remarriage situation more difficult for divorced parents than for divorced adults who have no children. Co-parental issues previously referred to—custody, visitation, financial arrangements, and the feelings of *everyone involved*—have to be dealt with realistically. An increasing proportion of American families are now "blended families," made up of "his, hers, and their children." Traditional conjoint marital therapy should be expanded into remarital premarital family therapy in these instances so that all the members of the new family systems that will be created by remarriage may become positively involved with one another and competencies developed for this new way of living.

GRIEF THERAPY

In the preceding sections, we have discussed marital therapy dealing with divorce issues. Some professionals believe this should represent a totally new specialization. Similarly, grief therapy—therapy with persons having difficulty dealing with their grief—is considered by many to also represent a new specialization. Grief arises at the time of death, separation or divorce, and also at times of tragedy, such as a severe accident, or upon the diagnosis of a terminal illness. Ordinarily, grief may be considered both a normal and a beneficial human emotion. It is considered in this section with the assumption that special grief therapy is to be recommended only when the person, couple, or family cannot cope with their grief utilizing their normal systems and methods of coping with stress, hurt, and loss. The marital therapist with a general practice, however, needs to be aware of some of the unique aspects of grief since periodically he or she will meet clients having particular difficulties with handling this.

Anticipatory Grief

Kübler-Ross (1969) has written of five stages that people go through when they are anticipating profound grief. First is the stage of *denial and isolation.* Because the person cannot consciously cope with the knowledge of a feared event, he or she protects him- or herself by denying the fact or possibility of the loss. The second stage is *anger.* This may or may not be acted out, but therapists need to accept it as real, valid, and understandable. Third is the *bargaining* stage. Devoutly religious people, for example, may try to bargain with God. "Spare my mother's life now and I will never miss going to church again," they may say during their prayers.

This bargaining is often common in predivorce maneuvering when a person fears catastrophe if the divorce occurs, so he or she is willing to bargain for almost any-thing—except that which is most feared. For example, a person may say to his or her partner "if you stay here and don't divorce me you can do whatever you want." The fourth stage is *depression*. When a person experiences a death in the family, major support systems made up of other relatives, friends, neighbors, and fellow workers usually come forth to lend help and solace. This support is much less common, however, for the person grieving over a divorce; friends and relatives may take sides or, even in the most positive circumstances, they often don't know what to say or do to reduce the grief. Finally, according to Kübler-Ross, is the fifth and final stage—*acceptance*. During this stage the grief is finally resolved realistically and the person can move ahead with his or her life in a more positive manner.

Acute Grief

People experiencing sudden or acute grief react somewhat differently. They are first hit by emotional shock and frequently become numb and unable to plan for themselves. They may even need supervision so that they will not place them-selves in jeopardy. As they move through this stage, their emotions become very volatile and their anger may pour forth vigorously. Guilt emerges, and the person may repetitiously say, "I should have . . . " or "What if I had . . . " as they try to magically undo what has happened or is happening. After this process of compul-sive, guilt-ridden thinking, loneliness sets in and, particularly in cases of death, survivors may actually search for the deceased as if he or she were still alive some-where. All sorts of things and events which symbolize the person that has been lost begin to symbolize the loss—a song, a favorite scent, an article of clothing. Relief from these processes may come with death if the cause of grief has been a terminal illness. But even death with its relief may bring more guilt. Eventually, as was true in Bohannan's last stage of divorce and is true in anticipatory grief, the whole process completes itself, allowing the survivors to re-establish themselves as healthy, independent persons who can once again be productive and happy.

Therapeutic implications. Therapists can expect clients to react to grief ex-periences in the same uniquely individual manner with which they face other crises in their lives. Those with strong egos and who have been leading constructive lives will ordinarily cope with grief experiences with deep and profound feelings of sad-ness but with a minimum of disruption in their lives in terms of the length and the severity of their temporary incapacities. Other clients, those with more fragile egos who may have been experiencing difficulties coping with life even before they met up with tragedy, will be far more severely impaired in their feelings and functioning and will remain so for longer periods of time. As is always true when dealing with depressed persons, marital therapists need to be watchful of increased suicidal risks during periods of strong grief for their clients.

IMPLICATIONS FOR MARITAL
THERAPY OF DIVORCE
AND GRIEF

Countertransference Problems

We have touched on some of the unique aspects that therapists must consider in treating persons involved in divorce and grief processes. One of the major implications for the marital therapist in these areas is that of countertransference. Always an issue in any therapy, countertransference becomes especially powerful when the therapist is treating clients experiencing intense psychic pain and conflicting loyalties. It is difficult for some therapists to avoid taking sides in divorce issues. However, it is critical to the outcome of therapy to comfortably relate to *both* marital partners—even when they are involved in a destructive process with each other. If a therapist cannot handle his or her feelings toward one or the other of the partners, referral of those individuals to another therapist is necessary. If this occurs frequently, the therapist should investigate the matter with a supervisor or consultant because unconscious factors may be operating that limit the ability to be of help to clients. Some therapists are drawn to marital therapy because of unconscious needs to "save" marriages. Working with couples going through divorce will activate their unconscious conflicts and, if these are untreated, may ultimately frustrate clients' needs and wishes. A clue to this phenomenon may be repeated feelings of frustration or impotency on the part of therapists when their clients divorce.

Divorce Can Be Healthy

A common error made by some therapists is to assume that everyone who divorces is, ipso facto, immature, narcissistic, and badly in need of individual psychotherapy. Perfectly healthy "normal" human beings can and do divorce each other. Often it is not that the person or persons have "failed" but rather that the marriage relationship itself is no longer viable. No matter how mature and well prepared the couple are when they marry, no matter what religion they follow or how much "in love" they are, no one can predict with any absolute certainty that a specific marriage relationship will continue to fulfill each of the partner's various needs year after year. These persons need to be reassured that they are "OK" and that, difficult though divorce may be, they still have worth and value as individual human beings. At the same time, it should be cautioned that a divorce may very well result from individual psychopathology in one or both of the partners. In these instances, therapists should make firm efforts to encourage these persons to enter individually oriented psychotherapy. These are the persons who are often divorce repeaters, and they can benefit greatly if they can overcome their intrapsychic problems.

Dangers in Premature Separation

Caution might also be offered to couples contemplating divorce regarding the issue of "premature" separation. Some therapists have recommended trial separations early in the therapy process as a means of helping the partners confront what being apart may mean to them. On the surface, this technique looks appealing, but a very real danger exists—that involved in what amounts to a public announcement of the couple's difficulties. As soon as a husband and wife are physically separated, a new and complicated system consisting of friends and relatives begins to intrude into the whole process and sides are taken, conflicting advice is offered, and a couple's private decision is turned into a public process. In general, early physical separation should be encouraged only when such severe tension exists that irreparable harm may be done if the partners continue to live together. Often this reduction can be obtained with minimum public intrusion by the time-honored tradition of temporarily sleeping in separate rooms, or going on an extended separate trip.

"Expert Opinion"—A Caveat

The foregoing raises another implication of divorce cases for marital therapists—whether or not they should share with couples their own judgments about the potential success or failure of the marriage. Couples often want to know their therapist's impressions, and it would seem that they have a right to know. After all, the marital therapist is expected to be knowledgeable about both marital success and marital breakdown. At the same time, one should recognize that many therapists feel very strongly about clients' rights to self-determination; also, the views of therapists, *because they are perceived as experts,* may carry unusually great weight in couples' decision-making processes. Therefore, if the therapist does choose to share his or her professional impressions when asked for them, he or she should do so with great caution. Earlier it was pointed out that no one can predict with absolute accuracy who will succeed in marriage, and the same is true for predicting divorce.

One rule of thumb therapists may choose to follow when pressed for "expert opinion" is to first ask each of the partners: "can you say *to yourself* that you have done *all you can* to maintain the marriage—or *all you want to do* to maintain it—and still want a divorce?" A "yes" by the individual client suggests that the person has reached the limits of his or her motivations or abilities and can probably move ahead with the divorce with a minimum of regret or guilt later on. When couples reach this point and when the continuation of the marriage appears either totally destructive to at least one of the partners or totally impossible from a systems perspective, then it would seem helpful and appropriate for the marital therapist to support reality and good mental health by sharing professional observations that divorce may be both inevitable and the healthy thing to do. For these same reasons, there may be times when therapists can validly advise *against* separation or divorce if they sense that the partners are primarily impulsively acting out instead of genuinely giving up on their marriages.

The Right to Divorce

All of the foregoing implications suggest that modern marital and divorce therapists should be "pro-divorce" in the sense that they support the right of adults to live their lives in accordance with each individual's own needs and wishes as long as these do not unduly damage others' health and well-being. The denial of one's right to divorce or to stay single or to remarry would appear to be an archaic carry-over of a punitive value system. That system originated when the human life span was much shorter and when societies would be excessively weakened if permanent, lifelong monogamy were not enforced by strict and punitive measures. This is not to say that the institution of marriage is not valued and not extremely important. Quite the contrary. Marriage can be—and should be—a positive, self-affirming relationship. When it ceases to be this, it becomes cheapened and degraded by attempts to punish by forcing people to stay married.

Special Training in Grief Therapy

The implications for marital therapists of grief therapy would appear to be less complicated than for those concerning divorce therapy. The experiencing of grief and loss are normal parts of living and therapists must be prepared to deal with them. Because so few training programs pay much, if any, attention to grief, however, it is highly desirable that therapists take advantage of post-graduate workshops and other sources of special training in order to develop their understanding and abilities to deal with these subjects. So far two groups have dominated the field of grief therapy—the clergy and funeral directors—but in a few urban areas specialized nonsectarian therapists are beginning to be recognized. They deal primarily with death and dying, two "taboo" subjects for our society. Marital therapists may find these specialists especially helpful in continuing education workshops or in accepting referrals for both crisis counseling and ongoing therapy with bereaved and grieving persons.

CASE EXAMPLE:
SYLVIA AND BILL GURNEY

Background

Bill and Sylvia Gurney represent one special type of divorce therapy situation: where marital therapy results in a couple's reconciliation and decision to keep their marriage. Other cases that may be considered as having achieved similar successful therapeutic results are those in which a divorce is obtained and each person successfully moves ahead with his or her separate life. The case of the Gurneys is presented here because they illustrate how even short-term therapy performed at a crucial time may lead couples to take a "second look" at their marriage before they make the final decision to divorce.

When Mrs. Gurney phoned for an appointment, she said she and her husband had been referred by the court where she had filed for divorce. She was hesitant about the cost of therapy but rejected referral to a sliding-fee clinic. An evening appointment hour was arranged for Sylvia and Bill with the understanding that each would be seen both individually for a private session and together for a conjoint session.

Session 1—Initial Evaluation

Individual interview: Sylvia. Sylvia turned out to be an articulate woman in her mid-forties, neatly dressed, and very controlled in her emotions. She explained that they had canceled a preliminary divorce hearing after they obtained the appointment with the therapist. A year-and-a-half before, she related, she had canceled an earlier application for a divorce when Bill promised to accompany her for marital therapy. He had reneged on his promise at that time, however, and hadn't mentioned it again. Shortly thereafter, Sylvia had had a hysterectomy and the whole matter of divorce or therapy was dropped. However, she believed that things were still bad between herself and Bill, so she finally called a lawyer about refiling for divorce. When Bill learned this, two weeks before this evening's appointment, he again requested that she drop the divorce action and that they both go for marital therapy. She had agreed to do so, but was quite clear that she didn't trust her husband's motives in seeking therapy at this time.

Sylvia described the Gurneys as a "typical" middle-aged family. They were in their mid-forties, had been married for twenty-one years, and had three children: a daughter, 20; a son, 15; and a younger son, 9. Bill had his own television repair business which he ran out of their home. From Sylvia's perspective, their troubles had come about primarily because of their friendship with another couple, Robert and Geraldine. This friendship had gone on for several years. Robert was an electronic parts wholesaler with whom Bill regularly did business. The other couple enjoyed a higher scale of living than the Gurneys did and had, on various occasions, even loaned the Gurneys money to purchase some household items and a truck for Bill's business. The major issue for Sylvia, however, concerned her negative feelings about the way she believed Robert and Geraldine dominated the Gurneys' life—especially Bill's. There were numerous daily phone calls, joint weekend and vacation trips, and Bill stayed late at the other couple's many evenings while helping them perform a variety of home repair jobs.

What particularly incensed Sylvia was the complete domination that she felt Geraldine had over Bill and how she often playfully "pawed Bill all over." When Sylvia complained to her husband about this behavior, he angrily accused her of imagining things. She said she really didn't think Bill and Geraldine were having an affair, but felt that Bill, Geraldine, and Robert left her out of a lot of things. She felt like "so much excess baggage" at times. When the therapist attempted to clarify and understand Sylvia's role in relation to the three others, she was rather evasive.

She perceived herself as a victim—a neglected, misunderstood person who was being isolated and left out of everything for the simple reason that she didn't want to "constantly" party and interact with the other couple. She alternated, she said, between never complaining and "going along for the ride" to "blowing my stack and yelling and screaming at my husband." Finally, almost a year previously, she had refused to see Robert and Geraldine any more, but Bill had continued to go over to their home a few evenings every week. She knew Geraldine now thought that she—Sylvia—was a "mean bitch," but she didn't care.

In response to the therapist's routine questions, Sylvia brought out that during the preceding summer, after she had refused to visit Robert and Geraldine any more, she and Bill had sought help at a pastoral counseling service near their home. They had been seen individually by one of the clergymen on the staff; Sylvia went for about twelve weekly sessions. Her counselor wouldn't tell her if Bill was continuing his sessions, however, and later she learned that he had quit after only two, "because it wasn't helping." She said her own counseling had been "interesting" but didn't result in any change in the marriage.

She said that Bill claimed he had always loved her and she sensed that he was now trying to be more of the husband she wanted him to be. However, her feelings for him were "shattered" and she felt she couldn't believe anything he said any more. In response to the therapist's questions, Sylvia said that she realized Bill was not likely to change and that he was a very stubborn guy. She apparently remembered quite vividly the minutest details of every insult and rejection she had ever experienced from Bill and seemed to derive both relief and pleasure from recounting these hurtful experiences. When questioned about why she was seeking marital therapy now instead of a divorce—in view of these unending negative experiences—she softened her demeanor and revealed her ambivalence and uncertainty. As long as there was no hope for change on Bill's part, she believed she had no alternative but to divorce him—in order to keep her "sanity" and self-respect. At the same time, she didn't have the faintest idea of what she and the kids would do without him. Thus her move toward divorce was being made out of hurt, rejection, and anger, rather than because she saw some appealing alternatives in leaving her husband.

Individual interview: Bill. Like his wife, Bill was in his mid-forties, plainly but neatly dressed, and looking every bit the small-business owner that he was. He briefly recounted the earlier plans for marital therapy that he hadn't followed through, plus his brief but unsatisfactory experience with pastoral counseling. He said he had spoken briefly with the family physician about their troubles, but his wife refused to do so. He felt that *she* had a problem with which the physician might have been able to help her. Bill claimed that he had looked forward to the present appointment but he was obviously cautious about its outcome.

Bill put the problems very succinctly: "She's never given me her full love and affection. I've tried to give her a good home and a decent living. . . . We've been married over twenty years and I've busted my ass to do well for her and the kids. . . . I've got friends and she thinks they dominate me." Sylvia, to Bill, was apparently "she"—not "Sylvia"—a hint of both their emotional distancing and of Bill's own discomfort with intimacy. Early in their marriage, Sylvia had complained that they had "nothing in common." Then and now, he felt she was selfish, demanding, and unfriendly. Personally, he enjoyed friends but his wife complained that he treated his friends more thoughtfully than he treated her. Years ago, Bill indicated, he had realized that "every little thing" upset his wife so he developed the pattern of withholding many of his own feelings from her so he wouldn't upset her. He portrayed her as "childish," explaining how she would reject him sexually if she felt the slightest bit angry. "Three months this time she's been sleeping in the other room," he complained.

When asked how he felt toward his wife, however, Bill insisted that he loved her. Immediately thereafter, he returned to telling the therapist how he felt rejected and neglected constantly by her. Without breaking any confidences, the therapist said he understood that the Gurneys might have some issues about another couple. Bill opened up and spilled out his frustrations about his friendship with Robert and Geraldine. He felt his wife blamed all their troubles on the friendship with this other couple, but he didn't believe that was accurate. He took responsibility for being at the other couple's house "too often and too late," but he was clearly defiant about not caving in to his wife's demands that he abandon this couple that meant so much to him. He portrayed his wife as not getting along with "anyone," including her own mother. "Everybody's wrong but her . . . I have to constantly be the peacemaker." He didn't want a divorce, he strongly maintained, but at the same time, he felt pretty hopeless about his wife changing in any constructive ways.

Conjoint interview.   When Sylvia and Bill Gurney were interviewed conjointly, immediately following their individual sessions with the therapist, the atmosphere was tense. Sylvia acted very distant and aloof while verbalizing how much she had been neglected by Bill. Bill, on the other hand, fell into his self-described role as peacemaker and was by far the more positive of the two in respect to expressing affection for his spouse and wanting the marriage to succeed. The therapist, for his part, openly acknowledged the precariousness of the Gurneys' marriage. Obviously, *if* they chose to hold off on the divorce and stay together, they had four potential "options" facing them: (1) Bill would have to change a lot in order to better satisfy Sylvia; (2) Sylvia would have to change a lot in order to better satisfy Bill; (3) they would both have to make sincere, consistent efforts to better meet their partner's needs and expectations; (4) they could stay together and continue to muddle along until one or the other of them finally could take no more and divorce would then become a necessity. Sylvia and Bill were thoughtful and rather subdued upon hearing the alternatives identified by the therapist. They decided to discuss it and call back if they wished to proceed with therapy.

Therapist's observations.   It was the therapist's impression that even though the marriage had lasted for over twenty years, it had rarely, if ever, been entirely satisfactory to either of the Gurneys. Sylvia was an ungiving, demanding, verbal person who needed regular reassurance that she was loved, even if she rarely gave much love herself. Bill, whose enormous belly indicated that he sought to sublimate his needs to be given to both through friends and food, felt unable to cope with his wife's incessant demands and had long since retreated to safer and more rewarding sources of personal gratification. Sylvia had accepted their relationship with Robert and Geraldine initially because they had had good times and it brought fun into her otherwise rather dull life with Bill. Bill, even though he knew his wife resented his continued contacts with the other couple, maintained that friendship, because it fed his ego and he felt his wife was both unfair and inaccurate in her complaints about being "swallowed up" by Robert and Geraldine.

Clearly, neither Sylvia nor Bill was giving each other the recognition and caring messages and experiences that most couples expect in marriage. Effective, open, honest communication between the two hardly existed and there was a stalemate. Sylvia's filing for divorce forced both of the Gurneys to finally face up to the seriousness of their situation. Sometimes a divorce filing is a manipulative gesture, one designed to bring attention or change rather than one designed to end a marriage. Sylvia had gone through that phase earlier—now it appeared that she was very serious in her intentions. The marital therapy assessment sessions and the feedback received from the therapist highlighted this fact. While initial evaluation sessions are sometimes a painful experience for everyone, their virtue comes from the fact that the therapist, unlike the role an attorney might take, has a more neutral function in supporting either a move to divorce or a move to reconsider such a step. The decision about what should be done—as always in therapy—rests entirely with the clients, however.

Session 2

Ten days after their first session, Sylvia Gurney called back and requested marital therapy for both of them. During the conjoint session near the end of their initial assessment appointment with the therapist, treatment by conjoint sessions exclusively had been recommended. No secrets appeared to exist, their interaction was a major concern to both of them, and both their finances and their attitudes appeared to rule out individual sessions combined with conjoint sessions. (This compromise with the therapist's ideal recommendations—that of combining individual and conjoint approaches—often has to be made on just such realistic considerations as time, money, and client attitudes.)

When Bill and Sylvia appeared for their second session, both appeared much less tense. Rather than focusing directly on the question of whether they should or should not go ahead with their divorce—as might have been expected—they decided to concentrate on their daily interactions. Sylvia felt more disturbed when she thought Bill was ignoring her feelings and wishes, especially in preference to the other couple, Robert and Geraldine. Bill said little about his wife's comments concerning his "style," but emphasized how painful her anger was for him. He had grown up in a "fighting family" and early in life had adopted the defenses of suppression and retreat. He knew he was that way but saw no alternatives in dealing with Sylvia's anger.

The therapist helped Sylvia explain to Bill (insight) how abandoned she felt when he retreated; in turn, he helped Bill realize that Sylvia's anger came from both fear of rejection and not getting his love. During this session, the Gurneys mentioned that Sylvia usually handled the phone calls for Bill's TV repair business. Callers were often upset and made impossible demands for faster service than Bill could possibly provide. Bill, however, as part of his passive resistance to his wife's domination, refused to call these irate customers back and instead, serviced their televisions when he chose to. In the meantime, they often called back repeatedly to complain—and Sylvia was the one who had to fend off their rage. Thus, to the "normal" husband–wife interactions many additional opportunities were added for fighting and seeking to control each other. The therapist recommended different telephone arrangements—such as the use of an automated answering machine—but Bill felt Sylvia did a far better job with "his" customers than any machine could do.

Therapist's observations. Couples complain, but when a therapist tries to alter their systems, they may sabotage the therapist's suggestion. Marital couples often unconsciously throw monkey wrenches into suggested solutions, and the Gurneys demonstrated this very clearly.

A recurrent theme in this second session was the repetitious replaying of old hurts and frustrations. Working with couples contemplating divorce rarely gives the "luxury" of an opportunity to do longer-term, personal psychotherapy. The therapist must pragmatically concentrate on change—change in attitudes and change in interactions. He or she must try to determine whether or not there is any motivation on the part of either partner for change, or whether there are indeed any capabilities for doing so. In the case of Sylvia and Bill, the therapist utilized confrontation to "challenge" change. Pointing out that neither partner was accepting the other *as the other really was,* the therapist pushed Bill and Sylvia to try to repress the past as much as they could and to concentrate on the here and now. By focusing on the present, they might discover for themselves whether or not they had the ability to relate more positively to each other and, if they did, whether their combined intrapsychic and interpersonal systems could "accept" a more positive relationship. If one or both simply would not—or *could* not—try to relate more positively, this would appear to be a negative omen about continuing the marriage. Working in this time-limited fashion, therapists utilize the marital history as well as the psychic and familial histories of both spouses to set up situations that will enable the couples to test out their individual and collective capacities for change. Sylvia and Bill agreed to "consider" these possibilities before they returned for their next therapy session.

Session 3

At the start of this session, the Gurneys appeared to be in a good mood and Bill engaged in considerable humorous banter with both his wife and the therapist. (Such banter may constructively ease the tensions that invariably exist in these sessions, but it may also serve other purposes, such as manipulating the discussion away from anxiety-provoking issues or attempting to demonstrate to the therapist how funny and friendly a client is—in marked contrast to the unsmiling partner.) The Gurneys had talked together this week about the last therapy session and the changes they both desired, especially in each other. They complained that their lives were "too busy" to have much time and energy just for themselves. Raising three kids and operating a home-based business that generated phone calls at all hours kept them constantly on the go. This was challenged by the therapist. (Some couples respond negatively to confrontation and challenges. Therapists have to make constant decisions about whether a challenge will motivate or anger any specific couple.) In effect, the therapist asked, "If you don't care enough about your marital relationship to give it a high priority in your lives, how can you expect to feel good toward each other?"

Therapist's observations. Children and work *are* demanding and time-consuming. But what are partners' obligations to themselves and to each other? Americans still appear to be so indoctrinated with the idea that it is better to give than to receive that they often suffer guilt if they wish to derive personal pleasure and rewards from their own actions—including their actions with their husbands and wives. In sharing these views with the Gurneys, the therapist was attempting to use his authority role to "give them permission" to work on their marriage instead of always concentrating on being good parents or great businesspersons.

Also focused on during this session was the pattern by which both Sylvia and Bill often retreated from each other without directly addressing the issues between them. Bill had portrayed himself as the "peacemaker" who retreated to avoid conflict, but it became equally apparent that Sylvia also used retreat—such as from sex—both to avoid something she regarded as undesirable at that moment and also to punish her husband by refusing to "make love" with him. Both the Gurneys were quite verbal during this session and were able to both verbalize their own feelings *and to listen to* their partner's feelings without counterattacking every time a negative feeling was exposed. Psychodynamic marital therapy often relies heavily upon these two principles—that of couples gaining insight into their own and the partner's emotional needs and that of utilizing generalization—that is, helping couples find out that if a positive communication and/or interaction can occur within the protective setting of the therapist's office, it can "generalize" or spread out and occur at other times and during other issues concerning the couple's relationship.

Session 4

This session, on the surface, appeared to have little direct relevance about whether or not the couple should stay together or divorce. Implicitly, however, it seemed that the Gurneys were quite united—in frustration and irritation with their 20-year-old daughter. The daughter had a job and lived at home with them but she paid only modest rent, and "bellyached" whenever she was asked to help with routine household chores. Bill complained that she didn't pay them enough rent and Sylvia complained that the daughter did not help with household chores. The therapist could have chosen to initiate some family therapy sessions at that point by having all the children enter therapy with the Gurneys. However, the major reason that marital therapy had been sought was the issue of divorce or continuing the marriage. The highest priority, therefore, was to continue to concentrate on the Gurney's marital relationship. Family therapy would have been recommended from the very beginning if the children were the prime *cause* of the marital strife—or it would have been recommended if they appeared to be needing help because of the strife. Neither situation seemed to exist at this time with the Gurneys, however. Both Bill and Sylvia aired their frustrations, but the therapist helped them see that they were displacing many of their marital hurts onto issues of "discipline" and unrealistic expectations of their children. At the same time, the therapist emphasized that they *did* have numerous concerns in common—even if they were sometimes negative ones.

Session 5

Bill started off this session with a whole series of jokes and gibes directed at both his wife and the therapist. Sylvia's response to her husband was essentially reciprocal. They both seemed to enjoy this game. Apparently, they often used "good-natured" sarcasm as a way of relating to each other in a positive, but not too close, fashion. The therapist's comments about their good mood led immediately to the issue of divorce or not. Sylvia talked about how desperate she had felt when she filed her legal papers but how she now believed that divorce was not an answer. Both of the Gurneys were quite open with each other about sharing their former negative feelings and their individual perspectives about their marriage. They were able to do this in a sharing—but not attacking—manner in order to help their partner and the therapist fully understand how they had felt. Then both, again with the therapist's support and direction, were able to share their negative thoughts about each one's own attempts to handle the marital battles and to take personal responsibility for themselves. This process of sharing one's own "bad points" in conjoint sessions reduces blaming when each partner no longer feels he or she is being unfairly accused of being totally "at fault" for the difficulties.

During one part of the session, Bill tried to get Sylvia to compromise about her refusal to visit his mother's home for a family occasion. Sylvia reacted by getting irritated and repeatedly cutting Bill off—moves that clearly led him to start to retreat from her. The therapist immediately "replayed" what had just occurred in the session (a videotape of the interactions would have been the ideal way of handling this, but this option was not available) and was able to help the couple come to grips with Sylvia's sabotaging of her husband's efforts to find some middle solution to an emotionally laden dilemma. When Sylvia fired back that the therapist would have to "really know" her mother-in-law to understand why she resisted visiting her, the therapist ignored that issue and chose to concentrate on the process—or, more specifically, on the destructive nature of the process—that had occurred when Sylvia had adamantly refused to compromise or help find a solution to the problem. While the therapist was doing this, Bill might have tried to "gang up" on Sylvia at the very moment she was feeling rather isolated and uncomfortable. Bill did not do this, however. Had he done so, the therapist would have handled it by refusing to let him attack his wife when she was struggling to overcome an unconstructive habit pattern on her part. At such moments, clients need support, not vilification. Before leaving, Sylvia said she would "think about" the therapist's comments.

Session 6

When the sixth session commenced, it appeared that regression had occurred. Tension was high, especially in Bill's looks and words. The therapist encouraged Bill to share his feelings openly and, in effect, to protect his relationship by protecting himself. Bill refused to do so. This led Sylvia to pronounce that her husband and their marriage were both hopeless cases. Tears flowed as she lamented that nothing had changed. Bill became even more uncomfortable in the face of his wife's obvious distress, and tried to minimize their difficulties, but finally shared that he had experienced a bad day all around. The therapist said he felt that this was precisely why Bill *should* share his feelings with his wife. When he just acted irritable without explanation, she could easily—and perhaps erroneously—assume that his downcast mood was being seen as her fault. Bill was able to move on this statement and explained that "When I was a kid, no one listened to me." Thus he had carried his childhood expectations into his adult life. The therapist said he believed that Sylvia *did* care about her husband's feelings (placing her under some calculated pressure to affirm or deny this), and Sylvia said she "wholeheartedly" agreed. Both the Gurneys were then able to talk about their mutual concerns for each other's feelings, thus reaffirming that divorce was not what they primarily wanted.

During the session the couple also spoke of their intentions to open a store. Sylvia would run the store and Bill would handle the service and repair business. The therapist spoke openly of his discomfort about their mixing business and marriage, especially at the present time, but they felt confident about their ability to handle both.

Session 7

This session came immediately after Bill and Sylvia's wedding anniversary and both were in high spirits. Sylvia spoke of the nice flowers Bill had given her but Bill, in characteristic style, said the best present he had received was in her not "harping" at him that day. Most of this session centered on their plans to open their own TV store and the implications this might have for their marital relationship. The therapist was "uncomfortable" with Sylvia's attitude about how Bill would have to follow her orders for service and repairs under such a new setup, but Bill said he'd just ignore her if she got "too unreasonable." Neither, however, felt this would be an insurmountable problem, especially if they were able to communicate more openly and constructively.

Session 8

Two weeks had elapsed since the last session, and the Gurneys announced that they were "cured." They were in a very light-hearted mood, full of jokes and talk about an upcoming vacation trip they had planned. When the therapist sensed that the Gurneys had gone as far as they could—or would—in respect to dropping the idea of divorce and in handling their marriage more constructively, he shifted the session to a review of where they had been when they started therapy, what each had contributed to the changes that had occurred, and what they each perceived as being very important issues for them to be sensitive to in the future. (Such a review contributes to the ending process and helps to emphasize insight, change, and positive interactions between partners.) Sylvia emphasized how bitter, alienated, and discouraged she had felt when she applied for divorce. She believed therapy had helped her understand her husband better—and even more important to her, she believed the process had helped Bill become more understanding and sensitive to her feelings and needs. Bill, unwilling or unable to handle his positive feelings for his wife in an openly warm and gentle fashion in the therapy office, insisted that all was well in their marriage because "I told you (the therapist) in the beginning that everything would be OK if she would only shut up and do what I told her to." Some partners would obviously react very negatively to a statement like this, but Sylvia only laughed and said the feelings were mutual.

SUMMARY

The reader should be cautioned again that marital and divorce therapy are not to be construed as synonymous with conciliation therapy. In the case presented here, the Gurneys did become reconciled and this will be the result in many cases. At the same time, there should never be any efforts on the part of the therapist to exclusively emphasize reconciliation if both partners do not wish it. This holds true for two basic reasons: (1) It is unethical for therapists to attempt to manipulate clients to subscribe to the therapists' own value systems; and (2) reconciliations that are not ego-syntonic with the emotional needs and wishes of *both* partners are probably doomed to eventual failure anyway. Therapeutic efforts that attempt to ignore these facts can only result in a postponement of the inevitable and perhaps an increase in the psychic damage done to all members of the marital and family unit.

CHAPTER NINE
GENERAL
MARITAL PROBLEMS

BACKGROUND

The institution of marriage provides an extraordinary number of areas and opportunities for conflict to arise between husbands and wives. Most couples, even happily married ones, experience difficulties with each other of one type or another almost every day. In preceding chapters, we have examined some of the major areas of marital conflict, but the areas that have been covered are by no means exhaustive. Regardless of whether couples present themselves for therapy over the issue of extramarital affairs or arguments about how to discipline their children, most couples demonstrate simultaneous problems in several areas of their relationship. Couples who claim to only have one problem in their marriage are rare. They may have one *overwhelming* problem, but the probability of a ripple effect into other areas of their relationship is always present. In this chapter, therefore, we examine some other common problems that couples experience and that often become major foci in marital therapy.

FINANCES

Money: It Means Power and Love

Family researchers often argue about whether sex or money is the number one area of marital conflict for Americans. In Chapter Four we discussed sexual conflicts; here we shall examine financial ones. For many marital therapists, and for virtually all those in private practice, money issues are not so much a matter of not having money, such as is true for the very poor, but rather center around the control and use of money in the marriage. *Who* spends it? *When* do they spend it? And *what* is it spent upon? In American marriages, money means power and money also means love. Power arises from decisions about "essential" versus discretionary spending. Who defines the terms? Are Junior's orthodontic braces "essentials"—or "luxuries"? Do couples "have to" have new bedroom furniture or are parental hand-me-downs adequate? Are savings accounts to be viewed as reserves for unanticipated emergencies such as sudden expenses from illnesses—or are they disguised forms of vacation funds that may be emptied each year? In answering these questions, couples face the same dilemmas they experience in conducting their marital sex lives: Whatever one spouse does directly and incontrovertibly affects the other person. This single feature may explain many of the clashes over marital finances.

In addition, money is tied up with the concept of love. "Stingy" partners are viewed as ungiving and uncaring. Purchasing a birthday gift for one's spouse at a discount store doesn't show as much "love" as purchasing the same item in an expensive specialty shop that charges twice as much for the same item. Complicating the whole matter of marital finances is the fact that values about money and its usage are established early in people's lives. These values derive from individuals' childhood experiences and the models in their families of origin. Marry a "spender" to someone from a "saver" type family and one has all the necessary ingredients for perpetual clashes about the "proper" use of money. In this scenario, there is often no "right" and no "wrong"—just "his" way and "her" way of handling the family finances.

The checkbook saga.   This is not to overlook the fact that Americans in general are often very ignorant about consumer education. Young couples about to marry often have little, if any, grounding in budgeting, how to obtain and handle credit, and what it will actually cost them to maintain a household. A classic example of this is the saga of the checkbook. Therapists repeatedly hear how the checkbook becomes a common center of marital strife. If the checking account doesn't balance, the person doing the bookkeeping is obviously "dumb, moronic, and incompetent." After a pronouncement like this in the heat of a marital argument, the defendant often throws the checkbook at the accuser, challenges him or her to "prove your superior intelligence by keeping it balanced!" and marches off in a furious huff. The accuser now becomes the defendant and must be extremely careful to keep the checkbook balanced because now he or she is the one on trial. Some couples swap these roles every few months without ever consciously realizing the power struggle they are involved in.

Who controls the purse-strings?   In the past, many households were male-dominated and this was clearly demonstrated in the area of financial control. Wives were given household or personal "allowances" and had to bargain with their husbands for every cent over their allotted quotas. The advent of wives working for pay outside their homes, among other things, has shifted this power control. Husbands often have to adjust to this fact—whether they like it or not. Husbands unsure of their masculinity or deeply indoctrinated with traditional values of male superiority may find the concept of equalitarian control of marital finances deeply disturbing. Adding to these sex-role conflicts have been the modern issues of electronic money and credit cards. The American economy is said to be completely dependent on credit, and certainly married couples represent prime examples of this fact. Credit cards, electronic fund transfers, machines that dispurse money twenty-four hours a day—all seduce many families into a never-ending routine of "spend now, pay later." This system lays a deadly trap for those couples who are so impulse-ridden that they cannot control their urges to overspend. Marital therapists who encounter compulsive spenders should consider referring them to specialized consumer counseling services where there are people who are trained to treat such neurotic behaviors. In addition, referral for consumer education through a local adult education or community college program may be helpful. Encouraging couples to read lay magazines such as *Consumer Reports* may help many clients, but will not cure the immature and the compulsive spenders.

RELIGION

Source of Stability or Conflict?

Historically, family relations textbooks and earlier manuals on marriage counseling placed great emphasis upon religion as a source of both marital stability and marital conflict. Interfaith marriages were repeatedly studied and listed as something to be assiduously avoided by couples contemplating marriage. In more recent times, however, the role of organized religion in American society has been undergoing such profound change that it has become increasingly difficult to generalize about its impact upon marital strife. One fact appears to be unchanging, however. Religion becomes the cause of strife in marriages primarily when husbands and wives find themselves differing with each other over their religious beliefs and values. This problem can arise within intrafaith marriages just as well as within interfaith marriages. A continuing example of this concerns the role of male–female relationships as taught by various religious denominations and clergy. Sitting in their church or synagogue—or in front of their television screen listening to their favorite "electronic church" orator—husbands and wives may consciously hear the same commandments laid down to them about how they should trust each other, but each one will "hear" and interpret these dogmatic messages in basically ego-syntonic ways; i.e., they each hear what they want and need to hear. These conflicting messages often touch all areas of married life—love, sex, birth control, child-rearing, education, and one's duties as a citizen. When marital partners then attempt to conduct their marital roles in accord with what they believe their religion teaches, they often run into direct conflict with their partner's understanding of the same spiritual message.

Religion remains for probably the majority of Americans a major source of guidance concerning the whole institution of marriage. Marital therapists should be aware of the religious beliefs and teachings of their clients and must take these value systems into account in understanding clients' total life situations. The therapists, as individuals themselves, may or may not agree with clients' particular religious beliefs, but ethically, they must respect them. In addition, it is impossible to establish the rapport necessary for a positive therapeutic relationship if clients and therapists cannot accept each other's differences, including their religious beliefs.

DRUG DEPENDENCE

One of the most common sources of personal problems for married couples is the whole issue of drug dependence by one or both members of the pair. For adults, alcohol has traditionally been the drug of "choice," but in more recent years this pattern has been shifting as the use of marijuana, cocaine, and all kinds of pharmaceutical prescription-drug abuses have become widespread throughout all segments of society. These problems have arisen because drugs represent traditional methods of attempting to escape from one's troubles and because modern transportation and communication systems have both aided and encouraged their abuse. In performing routine marital therapy, one becomes aware of these problems as clients relate their stories and conflicts. Often the married partners are intellectually aware that one of them has a drug problem but both have successfully repressed this fact. This is especially true for the abuser him- or herself, because denial is one of the most frequent characteristics such a person demonstrates. Interpretation to a person that he or she has a problem with drugs almost inevitably arouses resistance. Often the partner colludes with the abuser and actively maintains the charade that no problem exists. In these cases, marital therapists will have to utilize their own clinical judgments as to whether marital therapy should continue or whether a therapeutic stand should be taken that may indicate specialized treatment for the drug addiction before marital therapy can continue. A significant factor here is whether or not the marital therapist is also trained in drug counseling. If so, he or she may choose to combine both therapeutic approaches; if not, referral becomes necessary.

PERSONALITY FACTORS

Compatibility, changing needs. Throughout this book, repeated references have been made to numerous issues concerning personality problems that clients in marital therapy may possess. An earlier statement was made to the effect that the "average" client in marital therapy is usually a reasonably healthy, "normal" person. Assuming that this statement is correct, allowances must still be made for the widespread incidence of what can best be described as specific personality traits that cause conflicts in marriage. Some of these relate to basically incompatible pairings—such as two excessively domineering persons married to each other. Others relate to personality needs that change with the passage of time. The macho man who desired a sweet, dependent, "little-girl" type of female during courtship and early marriage often becomes tired of her dependency as the years pass and then begins to complain that she should be more "grown-up" and independent. Therapists are often struck by the results of the old courtship theory of complementarity—how opposites may attract, but how poorly these same opposites often wear over time.

Emotional maturity.   An examination of divorce statistics reveals that marriages contracted by teenagers have marital failure rates several times higher than is true for those who marry in their twenties. A prime reason for this—albeit not the only reason—is that teenagers by definition are not yet emotionally mature adults. Marriage requires both partners to be emotionally mature. Immature persons are characteristically impulsive, narcissistic, stubborn, needy, insecure, and unable to genuinely give or receive love. Chronological maturity obviously does not guarantee emotional maturity, so therapists will often find older clients who suffer from immature behavior patterns. If immaturity exists in both partners, marital success is even less probable. These persons need to mature before they can begin to fully understand and accept their partners—especially their partner's "faults" or shortcomings.

MENTAL HEALTH

Appraisal necessary.   Therapists also need to appraise every client's degree of mental health. Individuals who are severely neurotic are always somewhat incapacitated in their ability to function as marital partners. Given the widespread incidence of psychoneurotic traits in our population, however, therapists must exercise careful judgment about when a neurotic disorder is severe enough to justify individual psychotherapy as opposed to regular marital therapy. An important variable in arriving at this decision is the degree of tolerance of marital partners to their mate's neurotic condition. Some individuals put up with neurosis in their partners quite comfortably, and individual therapy in these instances is optional. When the neurosis clearly and consistently interferes with positive marital interaction, however, the need for individual psychotherapy increases. For example, a wife may comfortably (although sometimes irritably) tolerate a husband who must compulsively count the cracks in the sidewalk when they stroll through the park, but she may have a considerably more negative reaction if he has a cleanliness fetish that requires him to take a 60-minute bath every time they decide to have sexual intercourse.

Mental illness.   Marital therapy is sometimes requested when one of the partners is mentally ill. This is particularly true for therapists employed in mental health settings. This needs to be considered from two different aspects: first, when the psychosis develops after marital treatment has commenced; and second, when a partner is actively psychotic before marital therapy begins. In the first situation, the marital therapist must decide, when the psychosis develops, whether to refer the couple for psychiatric help exclusively or whether marital therapy can continue while concurrent psychiatric help is obtained. Numerous factors enter into this decision—the type and degree of psychic impairment caused by the psychosis, the strength of the marital unit, the motivations of the identified patient and of the spouse, and the professional training of the marital therapist. If the therapist is also trained as a psychiatrist or psychologist, then he or she is unlikely to refer the clients elsewhere just because a psychotic break has occurred. On the other hand, marital therapists not qualified to treat mental illness will find referral a necessary step.

In the second instance, when referral for marital therapy is made for persons who are already diagnosed as having a psychotic condition, such as often occurs in psychiatric day-treatment programs, marital therapy can occur, but usually under two conditions: (1) The marital therapy concentrates upon reality factors in the marriage; and (2) the marital therapist has regular access to the psychotherapist responsible for the "patient's" mental condition. The psychotherapist must remain responsible for any medications and for the overall management of the psychiatric disorder while the marital therapist attends to the problems in the marriage itself.

MONOGAMY AND MONOTONY

Listing monogamy as a source of marital conflict may not, at first glance, appear to make sense. Marriage equals monogamy under our American system. But all too often, monogamy also equals monotony for countless married couples. In Chapter Three, while discussing extramarital sexual relationships, it was pointed out that monotony is frequently a factor in motivating married persons to seek sexual excitement with people other than their legal partners. Here we will consider monotony that disturbs marriages but that does not lead to infidelity. That is not to minimize its danger, however.

The continuum of declining satisfaction and involvement.   Cuber and Harroff (1965) divided American marriages into five categories: *Total, Vital, Passive Congenial, Devitalized,* and *Conflict-Habituated*—in that order of declining satisfaction and involvement. Couples suffering from monogamy monotony probably fall into the *Passive Congenial* and *Devitalized* categories. They do not openly fight a lot; they appear to their relatives and friends to be reasonably happy and settled couples; and they often have existed in their monotony for long periods of time before they seek therapy. Their marriages, however, have lost much of their original vitality and they have settled into the proverbial rut. Marital therapists, accustomed to loud anger and tears during sessions, sometimes find these clients perplexing and try to "dig" for underlying marital pathology that they assume must be there. It may not be there. In the words of one wit, "If it ain't broken, don't try to fix it."

However, therapists need to be cautious about dismissing these clients' needs too hastily. If love is a flower, without good soil, sunshine, cultivation, and nourishment, it will wither and die. Monotony assists this destructive process. Slowly, little by little, a dull marriage can cause marital partners to feel disinterest, separateness, and isolation from each other. These couples need a type of marital therapy that makes them aware of the insidious process of monotony, and they need to learn ways to successfully combat their slow slide into marital oblivion. Among other things, they need some excitement. It is indeed true that "the couple that plays together stays together."

IMPLICATIONS
FOR MARITAL THERAPY

Each of the common types of marital disharmony covered here has its own unique implications for marital therapy. Financial problems, the first problem area covered, often involve highly symbolic behavior and power struggles. When therapists hear the familiar "We always fight over money" refrain, they must ask further questions about just what it is that the clients are fighting about. Is it financial mismanagement, ignorance, power plays, sexism, or clashing values on the use of money? Sometimes bibliotherapy is called for, particularly for very young clients, in order to improve clients' basic skills in conducting financial affairs. More often, however, the arguments over money represent only the tip of the iceberg, that which is visible and easy to see, while the underlying psychodynamic and relationship issues are hidden in the dark waters underneath. Therapy here should be directed at identifying the "real" issues (patterns of thoughts, feelings, or behaviors) and helping the couples to confront them openly. Often, as so frequently occurs in marital therapy, compromises may be worked out that minimize actual conflict over money handling and permit couples to relate to each other more positively. Some couples, for instance, "program" the handling of the dangerous checkbook-balancing responsibility and allot each person six months of "duty" each year—with the partner agreeing not to "butt in" when it is not his or her turn. Other couples abandon their joint checking accounts in favor of separate accounts, with each person having total control over his and her own checks and expenditures. Obviously, these techniques require negotiations over major expenditures like house and car purchases, vacation costs, and the like, but the marriages benefit by reductions in the frequency of conflict possibilities. When the issues turn out to be clearly symbolic of interpersonal issues, however, therapists should be careful not to be seduced into accepting simplistic, behavioral "solutions" about money issues that only temporarily reduce the tensions without touching the underlying basic problems.

Religious conflicts, like those involving finances, need first to be examined for their obvious or apparent causes as compared to their underlying latent reasons. Religion is a highly personal matter for most adults and is closely tied to each individual's self-esteem and sense of identity. When one partner rejects or makes light of his or her mate's religious beliefs, it is experienced as a personal rejection. As always in marital therapy, therapists need to repeatedly emphasize sensitivity to partners' feelings as a recurrent, constant goal. This is especially true in religious matters.

Another common religious conflict occurs when there are genuine, incontrovertible differences over religious beliefs affecting both partners, such as birth control or the religious training of the children. If the husband and wife belong to the same religious denomination, it may prove helpful to have them discuss these matters with their local clergyperson. When they are of differing religious persuasions, the marital therapist may attempt to teach them "negotiation skills," which will also be useful in other areas of their relationship. In addition, referral to a pastoral counselor outside their local area may be helpful.

Drug-related problems are not ordinarily within the purview of marital therapists and are best treated by special drug counselors. In addition, groups such as Alcoholics Anonymous and Alanon can be invaluable in helping addicted persons and their families, at least in the case of alcohol abuse. Marital therapists, therefore, will find that their primary tasks rest with identifying cases of substance abuse and making a referral of the person(s) to a drug treatment program. This is ordinarily a very difficult process. Because of their often longstanding use of denial and rationalization, drug-dependent persons are often "experts" at minimizing their pathology. Therapeutic work with the marital partner becomes an absolute must in these instances. The nonusing partner's tendency to distort reality concerning his or her partner's illness must be openly challenged and confronted. When this person, too, makes habitual use of denial and rationalization in regard to the partner's drug usage and its effects, there may be little that the marital therapist can do to help the couple. Supportive help could be extended to them, but this would be primarily palliative in nature and would be unlikely to resolve anything. At the same time, it should be recognized that many marital therapists are working with couples in drug treatment centers and hospitals. Their marital therapy services are similar to those performed by marital therapists dealing with marriages in which one partner is psychotic; that is, they focus primarily upon the "usual" issues of marital relationships and deal with the drug-abuse issue only as it directly relates to the marital interaction. In this respect, therefore, their role is not unusual; it is just that their clients have some unique problems. Group marital therapy made up of three to six couples may also prove helpful with these marriages.

In treating couples with problems of *psychosis, drug dependence, and severe personality problems,* particular care must always be exercised in respect to both "labeling" and to therapeutic "triangling," in which the therapist appears to identify with the "well" or "normal" person rather than with the "sick" or "crazy" one. Sometimes it would seem almost impossible for the therapist to handle such a situation with perfect impartiality. Feelings of partiality invariably arise as soon as a label is issued, but assigning a label is necessary, much as making a diagnosis, in order to complete a referral or to satisfy an insurance company claim sheet. The client being referred may be expected to feel that the therapist rejects, blames, and dislikes him or her. In many cases, marital therapy may not be available in these special treatment programs for "well" spouses, and they should be offered the opportunity to continue in treatment with the therapist who made the referral of the partner. This unavoidably exacerbates the referred client's negative feelings, especially if that person has any markedly paranoid tendencies; the situation must be closely monitored to insure that the benefits derived justify the tension created because of these factors.

Psychiatric and drug-dependence treatments are still commonly viewed as disgrace-tinged admissions of personal imperfections. Clients sometimes deliberately search out marital therapists for treatment of these conditions because marital therapy may be viewed as less threatening and more socially acceptable than treatment for "craziness" or a drug problem. Therapists who are not skilled in these specialized treatment modalities should remain firm, however, regarding both their own treatment limitations and the clients' needs. "Giving in" because one feels sorry for the clients' fear and shame is both unethical and unprofessional.

SUMMARY

In summary, marital therapy, regardless of the problems clients have, is a professional process based upon knowledge of individual and marital psychodynamics and systems. Therapists constantly strive in their work to obtain clear understandings of the fundamental causes of these conflicts and to assist clients in resolving them. Marital therapists are guided in their work by their specialized training and by their psychological and treatment orientations. Regardless of his or her adherence to a particular school of thought, the marital therapist strives to help persons suffering marital distress so that they may resolve their problems without impairing their individual mental health functioning. Good *mental* health for clients, therefore, as well as good *marital* health, is a prime concern of contemporary marital therapists.

CASE EXAMPLE:
STELLA AND DON BURNS

Background

Don and Stella Burns represent the type of marriage difficulties a "typical" couple might bring to therapy. They were referred to the therapist after Stella called their family physician for help. He referred them to a local public mental health clinic where, in turn, they were referred for private therapy because their combined income exceeded the clinic's income limits. The Burns illustrate the "ripple effect" discussed earlier in which problems in one area or subsystem of a marriage spread out and impact on other facets of the couple's relationship. They also demonstrate that chances for rapid improvement in a marriage are best if couples enter therapy before extensive and prolonged conflict has arisen.

Session 1—Initial Evaluation

Individual interview: Stella. Stella, age 29, was a tall, slender, soft-spoken young woman, neatly dressed in a stylish suit as befitted her role as an accountant. She said she didn't know quite what to expect from therapy because neither she nor her husband had ever had any form of psychological help before. She hoped that the therapist could give them some "unbiased opinions" about their marriage. She expressed belief that there was much good about their marriage—but also there were many dissatisfactions.

Stella and her husband, she said, were very different vocationally. Her work as an accountant for a large corporation was going very well and she made more money than her husband did. His work as a self-employed craftsman building high-quality furniture in a shop at their home was "surviving," but at a great cost to their marriage, she believed. He put "everything" into his work—time, energy, attention, and money. The net result, Stella said, was that he often felt "too drained" to do anything with her and she felt lonely and neglected. She portrayed Don as a self-contained, soft-spoken person who valued his independence and liked to be by himself. He didn't express his feelings readily and had never been a "doting" husband— something she would have liked him to have been. Even sex had become a "sometime" thing and often occurred only when Don had finished some project in his shop and Stella could talk him into it. Often she was inorgasmic, but her husband never said a word about that. He told her he loved her, when she asked him, but rarely volunteered any such sentiments. This pattern had been going on for much of the six years of their marriage and she felt she was losing respect and affection for Don as a result.

Sensing that Stella's loneliness might have made her vulnerable to other men's attentions, the therapist inquired about this. She admitted that she did have "a problem" there. It involved a man at work "but wasn't sexual." She tremendously enjoyed talking to Ray (her male friend) and found herself feeling very sexually attracted to him. She felt guilty about the relationship and was thinking about not seeing him any more; this was a difficult goal since their work brought them together frequently. Don knew about this other man and was hurt about the relationship, but had not pressured Stella to break it off. As she talked about Ray and other men to whom she had felt attracted, Stella's strong ambivalence was clearly evident. She liked many things about her marriage to Don and said she believed he cared deeply for her—but she was also feeling both excited and threatened by her attraction to other men and by the dullness of life with her husband. Don had told her that she "didn't understand" him and his goals in life. Stella said what she did not "understand" was just where *she* fit into his life. She spoke of the many ways in which they differed—for example, he loved the out-of-doors; she loved knitting and attending the theatre. She felt Don was very self-indulgent and "always" buying himself trinkets like skis and cameras. She was feeling very accepted and understood by Ray, her "friend" at work, and very ignored by her husband. She saw no "ideal" solution to the situation but felt they were headed for trouble if something didn't change.

Individual interview: Don.   Don, age 31, was a quiet, neatly dressed young man who appeared to be in strong control of his emotions. He said he believed the marital problems stemmed from the fact that both he and Stella were strong people, "loners," and ambitious persons who were working very hard at their respective careers. He and Stella didn't argue often, largely because that would bother him. Also an issue, he felt, was the fact that they had different family backgrounds. His family members had always owned their own businesses; Stella's were salaried people. He enjoyed being thought of as a conservative, a loner, highly individualistic, and creative. Stella, on the other hand, had been raised to be dependent on others. He knew she had been forced to adjust to his "independence," but believed she had done well with this task.

Don said he loved Stella deeply, and thought she loved him also. She had expressed her unhappiness with his low level of overt demonstration of affection and they had "talked about it." Sex was a "bit of a problem" because of Stella's low orgasmic frequencies, but Don saw this as more her problem than his. He "couldn't remember" the last time they had had intercourse but thought it had been "recently." The actual referral for marital therapy had come after Don had rejected her overtures for sex one evening when they were late getting ready to go out to a dinner party. He had felt that it had been more important to be on time and Stella "blew up." Don was aware of Stella's attraction to her "friend," Ray, because she had discussed it with him. Outwardly he was calm about this, but he agreed he'd probably feel hurt or angry if she actually had a sexual relationship with Ray. The therapist feigned incredulity at Don's even-toned recital of Stella's obvious interest in the other man, but Don insisted that, at the worst, he had only felt "somewhat bothered" about it. Without revealing any of Stella's story about Ray, the therapist openly confronted Don in this first individual assessment session about how unrealistic Don appeared about his wife's outside interests, especially given her obvious pleas to Don for more affection and attention. Don, however, did not appear moved by this confrontation.

Conjoint interview: therapist's observations. During the conjoint session, the therapist moved rapidly and forcefully to confront the Burnses with the danger their marriage was in. He pointed out that both of them overcontrolled their feelings, made extensive use of rationalization, ignored their respective needs for their partner, and treated Stella's interest in her co-worker, Ray, as little more than an interesting issue. (This matter could be openly discussed because they had both brought it out during the conjoint session.) The therapist was emphatic about the need for marital therapy, although the choice was up to Stella and Don. In typical fashion, both listened attentively but calmly and said little in response.

Don and Stella Burns impressed the therapist as being a bright young couple, both of whom had compensated extensively through their occupations for the lack of consistent, satisfying, affective marital interaction. This was especially true for Stella who was clearly and consciously on the verge of having an extramarital sexual affair. It was not easy in this initial assessment session to determine whether Don was a man with rather low sexual and affectional needs or had "normal" needs and was unconsciously acting out his anger at his wife. Both the Burnses reported enjoying good health and held considerable positive feelings toward their marriage and toward each other. Their "rut," however, appeared about to do their marriage in if something more positive between them didn't occur—especially for Stella.

Don and Stella later discussed their assessment session between themselves several times, but it was almost three weeks before they called to schedule regular appointments.

Session 2

Conjoint interview. Usually the conjoint session starts with a review of what has occurred with the couple since the previous session, and this is particularly true of the first conjoint session following the initial assessment. A couple's decision to return and agree to regular sessions ordinarily indicates some kind of commitment to the process of therapy, although not necessarily to their marriage. Sometimes the only thing they agree on during this second session is that they agree on hardly anything, but they do not want to be "stuck" where they are. Typically, they also reveal their interaction patterns and their defenses in the way they handle the time between sessions as well as the session itself.

Stella and Don were no exceptions. When the therapist inquired about how they were feeling that evening, Stella replied with statements about her feelings, Don with descriptions of his behavior. Stella wasted no time in openly discussing her dissatisfaction, her desire for more attention, Don's lack of romance, and her feeling "used" because he seemed so indifferent to her sexual frustrations. Don said little but smiled and chuckled occasionally as if to convey that his wife was "pretty emotional" while he was totally committed to his craftsmanship and work.

Individual interview: Stella. Stella spoke vigorously and rapidly about her frustrations with Don. Recently she had been revealing more and more of her feelings to him, but with few positive results. She felt he was very selfish and overly committed to his work and hobbies. As a young, skinny girl growing up, she said, she had been very shy and insecure. More recently, she had been feeling more self-confidence and excitement with life, but not with Don. She had thought about her "friend," Ray, a great deal. She talked about what a great listener Ray was—while she felt lucky to get even a grunt out of Don. It didn't take any interpretation from the therapist to help her see how "far" she had already emotionally moved out of the marriage, even though intellectually much of her was still wanting it to succeed. She told how she was willing to have Don spend a considerable amount of money in the next year to get some more education in woodworking and design skills. That would improve his earning capacity—so that if she left him he wouldn't be in a desperate financial condition. Her ambivalence was strong.

Individual interview: Don. Don revealed a candid and realistic understanding that his wife literally "had one foot outside the door" of their marriage. He sensed her swings from affection to aloofness but felt powerless to influence them. This alleged inability on his part to influence his wife's feelings about him was not accepted by the therapist, and he expressed his belief that Don was making few conscious efforts in that direction. Don only shrugged his shoulders at this.

Session 3

Conjoint interview. In the conjoint session, it became apparent that Don talked more about his feelings during individual sessions with the therapist than he did when his wife was present. (This is a typical pattern and suggests psychological blocking due to anxiety or anger—or both.) Nevertheless, they both reported talking with each other more at home than usual, in accordance with the therapist's encouragement to do so. They emphasized how little they seemed to have in common. The therapist concentrated on Don's feelings about this, alternately challenging him and then openly supporting him to encourage his discussion of his feelings. Two primary "findings" emerged: Don often didn't know *what* Stella wanted, and he did feel "upset at times" over some issues between them. (Pushing reluctant clients to share their feelings in front of each other, with the therapist present to "protect" them, often helps remove these barriers to self-revelation.)

Individual interview: Don. (When changing from conjoint to individual sessions with couples, the therapist often alternates who "goes first" individually to minimize triangulation.) Don talked mostly about Stella. He saw her as lacking friendships and as being rather socially aloof. He disliked these traits in her and portrayed himself as being more friendly and accepting of other people. He discussed how this pattern put special emphasis on the marital relationship for Stella and resulted in heavy "responsibility" for Don to meet all of her needs in this respect. He wasn't always willing to give so much of himself to her, he felt.

Individual interview: Stella. Stella focused primarily on her relationship with Ray. During the preceding week she had told him that she would not see him "socially" any more because she was feeling very guilty and frightened about the relationship. The therapist acknowledged her sense of loss and ambivalence about taking this step. He recognized that the current crisis in their marriage did have much to do about her feelings, her needs, and her uncertainties. Stella completely agreed that she appeared to have been the one most dissatisfied with the marriage, but she was unable to clearly articulate what she did want in her relationship with Don.

Session 4

Conjoint interview. Again during the week, the Burnses had talked more at home about their feelings and their relationship. Stella, in particular, had been thinking about her discomforts with other people, especially her female peers. She had recently read a book on being your own best friend and it made her realize how important one's childhood experiences are in respect to influencing one's adult feelings about self and others. As the oldest child of four, she had sensed considerable pressure from her parents to achieve—and she knew this fit with her occupational success, although she also wanted to be successful as a wife, she emphasized. Interestingly, Stella and Don had made arrangements to get away during the preceding weekend and had enjoyed a fantastic time at the seashore. "All play and no work!" they beamed.

Individual interview: Stella. Stella used her individual time with the therapist to look at several aspects of her growing-up process and how these things influenced her now. She expressed many feelings of obligation—the usual "shoulds, oughts, and have-to's"—which represent internally generated pressures that people feel when they have introjected family and society injunctions to work hard and do well. More individual therapy time was recommended so Stella could discuss this with the therapist because her motivation to better understand and accept herself was high. She readily accepted this suggestion as well as the therapist's requirement that this increase in individually oriented therapy be "cleared" with Don. She viewed much of her boredom with their marriage as stemming from her boredom and uncertainties about herself—in spite of her many accomplishments with her education, her career, and their attractive house in the country.

Individual interview: Don.   It was difficult for the therapist to keep Don consistently focused on his feelings with his wife and marriage. Therefore, the session consisted of Don talking about his work and his frustrations. He felt torn between having to work to earn money versus his "creative" interests in design. The session ended with the therapist repeating his reminders about both Don and Stella needing to give consistent thought and attention to their priorities and their emotional needs (a salutory goal but often a waste of breath that only makes the therapist feel better!).

Session 5

Conjoint interview.   The session was devoted almost entirely to examining the possibility of Don giving up some of his time and income so that he could take the additional studies that he strongly wished to do. He was hesitant both because of finances and marital pressures. Stella acted somewhat detached during this conjoint session, later revealing in her individual session that Don "always" feared making changes or trying anything new because he was so apprehensive about failing or being rejected. (Was Stella projecting—or had Don been projecting when he earlier complained about her insecurities? Were they both projecting? Or were they both accurate? Therapists often have to live for awhile with diagnostic ambiguities—and that was true in this situation.) The therapist openly supported Don's taking the studies because Don obviously wanted to, it was to his clear professional advantage to do so, and the outcome of his marriage did not hinge on this single issue.

Individual interview: Stella.   This had been a previously agreed-upon special time during which Stella could "work on herself," but it turned into a "complaint" session about how selfish she believed her husband was. He was planning to go off on a hiking trip with some friends soon; this trip would cost considerable money, and she resented that. The therapist accepted her anger and frustrations but encouraged her to express them where they belonged—on Don's shoulders. Obviously, the therapist pointed out, Stella often repressed and suppressed much of her negative feelings toward Don. This could lead to her displacing her anger into other areas of their relationship or to loss of love—or both. This interpretation brought out Stella's fear of Don's temper, something that had not been mentioned before. Sometimes he yelled loudly and sometimes he acted in a passive–resistant manner when he was angry, she said. Either way was unpleasant to her, so Stella usually refrained from pursuing an issue when Don became angry.

Session 6

Conjoint interview. This had not been planned to be exclusively a conjoint session, but it turned into one. Both Don and Stella were feeling discouraged about their marriage, Don's work, their poor sex life, her fatigue and irritability, his allergies, and so on. Stella questioned whether marital therapy was worth the time and money since they didn't seem to be getting anywhere. Perhaps the most significant part of this primarily negativistic session was Don's revelation to Stella that often he had felt like paying more attention to her but that he had become "gun-shy" because he anticipated her expected rejection. This was a new revelation to Stella, who until then had believed Don wasn't attentive primarily because he was self-centered and didn't care. Her insight into the fact that her own negative and demanding attitude had become a self-fulfilling prophesy opened her eyes, she said.

Session 7

Individual interview: Stella. Don was off on the hiking trip he had planned so Stella came alone for this session. During her husband's absence she had gone to an accountants' convention where, in her loneliness, her thoughts had been primarily about Ray—not about her husband. She discussed her ambivalence about Don at length; his many good qualities, his accomplishments in his work, and her fears that he would "fall apart" if they split up. She still had not fully disclosed to Don how dull she found him, especially sexually. During intercourse, her fantasies were usually of Ray, not Don, and this made her feel guilty. She knew she was highly orgastic during masturbation and had found that somewhat reassuring, but her goal was to have happier sexual experiences with a man. She also expressed some concerns about some longstanding feelings of fatigue. Because of these tired feelings, which appeared to be rather chronic in nature, she was encouraged to go for a long overdue physical exam to rule out any physiological factors in these complaints. It was fairly evident that at that point in the marriage Stella was doing a lot of complaining but offering very little of herself to her husband—this is a rather common "standoff." Intellectually, she realized she could potentially get Don to respond differently to her by changing some of her own behaviors, but her motivations to do these things were blocked.

Session 8

Conjoint interview. Don was full of enthusiastic descriptions of his hiking trip but wasn't very happy about his reception from his wife when he got home. She had been "damned bitchy," and he'd felt like going right back out the door for another trip. When the therapist inquired about Stella's handling of this specific incident, Stella responded irritably. The therapist mentioned that "one has to give in order to get," but she shot back in a hostile manner that she felt that was a "bunch of crap." She appeared very angry that Don had enjoyed himself so much on his hiking trip and she was in no mood to listen to the therapist "moralize about (her) responsibilities in the marriage." "In fact," she said, reinforcing her anger over what she obviously perceived as the therapist's insensitivity to *her* feelings, "let's skip next week's appointment." (This acting out should have been discussed further, but the therapist was probably feeling defensive at that time, since the records indicate that he ignored it.)

Session 9

Conjoint interview. The Burnses called for an unscheduled appointment because "everything was awful." The whole pattern had shifted. Now Don was questioning whether or not he wanted to—or *could*—tolerate his wife's "nastiness" anymore. He had become quite depressed and was having trouble sleeping, although he denied any suicidal thoughts. He had become "unsure" about how he felt toward Stella, but believed more and more that he couldn't continue in the marriage the way things were.

Interestingly, as is so typical in marital systems, Stella's mood had apparently shifted in response to her husband's. She was considerably more empathic toward him, apologizing for her negativism, "thinking" maybe she had been too self-centered, and repeatedly emphasizing that, while feeling on the "verge" of separation, she wanted their marriage to last. She had gone for her physical exam; both the exam and all lab tests were normal, and the examining physician had concluded that her chronic fatigue was due to the emotional tensions she was experiencing within herself and within her marriage.

During many of these highly emotionally charged interactions between the Burnses, the therapist said little. His presence appeared to calm their painful exchanges a bit, and so he allowed their discussion to go on uninterrupted. However, toward the end of the session he shared his deep concerns and his uncertainties about their respective abilities to make their marriage "work" in a manner that left them both feeling good and each person's integrity intact. He expressed his belief that it was important for married persons, before they actually split up, to be able to say, *each one to his- or herself,* that they had done *all they could,* or *all they wanted,* to make their marriage work. If they had reached that spot and could say "yes" to *either* of those two conditions, then they were probably ready to separate with minimum guilt and ambivalence. If they couldn't say "yes," in spite of their pain and hurts, they probably "weren't ready" to quit. The Burnses appeared extremely thoughtful about the therapist's candid expressions of uncertainty about their chances for marital survival with each other. By the time the session ended, the tension between them had decreased appreciably and both were discussing their seriously strained marriage more objectively.

Session 10

Conjoint interview. After hitting rock bottom, there is only one way one can go—up—and that is what the Burnses marital interaction had done by the time they returned for their next therapy appointment. After the previous sessions, they had gone home and seriously considered a trial separation. That had led Stella to reconsider her position further, and she had concluded that their marriage *was* important to her and that she wanted to keep it going. Don said he had been very depressed, but his mood had lightened as soon as Stella had announced her "decision." This revelation led us to focus on Don's anger and how he had suppressed anger ever since he'd gotten in trouble as a kid for fighting. With Stella, he felt he had repressed it until he blew up at her or until it came out through cutting, "put-down" remarks he often made to her at parties. He was supported by the therapist in his goal of trying to handle his angry feelings more openly and directly, especially with his wife.

The focus with Stella during this session was on her decision about not leaving the marriage and the "challenge" she faced—that of seeing whether she could emotionally accept Don *as he really was,* and not as she had tried to force him to be. While cautious about her long-range ability to do this, Stella was nevertheless highly motivated to try. Symbolic of their newly affirmed commitment, the Burnses were now having "great sex" every day and had gone on a camping trip the preceding weekend, in spite of Stella's previous resistance to such activities. Don was planning to reciprocate the "favor" by accompanying his wife to the theatre the following weekend.

Session 11

Individual interview: Don.   At the therapist's suggestion, both Don and Stella were seen individually during this session. (The therapist primarily wanted to "check out" their individual feelings in confidential individual sessions to insure that nothing significant was being held back in the conjoint sessions, which had become routine by now.) Don was in an upbeat, positive mood about their marriage. He also spoke with enthusiasm about his studies, which he would be starting soon, and about a vacation trip the couple would take before then. Again, the therapeutic focus was primarily on Don's continuing efforts to share his feelings—both positive and negative—with his wife consistently and openly so that she would not have to engage in "mind-reading" to know where she stood with him. Don appeared to be convinced that although it had been "scary" to share with Stella, it had "paid off," for it enabled her to both feel and react to him more realistically. That was, he said, both good and bad—but then, "that was also life."

Individual interview: Stella.   Stella continued to feel positive about her decision to keep the marriage. She was increasingly feeling more comfortable with her husband and accepting his "shortcomings" as a small price to pay for his positive points. She had not realized how she had "cut him down" with her acid verbalizations and was consciously making efforts to develop her abilities to share her negative thoughts—such as complaints that Don rarely helped her with the cooking—in a way that allowed them to stay issue-oriented instead of sinking into "you don't love me" attacks.

Session 12

Conjoint interview. This session occurred one month after the eleventh session as part of a tapering-off process after the Burnses began to feel more comfortable with the improvements in their marriage. They felt that one of the most important issues for them was to be constantly, but judiciously, more open in their intercommunications, as well as to make consistent, conscious efforts to remain sensitive to each other's feelings and wishes. The atmosphere between them during this session was open, playful, relaxed, and trusting. They were now "working on" making sex a more positive experience for both of them instead of Don "just getting his rocks off." Don was starting his studies the following week and both appeared content with that decision.

Session 13

Conjoint interview. This was a planned ending session that occurred about one month after the previous follow-up session. Things were "fine." Money was short with Don's reduced income, but Don and Stella were not complaining. They were communicating better, their fights were issue-oriented when they occurred, and they were both feeling and expressing their love for each other more openly, consistently, and enthusiastically. They "dreamed" about some of their long-range plans, including having a baby, but for now they were feeling busy and contented. No further therapy visits were planned, but both realized they could return to the therapist at any time if they wished to do so.

SUMMARY

Five years later, the therapist had occasion to contact Stella and Don on another matter. They reported that they were the proud parents of a young son, Stella was enjoying being "just a mother" for a while, and Don's business was going very well. Their marriage appeared to be sound and satisfying to both of them.

The Burnses marital therapy case was "typical." They started their therapy with some simple, ordinary complaints. Stella believed that Don wasn't emotionally giving to her; Don felt that they just had different ideas about marriage. Therapy "uncovered" a borderline extramarital affair, sexual maladjustments, depression, value conflicts over lifestyle, and a "near miss" with marital separation. Therapy focused on their respective feelings, their interactions, their intrapsychic issues as well as their interpersonal ones, and on some therapeutic education about what is required to keep monotony out of a marriage so that the marriage will function to both partners' satisfaction. The case also demonstrated how relatively "short-term" psychodynamically oriented therapy (thirteen sessions), utilizing the combined interviewing modalities of individual and conjoint sessions, can reverse a negatively reinforcing, downward-spiraling marital struggle and help it become an affirming system that tends to perpetuate itself.

PART THREE
PROFESSIONAL ISSUES IN MARITAL THERAPY

CHAPTER TEN
ESTABLISHING
AND MAINTAINING
A PRACTICE
IN MARITAL THERAPY

Marital therapy is performed in both organizational and private-practice settings. In the former, therapists are the employees of various organizations, such as governmental units, social agencies, religious bodies, or industries. When a therapist has a private practice, he or she is self-employed and performs services for persons or groups who pay directly for the services rendered. In the evolution of marital therapy as a specialized professional service, marital therapists—particularly those from the fields of social work and theology—historically were primarily employed by various organizations. By contrast, marital therapists from the field of medicine, a much smaller but highly significant group, were most often self-employed and in private practice. It was undoubtedly the greater prestige and higher incomes of these medical practitioners doing marital therapy that led clinicians of all types to gradually move toward becoming private practitioners. In addition, as shall be outlined here, private practice has developed out of specific needs of both therapists and clients, and, in many respects, differs considerably from marital therapy practiced under the auspices of an organization. The actual therapy—what goes on between therapist and clients—may not appear to differ appreciably but, in actuality, the impact of the "setting" has many implications for therapists and clients alike.

MARITAL THERAPY
IN ORGANIZATIONAL SETTINGS

The Organization as Employer

Marital therapists in organizational settings may be employed by governmental units, such as cities, states, the federal government, and/or combinations of these, or by agencies funded by religious bodies, charitable foundations, and so forth.

Here we shall ignore any differences, except as noted, and consider all such units as organizational employers of marital therapists. As employers, the organizations pay the therapists salaries to perform their work, provide them with various "packages" of fringe benefits (vacations, sick leave, medical insurance, holiday time, etc.), make provisions for the necessary physical settings in which to perform therapy (offices, chairs, desks, phones, heat, custodial services, etc.), supply them with support personnel (receptionists, typists, etc.), and are also expected to provide whatever clinical supervision and consultation the therapists may need. Usually, these organizations employ more than one therapist so working in these settings automatically brings with it a certain amount of professional companionship and also potential opportunities to supervise the work of other therapists. If the agency is connected to a college or university training program, opportunities to teach student therapists are also common.

Positives and Negatives
for Therapists

Studies performed on job satisfaction of marital therapists employed in organizations, as compared to those in private practice, suggest that there are positives and negatives, for therapists and clients alike, that are functions of the settings in which the marital therapy is performed. Therapists working for agencies particularly like their greater opportunities for forming professional networks, their sometimes greater financial security, and their opportunities for supervisory and training work. They report the negatives of agency employment to be minimal control over their working hours and schedules, as well as over the physical settings of their offices, longer work hours, sometimes excessive paperwork, administrative interference with therapy, limited salary ranges, the necessity of dealing with a less educated and less sophisticated clientele, and lack of control of certain treatment policies. The latter item may be especially crucial in sectarian agencies in which religious teachings about marriage, divorce, sexuality, and so forth may demand that the therapist abide by the employer's dictates or be fired (Krupnick and Humphrey 1980).

Advantages and Disadvantages
for Clients

A major benefit of agency practice over the private practice of marital therapy is the availability of therapy to those of low and moderate incomes who do not have insurance and who cannot afford the higher fees of private practitioners. The limitations of agency practice, from the client's perspective, include the inability to choose the therapist; the likelihood of treatment by therapists who tend to be younger and have less academic training and experience than therapists in private practice; and a loss of privacy because they have to be seen in public offices.

MARITAL THERAPY
IN PRIVATE PRACTICE

Growth of Private-Practice Trend

Professional associations. More and more, marital therapy is being performed in private-practice settings. Adopting the medical model, marital therapists have been moving in this direction at an accelerated pace since the 1960s. Illustrative of this change has been the growth of the professional association which started in 1942 as the American Association of Marriage Counselors (AAMC). In its earliest days, its members represented a mix of organizational and private practitioners, but the majority of the members now are in full- or part-time private practice. By 1960, almost two decades after the AAMC was formed, its membership still numbered only about 200. By 1970, one decade later, it had changed its name to the American Association of Marriage and Family Counselors (AAMFC), reflecting the increasing emphasis of the treatment of the whole family as well as of the marital unit, and it had grown fivefold to over 1,000 members. By 1980, the group was renamed the American Association for Marriage and Family Therapy (AAMFT), reflecting more accurately the function of its members—now primarily focusing on therapy rather than counseling. The AAMFT by that time reported a membership of over 8,000.

Another clear indication of the growth of the private practice of marital therapy has been the proliferation of public listings of its services in the "Yellow Pages" of American telephone directories. Originally, these failed to list marital therapy at all, and persons seeking such services had to look under "Social Service Organization" categories to search out therapists who were alphabetically mixed in with the Boy and Girl Scouts, groups for handicapped citizens, Community Funds, and so forth. Finally, the category of "Marriage and Family Counselors" came into general usage. Today, anyone seeking a marital therapist in the phone book may be confronted with the names of dozens of practitioners in major metropolitan city directories; this is a far cry from a category that was almost nonexistent before 1960.

Positives and Negatives
for Therapists

The private practice of marital therapy appears to offer therapists several advantages that they normally do not have when employed by organizations. These include higher status, higher income potential, control over their work settings and hours of practice, freedom to make their own decisions, reduced time pressures, more work satisfaction, convenient office locations, the ability to maximize their therapeutic skills, and the opportunity to treat clients from higher socioeconomic groups. Negatives of private practice for marital therapists include isolation from colleagues, unstable incomes and anxieties associated with this, problems of community acceptance, and the lack of "business" training therapists may need in order to be successful entrepreneurs (Krupnick and Humphrey 1980).

From the standpoint of marital therapy clients, the pluses of private practice include greater privacy, the freedom to choose their own specific therapist(s), the opportunity to obtain the services of older, more experienced professionals with more academic training than organizational therapists usually possess, and potentially more convenient office settings and appointment hours. The disadvantages consist primarily of the higher cost for private practitioners (prohibiting some people from obtaining their services), the associated failure of most insurance programs to offer marital therapy as a reimbursable benefit, and finally, the occasional lack of availability of private practitioners, especially in rural areas.

MAKING THE CHOICE: ORGANIZATION OR PRIVATE PRACTICE?

Organizational Setting Necessary at First

For a neophyte marital therapist trying to make a decision about whether to seek employment with an organization or to hang out his or her own shingle as a private practitioner, there are ordinarily no options. New therapists, with the ink still wet on their diplomas and training certificates, ordinarily need to seek employment with organizations in order to increase their skills under supervision and to acquire the knowledge necessary to be able to handle any problem brought up by clients. Professional accreditation associations such as the AAMFT recognize these facts by requiring extensive supervised experience for full clinical membership, the badge of presumed readiness to enter private practice. In addition, neophytes will ordinarily have great difficulty achieving the type of public and professional recognition that is necessary to obtain referrals and build a successful practice.

Job Satisfaction

It should also be pointed out that research performed by a colleague and the author (Krupnick and Humphrey 1980) seemed to indicate that when various demographic variables and characteristics of the setting in which they practiced were held constant, therapists in private practice reported that they experienced about the same level of job satisfaction as those employed in organizations. Job satisfaction for the various marital therapists studied was more closely related to factors such as age, training, years of experience, types of clients, and professional opportunities than to organizational versus private employment. For the marital therapist with sufficient training and experience to be qualified to enter private practice, therefore, the decision about which setting to choose will be made primarily on each therapist's idiosyncratic values and needs. For some, the higher status and potential higher earning power of private practice, among other things, will offset the greater responsibilities and demands that go with the role. For others, the greater opportunities for supervision and training, of closer association with colleagues, and perhaps of a "calling" to serve persons from the more needy socioeconomic groups will make employment in an organization a more rewarding career choice. Later in this chapter, we will discuss full- versus part-time private practices, as well as solo versus group practices; many marital therapists find these "combinations" of practice settings to be ideal compromises between organization versus private practice.

ESTABLISHING A PRIVATE PRACTICE

Once the therapist has elected to establish a private practice, several decisions have to be made immediately. Will the practice be full- or part-time? Solo or group? Where will it be located? How much financial risk is the therapist ready and able to take? These and more decisions must be made before any initial steps are taken—especially before the therapist resigns from his or her regular organizational employment situation.

Full-Time or Part-Time Practice?

For the more cautious (perhaps even the more realistic) therapist a part-time practice enables the person to "test the waters"—*and him- or herself*—before the total risks of a full-time practice are assumed. In fact, for many, a part-time practice coupled with regular employment in an organizational setting may offer an ideal permanent marriage of the two settings.

Part-time and organizational practice combined.   Obviously, a first step in establishing a part-time practice is to determine that the therapist has the energy, the motivation, and the personal time available for both full employment and a part-time practice. The attitudes and feelings of one's present employer and of one's family members also need to be taken into consideration. Some employers actively discourage their employees from "competing" with them. Labor laws and contracts may be the deciding factors here, but common sense dictates that employees faced with hostile employer attitudes regarding a private practice will either change employers, decide not to enter private practice, or, at the very least, establish the practice in a geographic area and in a manner that will clearly minimize any reasonable claims of competition and conflicts of interest. Similarly, the more personal decisions that relate to the attitudes of family members and partners need to be made in accordance with the feelings of all concerned. Therapists who jeopardize their own marriages by excessive absences and perhaps extra fatigue brought on by a part-time practice hardly make good models for, say, high-powered clients who may be neglecting their marriages in pursuit of greater income and glory.

Necessary investments.   Part-time practices may start small, but even then certain minimum investments of time, money, and risk are involved. Office space must be obtained, professional announcements must be sent, a telephone service should be arranged, and so forth. Perhaps the greatest virtues of the part-time practice combined with the regular organizational position rests in the lower amount of risk in terms of income, and the advantages of working in both types of professional settings.

The "transitional" part-time practice.   Another model of practice might be labeled the "transitional" part-time private practice. This may be undertaken when therapists do not feel ready or able, psychologically or financially, to assume the risk of going into full-time private practice immediately. The transitional phase enables them to determine their abilities and satisfactions and to better judge their private-practice potential before "cutting the silver cords."

The full-time practice.   The obvious advantages of full-time private practice are largely those discussed in the preceding sections—higher status, greater income, more satisfying clients, and so on. Even though therapists individually assume all the risks and all the responsibilities in a full-time practice, these are ordinarily held to be well worth their "cost" to successful practitioners.

Private practices, however, do not always succeed. Their failures add to the millions of "small business" failures that government surveys report each year. Sometimes these failures can't be anticipated—such as those that may occur because major economic downturns drastically reduce the ability of potential clients to pay for private professional services. Quite often, however, the failures represent therapists' failures to realistically appraise their own potential as well as the availability of sufficient demands for their services. In addition to a high capacity to tolerate risk—personal, professional, and financial—private practitioners need to be successful businesspersons and to continuously command the confidence and respect of their clients and their referral services. "Successful" work experience for a larger therapy organization, where clients can be shifted to different therapists if needed or where therapists do not have to depend on public good will and appearances to survive, may give false impressions about specific therapists' real potential to survive on their own.

Solo Practice or Group Practice?

The next decision one must make in establishing a private practice involves whether to go it alone or join with others to form a group practice. If there are no potential partners in the area, the decision is obvious. Group practice enables one to share certain risks and responsibilities, such as rent and secretarial and phone services; it also provides one with professional colleagues to reduce the oft-voiced complaints of isolation in solo practice; and sometimes it enables therapists to provide clients with several services in one office, such as marital therapy, vocational counseling, and psychological evaluations. Many groups are formed when older, more experienced therapists receive an excess of requests for therapy and welcome the presence of younger colleagues to treat these persons. A more contemporary reason for joining a group practice is so that marital therapists can qualify for third-party and insurance payments for their services; in these cases they must be supervised by or under the immediate guidance of licensed physicians or psychologists. (This is not applicable in states that license marital therapists and have freedom of choice laws, nor is it applicable in Canada.) The particular requirements for these arrangements vary from state to state, so each person must understand the regulations in force in the state in which he or she plans to practice.

Personality, therapeutic orientation important.   Equally important in reaching a decision about joining a group practice are personality and therapeutic orientation issues. Personality clashes among therapists practicing together can be just as draining and destructive as similar rifts among organizational practitioners. However, in private practice, the greater interdependence of the partners tends to minimize any such tensions. Some group practice practitioners employ outside "consultants" (therapists) to meet regularly with the partners in order to work out rivalries, squabbles over who may be getting the "best" clients, and similar issues. Differing therapeutic orientations among the therapists in a group may be viewed as assets— or as liabilities. Some therapists prefer to be associated primarily with those who share their own philosophical and psychological ideas about treatment. Others feel the exact opposite, find colleagues' differences stimulating, and believe that the availability of differing treatment orientations in one office strengthens what the group can offer its clients. These are individual choices, but it is essential that all members of the group reach consensus about them. Systems theories are real assets in diagnosing therapists' abilities to work with each other and should be considered in arriving at decisions about joining, changing, or leaving a group practice.

The Office

Location, cost, services.   Having decided to establish a solo practice, the therapist must arrange for office space. Decisions about this will vary greatly according to the geographical area in which he or she intends to practice, but numerous generalizations hold true almost everywhere. Decisions need to be made about location, costs, and services. The office should be located conveniently for both the therapist and his or her clients; there must be commuting and/or parking availability; the office must be in a safe and convenient location (issues are the dangers of muggers and fire, access for handicapped, etc.); there must be adequate services available (from air conditioning to nearby eating facilities, centralized custodial services, etc.). Cost is an important factor in selecting the office, as is "status." Cost and status considerations usually go together. An office is like a home; it projects an image of those who work and live there. Clients who utilize private therapists ordinarily pay higher fees and, in return, expect to be treated accordingly; thus comfort and attractiveness are expected in therapists' offices.

Some therapists seek offices in professional buildings also utilized by physicians and lawyers. They believe this lends them credibility and status and also increases their opportunities to become better known to these important sources of referrals. Other therapists, especially those who strongly resist the medical model of therapy, may deliberately choose a "neutral" building with no other professional offices. Some therapists prefer office space in shopping centers where people have easy access to all types of services. These also provide "good excuses" to clients who may wish to camouflage their real reasons for being there.

The Home Office

Pros and cons. One option for office space used by many therapists, especially those in part-time practice, is to establish an office in one's own home or apartment. This has both advantages and disadvantages. On the positive side, it almost invariably saves the therapist both time and money, as well as providing the ultimate in convenience if one dislikes commuting. The cost benefits derive from the utilization of space that is not needed for other purposes and also from tax benefits, particularly in regard to one's income taxes. This space, and its contents, must be utilized exclusively for one's practice, however, to qualify for these tax benefits, so tax laws must be scrupulously obeyed to avoid problems.

There are two other legal issues one must consider in respect to home offices: insurance and zoning regulations. *Liability for any injuries* clients suffer if they are injured on one's premises must be covered as homeowner's insurance policies do not ordinarily extend coverage when the home is used as a place of business unless a specific, extra premium rider has been paid and is in effect. Zoning regulations often permit professional offices to be maintained by a single practitioner in residential areas, but they always need to be checked out for the specific neighborhood and building.

Another plus for the home office is the opportunity to be near one's family (or pets, or TV, etc.) when appointments are suddenly canceled or open. This also relates to another positive point: home offices can help clients obtain a better sense of their therapist as a real person, a human being, and even as a marital partner and family person.

There is also a negative side to having a home office. It can directly intrude into personal and family spaces, a factor some therapists may dislike. Unless therapists are able to construct separate entrances and waiting areas, family members may resent the necessity for maintaining a certain amount of decorum around clients—to say nothing of reasonable quiet during office hours. This is a particularly difficult task for many adolescents and young children in the therapists' own families. Privacy for both clients and therapists' household members must be respected. Some clients have been known to object to home offices because "they did not feel professional," even though others value them for exactly the same reasons.

Subrenting Office Space

Still another form of office usage and location, especially for part-time practitioners, is that of renting another professional person's office during the latter's "off" hours. For example, physicians may be willing to rent out their consulting rooms during evenings or Saturdays when they might not ordinarily be expected to have their own office hours. Arrangements of this nature enable marital therapists to have many of the advantages of their "own" offices (location, furniture, waiting area, etc.) but with some limitations. The therapist, of course, must arrange his or her office hours around those of the other professional. It isn't possible in this situation to personalize the office with photos, diplomas, personal choices of color and furniture and so on. Also, it is often difficult to find other professionals who are willing to share their premises. However, when this model can be arranged, it is quite attractive and beneficial to part-time marital therapists, particularly those with transitional practices. If the practice thrives, this type of arrangement provides time to plan ahead for individual office space when a full-time practice becomes preferable. Finally, this arrangement permits the therapist to start a practice with minimum financial risks in respect to office space.

Office Facilities

Convenience, comfort, and privacy essential. The physical layout of the office needs to be planned to allow maximum convenience, comfort, and privacy. Privacy may be drastically reduced by thin walls, air conditioning or heating ducts, and excessively cramped quarters. Marital therapy sessions frequently involve loud voices and crying, both of which must be considered in planning for auditory privacy. Waiting-room chairs and receptionists should not be stationed immediately outside therapy-room doors, even if sound transmissions are unlikely, for they intrude into the clients' sense of psychological privacy.

In obtaining office furniture and decorations, as well as in planning color schemes, therapists will be guided by their own tastes (or pocketbooks, or interior decorators, or spouses!). A good interior decorator will ask how the therapist wants clients to "see" him or her. This sets the stage for the impression the therapist wishes to convey. Offices that are overly formal, stiff, and hygienically sterile may create negative impressions of the therapist for many clients, but so may offices that are too "mod" or "frilly" or "masculine" or "feminine," or what have you. Certainly one thing to be avoided in obtaining the necessary furnishings is the "Salvation Army Store look." Those who attempt to start their practices on the proverbial shoestring and whose office decor reflects this fact will find it hard to establish their credibility as well-trained professionals.

Records, phones. In addition to adequate and comfortable seating arrangements, offices require a certain minimum of space and equipment for storing records and for telephones. Records must never be stored where their confidentiality can be compromised, and this can readily be accomplished with the great array of file cabinets (with locks) available everywhere. Telephones are necessary for incoming calls, outgoing calls, and a source of referral through the listing of one's business phone in the Yellow Pages Classified Directory. Therapists cannot maintain their practices of marital therapy without adequate phone services. The immediate decision beginning practitioners must make concerns the *type* of phone services they will need. Minimal services consist of business phones that therapists answer themselves. This is the most economical type of phone service, but it also has some serious drawbacks. Who answers the phone when the therapists are out (at their "other" jobs or on personal business), or when they are interviewing? Unanswered calls mean lost business. Two major methods are utilized to overcome this—subscribing to telephone answering services or obtaining a personal electronic answering machine.

Professional answering services are usually available twenty-four hours a day, seven days a week. Here, receptionists can theoretically exercise some judgment in separating emergency calls from routine ones. These services vary greatly, however, in the tact of the answering personnel, their speed and reliability in obtaining messages, and in their costs. *Electronic answering machines* present a more economical method for these duties, especially for part-time therapists. They are also available twenty-four hours a day, seven days a week. They never answer with "Doctor's office—we're busy, one minute, please," leaving the agitated client wondering if the voice will ever come back on again. They may also be "called" by therapists from other phones almost any place in the world with simple, hand-held signal devices to obtain messages. Of course, these machines can also develop malfunctions, and some clients have strong aversions to the impersonal, recorded directions they give ("Leave your message in 20 seconds at the sound of the beep").

The waiting room.   Part of all offices should be waiting areas with provisions for hanging up coats and also with washroom and toilet facilities. The waiting area offers the therapist an opportunity to inform clients about his or her credentials (diplomas, certificates, etc., on the walls) and to educate them through the judicious display of materials dealing with marital therapy and related topics. Naturally, "lighter" reading material should also be available, such as up-to-date popular magazines, newspapers, and so forth. Client behaviors in waiting rooms can offer helpful diagnostic clues regarding their psychodynamics, especially their defenses against anxiety. Overtly anxious persons pace, depressed persons sit about lethargically and ignore their surroundings, and persons utilizing great repression or denial sit about engrossed in the daily newspapers as if they didn't have a care in the world. Observant therapists thus can gain additional diagnostic information from noting these waiting-room behaviors.

Public Relations

The printed announcement.   Once beginning private practitioners have completed the necessary planning for their offices, they are faced with the task of informing both public and professional audiences of their availability to provide services. The most time-honored and accepted method of reaching professional audiences is to send out printed, formal announcements to all prospective sources of referrals and to others that the therapist believes should know of the new practice. Individual tastes will dictate therapists' choices in these announcements, but it should be remembered that a written communication projects an image of the sender. In arriving at these decisions, therapists should consider printing versus engraving, light or dark print, the type of print, the color and quality of the paper used, and the "text." Minimally acceptable messages would provide information such as name, degrees, address, phone numbers, types of services offered, and perhaps office hours. For example, "Martha Doonesbury, Ph.D., announces the opening of her office for the practice of marital therapy in Suite 107, the Downtown Professional Building, 67 Main Street, Sometown, Ontario. Hours by appointment. Member, American Association for Marriage and Family Therapy." As in all things professional, senders should avoid hyperbolic claims and representations.

Announcements are ordinarily sent to potential referral sources such as internists, family physicians, pediatricians, obstetrician–gynecologists, psychiatrists, psychologists, attorneys (especially those who specialize in domestic law and belong to the family law section of the local bar association); also to United Fund clinics and agencies that may need to refer clients, public mental health clinics and hospitals, other practicing marital and family therapists, information and referral services, and selected clergy.

The therapist may choose to send similar printed announcements to referral sources when some major shift in services occurs—e.g., announcement of partnerships, of a move to new offices, of new services, and so forth. In effect, it is possible to justify any good reason that informs referral sources of new developments and also serves as a reminder to these same sources of the therapist's regular services. The old adage "out of sight, out of mind" should be remembered; referring professionals, like everyone else, can forget names and services of therapists if they do not have occasion to use them frequently.

Newspaper announcements. In addition to printed announcements of the opening of therapists' practices, some professionals choose to send a vita and photo to local newspapers, or even purchase ad space for the same purposes. Advertising used to be a "dirty word" to the ethics committees of professional associations, but legal changes and judicial decisions made in the 1970s have resulted in the opening up of these media. Advertising that informs consumers honestly about available professional services can be a positive force and not unsavory commercialism.

Personal contacts. In addition to making use of the printed media, marital therapists may also wish to arrange personal visits to selected professional referral sources and to public groups. There is no substitute for being able to sit down with other professionals and to let them experience the therapist directly. Often, friends and colleagues may be instrumental in arranging these meetings. In addition, many therapists find it helpful to become visible to lay groups in their area, particularly those that are in small or middle-sized communities. Organizations such as mental health groups, school parent–teacher associations, church and synagogue auxiliaries, business-related groups such as the Chamber of Commerce, and so on are constantly looking for interesting speakers on contemporary topics—and the marital therapist is a natural for these tasks. These opportunities, especially early in the therapist's practice, may be initially offered without charge; the publicity and good will engendered should provide ample compensation. Local radio and television shows also should not be overlooked as potential sources of help in educating the public about therapists' services, albeit indirectly.

It is almost always impossible to measure the exact cost-effectiveness of these various modalities that may be used to inform the public about therapists' practices. Some therapists may reject these public routes, either because they consider them "unprofessional" or because they do not possess the skills needed to do these tasks well. There is no single best way to let the public know of a new marital therapy practice, but one way or another, private practitioners must successfully inform the public and referral sources of their availability in order to establish a successful practice.

Referrals

Referrals are the vital ingredients of any practice of marital therapy. The preceding section on public relations covered ways and means of publicizing the opening of a new marital therapy practice. Referrals, however, must go on continuously as long as the therapist stays in practice. Once the initial phases of starting practices are completed, public announcements are no longer appropriate nor, it is hoped, are they necessary. It is difficult to anticipate precisely where any individual therapist's referrals will come from. The most common sources, however, are the related professionals listed in the preceding section; they will undoubtedly provide the bulk of the marital therapist's routine referrals. These sources are vitally important, and as such, should be respected, acknowledged, and cooperated with.

Acknowledging referrals. The marital therapist may choose to acknowledge specific referrals with phone calls to the referring person (or group), but this is time-consuming and is inappropriate for all routine referrals. It is possible to have small *acknowledgment cards* printed up, with space left in which the name of the referred clients can be written. These acknowledgments contain brief messages, such as "Robert Mondale, Ph.D., gratefully acknowledges the referral of _____ to him for marital therapy." Such cards are quick, easy, and inexpensive to use; they express the therapist's appreciation in a dignified manner, and they reinforce the referring professional's awareness of the therapist. In sum, they represent good business practices as well as being courteous expressions of appreciation.

Another practice sometimes followed is to send *periodic progress reports and closing summaries* of clients to their professional referral sources. These may be especially appreciated by the referring persons if they are involved in the total health care of the couples. However, in these cases, the therapist must first ascertain that the clients have given their written permission to release such confidential information, and that the referring source will use the reports appropriately. Unfortunately, not all professionals are sensitive to the highly emotionally charged material that is ordinarily contained in these reports, and the marital therapist must therefore exercise judgment and caution about *what* and *with whom* such information is shared.

Referrals by former clients. Once a practice has been underway for an appreciable period of time, one of the best sources of referrals are the therapist's satisfied former clients. These individuals know their therapist's skills and strengths intimately, so their recommendation of a specific therapist to a friend, family member, or colleague ordinarily carries considerable weight and merit. As noted earlier in this book, almost all prospective clients experience anxiety about whether or not a marital therapist will be able to help them. If they can identify with the positive therapeutic experiences of that therapist's current or former clients, they will find it that much easier to seek help. Another positive aspect of referrals that originates from current or former clients is that these clients, in effect, serve as "screening agents" and may save therapists from receiving inappropriate referrals.

Self-referrals. Self-referrals are also to be considered in the maintenance of a private practice of marital therapy. On occasion, therapists discourage these, believing that self-referrals are people who tend to be "shopping" and not seriously motivated. When referrals come only from other professionals and through former clients, grossly inappropriate requests for therapy are probably minimized. There is ordinarily no way to tell in advance what kind of clients self-referrals will become. Not everyone learns of a marital therapist through a friend or a professional person. The general public is fairly well informed today about the existence of marital therapists so it should come as no surprise that many couples who seek therapy do so without having been professionally referred and without any previous history of any type of therapy. While the therapist may have to provide these couples with some additional explanation about what is involved in marital therapy, they do not appear to be substantially different from other types of referrals and should be treated accordingly.

Referrals made to other professionals. The subject of referrals made by the marital therapist to other professionals was covered in Chapter Two. Numerous issues, including reasons for referral, confidentiality of records, and the types of services needed have already been discussed. It should be recognized, however, that referring clients to other professionals for specialized help often develops into a two-way street. For example, when a couple is referred to an internist because of some issues about somatic complaints that require diagnosis and/or treatment, a report should be sent to that physician. Once again, this will reinforce the physician's memory of the marital therapist's services—to say nothing of the assistance the reports may be in treating the somatic complaints. By conscientiously following through with these referrals, marital therapists are not only seeing to it that their clients receive the best possible care; they are also building good relationships between themselves and other professionals in their area on which they depend, in part, for referrals themselves.

Fees

The primary source of income for private practitioners are the fees they collect for the services they render to their clients. In contrast to physicians and psychologists, marital therapists' fees are not ordinarily covered by third-party insurance payments, with the exception of the federal CHAMPUS program and a small number of state and private provisions for this. It has already been pointed out that under some circumstances the marital therapist's fees may be reimbursable if he or she is under the direct supervision of a physician or psychologist. Clients and therapists who do not fit these criteria, therefore, must work out their own arrangements about fees.

Determining fees.   Two major issues must be considered in setting fees: How much should the charges be for each hour or session of therapy? How is the fee to be paid? Charges for marital therapy in private practice vary widely. Some therapists utilize sliding scales, charging different fees in accordance with couples' incomes and their existing financial responsibilities. This procedure has long been practiced by public organizations offering marital therapy, but these organizations are subsidized by governmental or private auspices and do not usually have to rely on client fees for the total cost of their services. The use of sliding or varied fees in private practice, therefore, would seem to be inappropriate except in unusual circumstances, such as when clients suddenly experience a totally unanticipated financial crisis in the middle of their therapy. In such instances, the therapist may adjust the fees temporarily, if he or she chooses. It will be entirely up to this therapist, however, to set his or her policies on these matters and to inform clients clearly about practices and expectations.

Inform clients immediately.   The fees to be charged for marital therapy should be set at the time of the very first interview. Clients have every right to know how much therapeutic services will cost and what the methods of payment will be. Beginning marital therapists often experience great ambivalence about fees. They recognize that fees must be charged if the practice is to survive, but they also may feel sorry for clients or may question the quality of their own services. When they are paid salaries to perform marital therapy for organizations, however, these same therapists are able to separate their salaries from their clients' fees—at least in their own conscious minds. (Often, in fact, in large clinics, therapists have nothing to do with fee arrangements. These are set by the clinic at the time of the first appointment, sometimes by an administrator, and then they are collected by the receptionist or are billed to the clients through the mail.) When these same therapists enter private practice, they often have to assume all the roles—receptionist, therapist, and fee collector. One consequence of this is that many new therapists end their first year of practice with clients owing them large sums of money. Because marital therapy often consists of only a few sessions, the professional relationships may be over with before timid and insecure therapists can bring themselves to bring up the matter of the bills. By then, satisfactory payment of the amounts owed may be out of the question.

Pay-as-you-go policy.   There is a very simple solution to problems of unpaid fees. Do what some therapists have done successfully for decades and what is increasingly being adopted in all types of professional practices—adopt a strict, pay-as-you-go policy. Once the fee is agreed to, it is paid immediately at the end of each session. Period. Prospective clients who cannot afford the fees and these conditions of payment can be referred to publicly subsidized organizations. Private clients usually do not object to the pay-as-you-go method because they do not accumulate bills and do not have to cope with transference guilt because of the money they might owe their therapist. Therapists who have adopted this method find that it is easy to administer, results in virtually zero loss of income, and does not burden them with negative countertransferences because of unpaid client bills. Therapists who let clients run up large sums in unpaid fees often end up having to turn these bills over to commercial collection agencies which, in turn, charge appreciable fees for their services when and if they are finally able to obtain payments.

A possible variation on the pay-as-you-go method consists of clients utilizing credit cards for their payments. Therapists are paid by the bank or credit company as soon as the therapy bills are submitted to them. These companies then charge fees for their services. Such procedures add to the overhead costs of running a practice, but many therapists believe that the costs (usually 4 to 7 percent of the amounts charged) are justified; this method is quick, easy, and someone else has to face the task of collecting the fees.

Fluctuations in cash flow. Fees, of course, directly determine private practitioners' incomes. Inasmuch as most marital therapists are used to being paid by salaries in their early days of practice, instead of depending on client fees, they often have paid little attention to necessary details such as numbers of appointments and cash flow. Consequently, they are often unprepared for the fluctuations that occur in respect to fees generated per week, per month, and per year. Examination of both organizational and private-practice records will reveal that referrals can vary widely in their frequency. In marital therapy, they often fall off during the vacation periods of the summer months, experience an upsurge in the early fall when life returns to normal, drop off again during the December religious holidays, and then resume a "normal" flow throughout the rest of the winter and spring months. Even a "normal" flow is highly individualistic and unpredictable, however. Neophyte private practitioners who are not mentally and financially prepared for these variations—the times when they "never" seem to receive any referrals, and later, when they may feel swamped by them—may find their worries, self-confidence, and their bank accounts all fluctuating widely, and often in diametrically opposed directions! Perhaps the best advice that can be given about this problem is: (1) to realize in advance that these fluctuations will occur; (2) to discuss them with a more experienced private practitioner and obtain reassurance that fluctuations do not spell failure, and (3) to realize that as one's practice grows, the impact of such variations on the therapist's ego, client load, and finances usually softens considerably with time and experience.

Business Details of Daily Practice

Insurance. Insurance is a necessary protection for private practitioners. It is needed for the usual coverages of fire, theft, and comprehensive damages to the office and its furnishings. Liability insurance should be carried also, for both rented and owned office space, to cover any physical injuries clients might accidentally sustain while on the premises. Finally, professional liability insurance should be considered to cover any possible malpractice claims. Malpractice insurance has been vigorously debated in professional circles, with some marital therapists recommending that it *not* be carried. They maintain that if clients anticipate that they might collect the larger amounts that most insurance policies contain, as opposed to simply being able to sue the therapist for that person's personal worth, they would be more inclined to sue on questionable grounds. Other marital therapists disagree and support the concept of malpractice insurance as one of the "necessary evils" of conducting professional affairs in the modern world. This insurance may be obtained through group policies in connection with some professional associations or through individual policies placed with individual brokers.

Record keeping.   Marital therapists must maintain two types of records: client records and business records. *Client records* contain all the vital information about each set of clients, including progress reports on their therapy. Ordinarily, the initial assessment interviews should be written up in greater detail than ongoing sessions because of the larger volumes of new material that therapists must absorb during these first appointments. After the first sessions, the therapist should maintain notes on each session, the particular issues covered, changes that emerged, and so forth. A quick review of the preceding session's notes before couples are seen for their next therapy visit is immensely helpful in assisting the therapist to quickly move to the core issues in the therapy.

In addition to the treatment records, which are commonly stored in standard manila folders, therapists may wish to maintain separate identification files on clients. These files provide quick access for case numbers, names, addresses, home and business phones, and dates of treatment. These should be kept close to a standard appointment book for handy reference in scheduling or changing appointments. Clients should be issued standard business appointment cards for each visit. These should be imprinted with the therapist's name, address, and phone number; and space should be left for the date and time of the next scheduled appointments.

Business records are a must for conducting a private practice of marital therapy. They are vital to insure the appropriate charging and receipt of fees, of recording all the necessary expenses for conducting the practice, and for tax purposes. In the professional training of marital therapists, the practical details of business records are almost universally ignored. The net result is that therapists often attempt to utilize in their practices the procedures and methods of accounting that they have followed in their personal financial affairs. When a practice is small, these methods may prove satisfactory, but they usually become totally inadequate as the practice grows larger. Here is where marital therapists-specialists, and professionals themselves should turn to other specialists—such as certified public accountants—for help. Accountants can help therapists develop their own record keeping systems, prepare their tax returns (federal, city, state; income, unemployment, workers compensation, Social Security, etc.), and advise them on retirement programs and other methods of handling one's professional income.

Secretarial services. Secretarial services are another vital part of operating a private practice. Part-time beginning therapists can rarely justify the expense of a regular receptionist and/or secretary. Options include the professional services that hire out typists and the employment of secretaries on a part-time basis. If therapists desire typewritten progress notes, dictating equipment will ordinarily be a great time-saver for this purpose as well as for routine correspondence.

Special equipment and expenses. In addition to the usual complement of chairs, desks, lamps, and the like for the office, therapists may also decide to invest in audio and video recording equipment for use in their therapy. The use of these specialized items is beyond the scope of this manual, but it should be emphasized that this type of equipment, plus any professional forms, books, test materials, journal subscriptions, and so forth, are all legitimate business expenses. In addition, the cost of attending professional meetings that relate to the maintenance of one's professional skills are also tax-deductible expenses. The total list of possible business costs that may be considered to be legitimate business expenses is so long and complex that therapists are advised to consult with both accountants and tax attorneys to fully understand and utilize these advantages of a private practice.

Consultants. In addition to the business and legal specialists referred to above, marital therapists who are neither psychiatrists or psychologists should consider obtaining the services of one of these specialists as consultants for cases in which there may be uncertainty about a client's mental status. Modern marital therapists are expected to be knowledgeable about many types of client problems, but they are also expected to be able to recognize their own limitations. Over the passage of time, a variety of clients who may be experiencing significant psychopathological conditions will present themselves for marital therapy. It is both prudent and helpful to be able to consult with a psychiatrist or psychologist qualified in these matters before such clients are referred elsewhere *or* accepted for therapy. Having the regular services of a psychiatrist/psychologist available is most helpful. This should be a person whom the therapist knows and in whose professional judgments the therapist has complete confidence.

SUMMARY

Marital therapy is practiced in both organizational and private-practice settings. Each setting entails certain benefits and certain liabilities for both clients and therapists. All marital therapists are expected to begin their practices working under the supervision of more experienced clinicians, and this ordinarily occurs in agencies and clinics where the therapists become salaried employees. A significant proportion of marital therapists today, however, are either full- or part-time self-employed private practitioners. They must be knowledgeable and skilled about both the therapeutic and the "business" aspects of conducting their practices. They must cope with public relations, referrals, fees, taxes, office space, and all the other matters that are germane to conducting a business in the modern world. Ultimately, the decision as to whether marital therapists will conduct their practices solely for salaried wages in organization settings or wholly or in part as individual entrepreneurs becomes a decision that can only be made by each therapist for him- or herself.

CHAPTER ELEVEN
PROFESSIONAL STANDARDS IN MARITAL THERAPY

The vast majority of marital therapy is performed by therapists who are responsible only to themselves or to the organization that employs them. In most states and provinces marital therapy is totally unregulated by legislative bodies; consequently, literally all types of persons are free to present themselves to the public as "marital therapists," to charge whatever fees they can collect, to do almost anything they wish to with their "clients," and to label their activities as "marital therapy." The public, therefore, appears to be literally at the mercy of the marketplace when it comes to determining professional standards in marital therapy. Fortunately, the situation is not quite that desperate, largely owing to the presence of the major professional accreditation and credentialing association for the field, the American Association for Marriage and Family Therapy (AAMFT).

PROFESSIONAL ASSOCIATIONS

American Association for Marriage and Family Therapy

AAMFT functions. As we have already noted in Chapters One and Ten, the AAMFT, which was organized in 1942, now has more than 8,000 members in the United States and Canada, with over forty state, provincial, and regional divisions. Its functions are sixfold: (1) To establish and maintain rigorous standards for its members' specialized academic training and supervised clinical experiences; (2) to establish and maintain the Commission on Accreditation for Marriage and Family Therapy Education, which examines and accredits training centers and academic programs in marital and family therapy; (3) to issue a scholarly publication, the *Journal of Marital and Family Therapy,* and a regular newsletter which covers issues and items concerning the AAMFT and the field; (4) to conduct regional, national, and international conferences in order to assist in the dissemination of new knowledge, techniques, and developments in the field; (5) to cooperate with other professional organizations in order to exchange information and to cooperate on matters of mutual concern, such as legislation affecting marriage and divorce; and lastly, (6) to provide the public with knowledge about matters relating to marriage and family problems and about the roles that professional therapists perform in preventing and solving these problems.

Licensure and accreditation. In the course of its history since 1942, the AAMFT has evolved from a small, predominantly Northeastern United States group of marriage counselors into the largest professional group in the world exclusively concerned with marital and family therapy. Its members have been in the forefront of all the major developments in the field, with some notable exceptions, and have represented the profession to public and legislative bodies alike. Because of the AAMFT's demanding membership standards, other professionals and the lay public have come to rely upon clinical membership in the Association as equivalent to licensure in those states and provinces which do not regulate the profession (see Appendix C). Its Commission on Accreditation for Marriage and Family Therapy Education is recognized by the U.S. government as the accrediting unit for the profession. In this capacity, it ensures potential therapists that the education and training they undertake will provide the breadth and depth of knowledge and skill that they will require in order to become practicing marital and family therapists. At the same time, it helps provide consumers with standards by which to judge the educational preparedness of the therapists they may wish to utilize (see Appendix A). The AAMFT's publication, the *Journal of Marital and Family Therapy,* was established in 1975. Within a few short years, it became the most widely read journal in its field and is served by a distinguished Board of Editors with international standing. The AAMFT's *Newsletter,* long an informal house organ, was restructured in 1980 and became a major force in the dissemination of information about the field as well as about the AAMFT.

Educational, legislative contributions. Professional conferences conducted by the Association experienced a rapid spurt in size and importance during the 1970s, reflecting the growth in membership in the AAMFT and in the profession as a whole, plus expanded formats and programming. These expanded conferences enable attendees to hear national and international leading theoreticians and tacticians expound on the latest developments in the profession. They also permit clinicians to attend workshops and institutes designed to update their clinical skills and knowledge. In its cooperative efforts with other professional groups, the AAMFT leadership works closely with physicians, psychologists, attorneys, clergy, family specialists, home economists, and family service personnel in promoting legislation and issues that have a direct bearing on the quality of marital and family life in the United States and Canada. In addition to the services already listed above, the AAMFT maintains a program of continuing education for its members and also a system of "Approved Supervisors." These approved supervisors are recognized as having the competencies and training required to provide clinical supervision to student and fledgling marital and family therapists in all types of settings (see Appendix B).

National Council on
Family Relations

While not an association directly concerned with the accreditation of marital and family therapists, the National Council on Family Relations (NCFR) is looked upon by many as a significant association for marital therapists. The NCFR's long-standing concern with research, theory, and teaching in the broad field of family relations has helped to stimulate much of the knowledge about marital and family relations that all marital therapists need to acquire. The NCFR serves some kindred functions with the AAMFT in its concerns about professional standards in counseling and teaching, the publication of its journals, its regional and national scholarly conventions, its cooperation with the AAMFT and related groups on matters affecting marriage and family life, and its assistance in the education of the lay public about family matters. Unlike the AAMFT, the NCFR does not require professional training for membership and hence represents a more diversified group of members. While it contains a section of family therapy, the NCFR has been best known for its support of academic programs for teaching and research in the family field. It publishes three major journals of direct interest to marital therapists: the *Journal of Marriage and the Family, Family Relations: The Journal of Applied Family and Child Studies* (formerly *The Family Coordinator*), and the *Journal of Family History.*

American Family Therapy
Association

In the late 1970s another professional association concerned with family therapy, the American Family Therapy Association (AFTA), was formed. Its founding members were primarily persons from outside the ranks of the AAMFT, tended to be from medical backgrounds, and represented professionals predominantly engaged in treating psychotic and other severely dysfunctional persons within the context of the family. Its initial leaders were individuals who had published widely in the growing field of family therapy, and several of these had developed their own unique treatment approaches for dealing with family problems. During its formative years, however, AFTA differed from the AAMFT in two significant ways: first, it did not become a clinical certifying group and it brought into its fold a very diversified group of persons in terms of training and academic preparation; second, AFTA placed major emphasis upon the treatment of the entire family unit, thus differing with the AAMFT's historical emphasis upon the marital unit. Its formation added considerable excitement to the entire field of marital and family therapy.

Initially, this appeared to be potentially destructive to the overall professional organization of the field, but as time has passed, AFTA has evolved into a group of theory builders, educators, and trainers who have brought vigorous leadership to these essential dimensions of the overall field.

Related Professional Groups

In addition to these three major professional associations, marital therapy has also been a matter of varying interest to several related professional groups. These include the American Psychological Association, the National Association of Social Workers, the American Personnel and Guidance Association, the American Association of Pastoral Counselors, the American Psychiatric Association, and some other, smaller groups closely allied with these fields. As the field of marital therapy grew, and especially after the broader treatment concept of family therapy was evolved, considerable rivalry often developed between the associations listed here and the AAMFT and AFTA. These rivalries had to do with both broad conceptual and theoretical issues and with pragmatic, political power issues of "turf," regulation of the field, and with the broader issues of the nation's total system of mental health care. These rivalries and differing emphases will undoubtedly continue for decades to come owing to the complex nature of health care in North America.

PROFESSIONAL JOURNALS

A regular responsibility of all professionals is to keep abreast of the latest developments in their respective fields. Marital therapists are no exception. All marital therapists, regardless of whether they practice in public organizations or in private practices, whether they are students or long experienced veterans, need to regularly read journals in their field in order to ensure that their clients will receive the advantages of new knowledge. Several journals exist to provide this information. Already mentioned has been the quarterly publication of the AAMFT, the *Journal of Marital and Family Therapy,* as well as the quarterly publications of the NCFR—the *Journal of Marriage and the Family, Family Relations: The Journal of Applied Family and Child Studies,* and the *Journal of Family History.* While the *Journal of Family History* may have less pragmatic appeal to the average therapist than do the preceding three, it provides fascinating coverage of issues and trends that help professionals better understand contemporary marital life.

One of the most prestigious journals in the field is *Family Process.* Founded in 1962, it has been served by an editorial board composed primarily of distinguished seminal thinkers. Until the *Journal of Marital and Family Therapy* appeared in 1975, *Family Process* virtually stood alone as "the" journal for all marital and family therapists. It remains as a must for all marital therapists to read. More recently, several new journals have been developed which deal with a variety of topics in the broad family therapy field. Some of these are primarily proprietary journals and others are published by small special-interest groups, all of which results in considerable unevenness in their quality and offerings. Two of these that are recommended for regular reading by marital therapists, however, are the *Journal of Sex and Marital Therapy* and the *Journal of Divorce*. In addition to those already mentioned, journals of related mental health groups often contain articles of interest to marital therapists. One outstanding example of these is the *American Journal of Orthopsychiatry*, published by the multidisciplinary group, the American Orthopsychiatric Association. Marital therapists may also consider subscribing to one of the newsletter-type services which abstract journals and books. These services help clinicians keep up with the major trends and direct their readers to materials of special interest which should be obtained and read in their entirety.

PERSONAL AND ACADEMIC STANDARDS

Personal Standards

Who determines the standards? Of all the issues surrounding professional standards in marital therapy, perhaps one stands out as the least studied and yet as the most controversial. That is the matter of the personal qualities of the therapist. *Who* should be permitted to train as a marital therapist? *Who* will make those decisions about which people will be allowed to train for this profession? *How* will they make the decisions? *What criteria* will they use? These issues are so controversial that they are, in fact, generally ignored by graduate admission and trainee selection committees except in very extreme cases. No research data appear to exist that tell us precisely what type of person makes the "best" and the most effective marital therapist. From what has been studied, as well as from years of teaching and supervisory experience, we are forced, therefore, to rely upon general consensus about what types of personalities are likely to be most desirable for work in psychotherapy in general and specifically marital therapists.

Specific skills and abilities needed. Therapists need to have skills that enable them to establish and maintain positive relationships with their clients. These are considered to be capacities for warmth, humor, empathy, "genuineness," and sensitivity to clients' feelings. Therapists need to be emotionally mature, well-integrated persons themselves with good self-confidence and with positive abilities to communicate clearly and directly with their clients. They need to have a high tolerance for ambiguity, for pain, conflict, and other psychic stressors, and for being comfortable with values and lifestyles that are different from their own. They need to be nonsexist, "nonageist," and unprejudiced toward the client groups they will be serving. They need to be open to life experiences, to emotions, and to change. At the same time, they need to respect and value the past where it has supported human growth and development. They need the courage to challenge forces and ideas that inhibit and hamper human interaction even when this makes their own position appear socially and politically unpopular. They need to value marriage as an institution but not be blinded to its limitations and its frequent need to adjust to new and changing conditions in the world. They must be advocates of marriage but not blind zealots seeking to impose their particular brand of husband–wife relationships on their clients. One could go on and on with this ideal list!

Screening candidates. In reality, many academic and training programs do not require personal interviews and personality testing for candidates seeking training but rely, instead, upon written references and experience resumes. At the other extreme, some programs require extensive personal interviews for candidates and accept only those they feel will best fit each particular program's philosophies about the treatment process. Some programs require, as part of the training, that all prospective marital therapists undergo personal and/or marital therapy themselves. These demands are made to help therapists better understand what the therapeutic experience is like from the client's point of view; to help therapists achieve insight and understanding into their own psychological and marital dynamics; and finally, to help with the personal and marital "readjustments" that invariably occur as one moves into training for the practice of psychotherapy.

Academic Requirements

The academic requirements that must be met to become a marital therapist have varied widely over recent decades. A lack of consensus remains on this matter, particularly on the part of the more traditional mental health practitioners such as psychologists, social workers, and psychiatrists, many of whom have not seen the need for any additional training on their part to practice as marital therapists. A contrary point of view is taken by the AAMFT, by the Commission on Accreditation for Marriage and Family Therapy Education, and by those state governments which license marital therapists. Appendix C contains the membership standards of the AAMFT, and these generally coincide, in respect to academic and clinical training requirements, with those of the Accreditation Commission. These standards represent well over two decades of evolutionary development since the AAMFT and its predecessors first began to develop standards and to "approve" training programs. They are based upon the concept that a professional association has a public obligation to ensure that its members will have sufficient and appropriate knowledge and training to render high-quality therapeutic services. Review of Appendix C reveals that marital therapists are expected to demonstrate that they have successfully completed graduate studies, with a minimum of a Master's degree having been awarded by an accredited institution in the areas of human development, marital and family studies, marital and family therapies, professional studies, supervised clinical work, and research methodologies. In essence, these standards require that the professional marital therapist know about human beings as individuals and as members of their social units and how they function throughout their lifetimes, as well as about the methods that clinicians use to treat these persons when their mental health is adversely affected by dysfunctional marital and family relationships.

Many persons are still unaware of the specific academic requirements needed to become a marital therapist, and so they seek their professional training in other therapy fields. In addition, numerous therapists who are already experienced in other areas, such as individual psychotherapy, often want to receive further training as marital therapists. To meet these needs, postgraduate training centers have been developed around the United States and Canada. These training centers do not award academic degrees and credits, but they usually offer both didactic classroom materials and supervised clinical training. Hence, for professionals in allied mental health fields who wish to shift careers or to supplement their existing skills, post-graduate training may be substituted provided it meets the Association's standards (see Appendix A). For persons with no prior training in any type of therapy and who lack appropriate academic content, an increasing number of colleges and universities are offering graduate programs that combine the necessary course content with clinical practical training. Graduates who earn Master's or Doctoral degrees in these programs are seen by many to represent the wave of the future for the profession of marital therapy. Several academic programs have already been accredited around the country (see Appendix A), and many more universities have either established comparative programs or are in the process of doing so (see Appendix D).

THE SUPERVISED PRACTICUM
AND CLINICAL EXPERIENCE

Supervision Is a Necessity

A marital therapist should be, above all, a skilled and sensitive clinician. Knowledge about marriage and interpersonal systems and about theories of therapy will be of little or no value if therapists have not developed their abilities to use themselves constructively in face-to-face therapy sessions with their clients. Marital therapy has often been described as an art as much as it is a science. There is only one method by which therapists can learn to use themselves professionally, and that is by practicing marital therapy under the tutelage and guidance of an experienced supervisor. All professions dealing with the healing arts recognize this principle, and marital therapy is no exception. There are two essential elements in this process; the availability of a representative supply of clients, and the availability of a supervisor.

The supervisory process in academic settings. In university training programs, arrangements are made for student therapists to work in a variety of clinic settings, often both on and off campus. These clinics provide marital therapy services to various populations in their respective geographical areas with the students performing a portion of the therapy. The clinics or agencies are responsible for providing clinical supervisors for the students, although sometimes the educational institution does this, or both may provide supervisors. These supervisors should not only be skilled and experienced therapists themselves, they should be knowledgeable and skilled in the process of supervision itself. Preferably, they should at least be equal to the supervisors who have been awarded the status of Approved Supervisor in the AAMFT (see Appendix B).

In regular, intensive sessions, the supervisors discuss what the student therapists are actually doing with their clients. A variety of modalities are utilized during these sessions. The supervisors may observe supervisees directly through one-way mirrors. Audio and/or video recordings of the supervisees' clinical sessions may be recorded and then played back for review and discussion during the supervisory sessions. Supervisees may be required to write up detailed clinical notes of their treatment sessions, and these are utilized for discussions. Finally, supervisees and supervisors sometimes serve as co-therapists with the same marital couple, and these sessions are later discussed. Regardless of which of these methods is utilized, the student therapists have the opportunity to learn "how" to talk and behave in their therapy sessions so as to maximize their therapeutic potential with clients. Periodically, progress reports on their professional learning and growth are developed with their supervisors. These are then shared with the students' educational institutions. At the end of the process, the supervisors submit their final reports, along with recommendations regarding the students' readiness to practice independently.

Postgraduate training centers. The supervisory process described above operates within clearly defined structures for supervisees, supervisors, universities, and professional associations. A second model that is widely used in the professional education of marital therapists is for supervisees to obtain their practicum and supervisory experiences on a postgraduate basis at the "freestanding" training programs discussed in the preceding section. The supervisory process itself at these training centers is very similar to that performed for university programs, but the postgraduate training centers usually bear the responsibility for the total process.

Direct contract for purchasing supervision. Finally, a third model of supervision and for gaining clinical experience is for supervisees to contract directly with supervisors, in a sense, "purchasing" supervision from them. This model is often utilized when, for practical purposes, it is not feasible for the supervisees to be directly enrolled in a university or postgraduate training program. It has been most commonly utilized by clinicians who were already qualified in related fields of psychotherapy and who wished to obtain the additional supervision and practicum experience required for them to qualify as AAMFT Clinical Members. Often they were already in private practice, and utilized their own clients for the learning and supervisory process. These arrangements are made directly with Approved Supervisors after the supervisees have qualified as Associate Members in the AAMFT, and progress reports are sent by the supervisors directly to the AAMFT Membership Standards Committee.

LICENSING

Licensing States and Efforts

Marital therapy clients, as well as related mental health professionals, are often surprised to learn that most contemporary marital therapy is conducted without any public regulation whatsoever. To date, only eight states in the United States

(California, Florida, Georgia, Michigan, New Jersey, Nevada, North Carolina, and Utah) have passed state laws to regulate marital therapy. In addition, Virginia has adopted an "umbrella" counselor law that regulates marriage counseling as a subspecialty. California was the first state to pass a law (1963), and Georgia had the dubious honor of being the first state to have its law repealed under "Sunshine" legislation. No provinces in Canada have licensed marital therapists, but differences in the Canadian health-delivery system partially account for this. Efforts have been made in many more states to pass licensing and/or registration statutes, but without success. The reasons for this situation are complex. Many legislators have maintained that there was no need for licensing laws because so few citizens, they believed, have been harmed by incompetent marital therapists. Some other mental health professional groups, fearing that licensing marital therapists would hurt their own vested interests, have lobbied vigorously against such laws. The outlook for any major shifts in this situation in the upcoming decade is poor; probably there will be few, if any, changes.

Public Regulation Lacking

This leaves the practice of marital therapy "wide open" in states and provinces without regulation. It is in these areas that therapists seeking some means of presenting themselves to the public as properly educated and trained in their field should seek to join the professional credentialing association for marital therapy—the AAMFT. Where legislation exists, however, marital therapists cannot practice and cannot publicly label themselves as marital therapists (or family or child therapists; state statutes vary on this) unless they have passed the necessary examinations conducted by their local state regulatory bodies. Loopholes are many, however, the most common one being that often only marital therapists selling their services directly to the public (such as independent private practitioners) are regulated. Marital therapists practicing under academic training auspices and those employed in bona fide nonprofit social and government agencies and clinics are ordinarily exempt from legislative restrictions. Thus, a rather peculiar set of values exists within state legislatures. They apparently feel that the public should be protected by licensing such diverse groups as barbers, foresters, TV repair technicians, antenna installers, plumbers, chiropractors, real estate salespersons, and street vendors who sell hot dogs—but not from unqualified marital therapists whose responsibilities are to treat the ills of the most basic unit in our modern society—marriage. Some state statutes *refer* to marital therapists (such as in Connecticut, where compulsory marriage counseling in marital dissolution cases may be ordered by the courts), but make no efforts to define their qualifications.

ETHICAL CODES AND CONDUCT

Professional persons are expected by their clients, by the public, and by their colleagues to conduct themselves and their practices according to certain ethical codes of conduct. Each profession ordinarily draws up its own codes so that the idiosyncracies of the particular type of practice may be taken into consideration. These codes set down certain broad ethical principles and often contain specific provisions for both enforcing the codes and imposing penalties when they are violated.

Special ethical obligations.   The practice of marital therapy is recognized as dealing with the most basic and most personal values and behaviors that individual persons and couples ever experience—their love lives, their sex lives, their feelings of trust, their egos and self-esteem, their sense of identity, and so forth. Because of the intensely personal nature of these issues, clients place great trust and confidence in their therapists. They must be able to believe that therapists will always act in the clients' best interests, will not exploit them, and will do everything they can to enhance their mental health and well-being. At the same time, a basic principle of all types of psychotherapy, including marital therapy, has been that of confidentiality. Thus, the work that therapists perform with their clients ordinarily takes place behind a veil of secrecy as opposed to being under the glare of public scrutiny. This type of a protective setting is deemed necessary for performing therapy but, at the same time, it always contains the potentiality for client exploitation and abuse. Throughout this book, it has been emphasized repeatedly that clients seeking marital therapy are ordinarily in a condition of high emotional vulnerability. A common experience in marital conflict is to feel deceived, devalued, and "used." If clients were to repeat these catastrophic experiences with their marital therapists, the damage to their mental health would be incalculable. Thus, regardless of any niceties or "high" principles one may feel should be observed by all professionals simply because they are "professionals," marital therapists have additional obligations to their clients to treat them ethically.

Dealing with misconduct.   In those states and provinces which do not regulate marital therapy, the professional associations' codes of ethics are often the only mechanisms by which aggrieved clients can seek redress for the wrongs they believe may have been inflicted on them by unethical therapists. Or, as it sometimes happens, concerned fellow marital therapists have to turn to their associations' ethics committees in order to deal with a practitioner they believe is practicing unethically. To have a practitioner brought before his or her peers on charges of alleged unethical practice is a sober matter, one to be viewed most seriously. In marital therapy, one's good reputation may be viewed as an extremely precious asset. To be accused and later found guilty of professional misconduct—a finding which ordinarily results in some severe penalty such as expulsion from the association—is perhaps one of the greatest negative sanctions that can be inflicted upon a professional therapist. Aside from the professional shame and damaged reputation that would likely come with such a penalty, legal charges against the therapist that might be brought by clients for the alleged misconduct could be strengthened if that therapist's professional society removed him or her for unethical behavior over the incident.

The therapist's ethical responsibility is great.   Appendix E contains the current Code of Ethical Principles for Family Therapists that binds members of the

AAMFT. A comparison made of this code with its predecessor codes will reveal this code to be broader in nature, rather than being highly specific and detailed. Modern legal developments resulting from the strong comtemporary emphasis upon the rights of individuals have forced professional associations to allow their members greater latitude in interpreting ethical behavior than was true earlier. A classic example of this was the AAMFT's earlier code which placed detailed limitations on its members' advertising, down to specific admonitions regarding how heavy the print type could be on members' telephone listings. Now individual marital therapists have to bear a greater burden of responsibility for their own decisions about what constitutes ethical behavior on their part toward their clients, their professional colleagues, and the public. In other words, today's marital therapists must, to a greater extent than ever before, internalize a valid set of ethical principles within themselves instead of relying on associations or regulatory agencies to tell them how to practice ethically.

CONTINUING EDUCATION

Education never ceases. When marital therapists complete their graduate education and the number of supervised clinical practicum hours required for membership in the professional association, they may believe that they have learned as much as any one person could possibly know about marriage, sexuality, family life, marital therapy, how to interview, and so on. Such is not the case, however. Two situations alone stand out as validating the need of every marital therapist to engage in continuing professional education for the entire lifetime of his or her practice. First is the fact that marriage is not a static institution. The twentieth century has witnessed a dynamic, never-ending series of changes in technology, in values, and in human relationships—every one of which has altered what therapists need to know about their clients' marriages and their worlds of reality. A second major criterion which dictates the necessity of continuing education for marital therapists is the never-ceasing development of new theories and techniques in the field. New theories, new therapeutic modalities, and new issues affecting the profession are constantly emerging. Therapists who remain ignorant of these changes are failing to provide their clients with the highest quality of therapeutic knowledge and skills. Such a situation would appear to be both unethical and professionally self-destructive for therapists and possibly harmful to clients.

Modalities of continuing education. Continuing education, now required of members by some of the more advanced clinical professional groups, may take place in a variety of settings. Marital therapists may enroll in university courses or training center seminars for regular semester or year-long offerings. Major professional conventions provide continuing education credits in recognition of the knowledge gained from attendance. Continuing education may be individualized by reading professional journals and books in the privacy of one's office or home. Workshops and institutes are regularly offered in most major metropolitan areas—and sometimes in exotic resort settings as well. "Electronic" continuing education is available through the medium of lectures on closed-circuit or cable television or through the use of prerecorded video or audio cassettes. Therapists thus may choose to satisfy continuing education requirements by spending vast sums to travel to far-off places to be educated—or they may use time spent sitting in their cars on the way to the office or in traffic jams by listening to lectures prerecorded on cassettes and played over the car audio system. Whatever the modality, wherever the setting in which it takes place, continuing education for marital therapists should be viewed as absolutely essential.

THE IMPACT OF MARITAL THERAPY UPON THERAPISTS' PERSONAL LIVES

Motivations to Be a Therapist

A subject of much interest to marital therapists, but about which very little has been written, is the issue of what impact the practice of marital therapy may have upon the personal lives of its practitioners. If marital therapists reveal their profession at social gatherings, certain questions and/or accusations almost invariably arise. "Are *you* married? What kind of a marital partner do you make? Do you practice what you preach? Oh, you're so lucky (to marital therapist's spouse) to be married to him or her . . . " and on and on. Many of these statements are made in jest or simply to carry on party conversation. But the impact upon the therapist's life—and the lives of family members—is inescapable and unique to this particular specialty; and it can be of considerable significance to therapists and their families.

Why do people aspire to be psychotherapists in the first place? Usually because they have a conscious wish to help people, they are seeking a vocation that will be satisfying to them and rewarding to their egos; and they wish to have the status and economic rewards that go with being professionals. For *marital* therapists, additional factors may be to compensate for their own parents' unhappy marriages, for the unconscious vicarious pleasures they receive from being exposed to other persons' intimate lives, or perhaps because they have a need to "sell" their own brand of marital interactions. Or, on the positive side, they may simply enjoy helping persons with the usual problems of marriage or prefer treating clients from a largely non-psychiatric population. Obviously one could extend this list of both conscious and unconscious factors endlessly, for every single marital therapist is motivated to perform this type of therapy by his or her own unique and unconscious motivations and needs.

The Marital Therapist's Own Marriage

Thoughts of the therapist's marriage. Marital therapists, especially when they first enter their work, find that listening to clients share their pains and their triumphs, their angers and their loves, evokes countertransference reactions to the clients and may also stir the therapists' fantasies into conscious thoughts. Therapists may think, from their own life experiences and from personal and marital therapy that they may have undertaken, that their own lives and marriages are in good order. But let them sit for fifty minutes with a couple vigorously arguing over who failed to show the other adequate love, sensitivity, and support, and their minds can easily wander to their own marriages, to how loving, sensitive, and supportive they are (or *are not*) with their own partners; guilt or determination or warmth may flood through their conscious minds. Suddenly, they realize they are failing to "be with" their clients and the latters' feelings.

Therapist's anxieties.   Clients may criticize their marital therapist because the therapist is single or divorced. The therapist can immediately diagnose these as obvious projections, but such criticisms may also initiate anxiety or guilt or worry for the therapist if the clients have unwittingly struck the therapist's vulnerabilities. Even when marital therapists' own anxieties are aroused by their clients, the therapists are expected to "act professional," to maintain their composure, and to refrain from unloading their own troubles onto their clients. Unfortunately, not all marital therapists are able to do this.

Misusing clients to solve one's own problems.   A frequent complaint one hears from clients about former therapists is that they seemed to have more marital troubles than the clients did. Some people report, "My therapist was constantly telling us about his own troubles!" Some therapists may do this deliberately in an effort to establish rapport and to remove any delusions the clients may have that therapists are superhuman. Others do it, however, because unconsciously they are trying to solve their own marital problems by playing at being therapists. They relate to their clients not as persons who need total therapeutic attention during treatment sessions but rather as if they themselves were fellow clients in miniature marital group therapy sessions. "You listen to me and then I'll listen to you" is their modus operandi. Marital therapists who consistently engage in this type of ventilation of their own problems obviously need therapy and better training—or perhaps they should not be in the profession at all.

Potential positive and negative impacts on therapist's marriage.   Marital therapists' reactions to clients' situations are not all negative, however. After particularly difficult sessions, therapists may find themselves favorably contrasting their own personal lives with those of their clients. Often, at these times, the therapists may feel particularly rewarded and fortunate about their own marital and other personal relationships. Therapists can learn from their clients how to avoid problems in their own marriages. They do not acquire knowledge just to share it with clients—they can use it and apply it to their own personal relationships. If certain principles of human relationships "work" for clients, they will likewise work for therapists in their own lives. Marital therapy can also sometimes have a negative impact on therapists' own marriages. Hours spent in performing therapy may be so emotionally draining that there is little psychic or physical energy left to be a congenial marital partner. A therapist may feel a need to use his or her partner as a sounding board and as an unofficial consultant and supervisor with whom he or she can discuss particularly distressing or puzzling cases. Some marital therapists' partners may enjoy this role—while others may be bored or distressed by it. Confidentiality has to be respected during these household discussions, particularly if the clients are persons known personally to the therapists' partners. Another potential stress point for marital therapists is that their own partners may not be therapeutically oriented. These spouses may find it easy to criticize clients who violate certain value codes and moralize about how "bad" the therapist's clients obviously are. Criticisms of this nature understandably place marital therapists in a difficult position.

Questions about therapist's marriage.   When clients ask their marital therapist, "what about *your* personal marital life?" a process is unleashed that frequently leads therapists to do considerable introspection about themselves. There are no rules that say marital therapists must be married—yet many clients feel this is a requirement to practice. These same clients often make the common assumption that if their own therapist is married, he or she must be *happily* married. Marital therapists' own marriages are very similar in their degrees of happiness–unhappiness as are the marriages of other adults with similar social characteristics. When clients raise these questions, therapists may answer if they wish to, but they should also ask themselves *why* the clients asked *these* particular questions *now*? The answers may or may not be significant to the therapy process, but should be examined.

Marital Partners as Co-Therapists

The positives.   In recent decades, the technique of co-therapy has been widely practiced, especially in training and research settings. One aspect of co-therapy is the issue of marital therapists who are married to each other working together as husband–wife co-therapy teams. Numerous values have been attributed to this practice. Clients are presented with a therapy team as "real-life" models with whom they can identify and whom they can emulate. Having both a male and female therapist may assist in achieving many insights not otherwise available. The fees for the co-therapist stay "in the family" and husband–wife teams can more easily correlate their joint working schedules. Moreover, having one's marital partner as one's co-therapist provides unique insights into therapists' individual countertransferences because partners can be expected to know each other very well. Sexual problems of clients may be especially helped by this particular approach, it has been claimed.

The negatives.   On the negative side, many husband–wife relationships are not equal. In Western society, males are likely to be more highly educated than women are, to hold more prestigious academic degrees, and to be the more dominant partner in the marriage. These arrangements may work well for the therapists personally, but many would question whether these represent ideal models of husband–wife interactions to present in marital therapy, or whether they are too "traditional" and sexist. Another issue for husband–wife co-therapists concerns the multitude of countertransferences that are activated when they treat couples. For example, a male therapist may react to female clients out of his own relationships with his mother and his wife (this occurs anyway), but his wife is also his co-therapist. This requires the male therapist to set a good model for *both* the male and female clients by relating to his own wife simultaneously on several levels at once—as co-therapist, wife, colleague, financial partner—perhaps even as the person who insulted his ego by beating him at tennis the day before. These pressures exist for male and female married co-therapists alike. Husband–wife co-therapy teams often report that they experience increased stresses in their personal relationship as a direct result of their co-therapy work. For example, disagreements over treatment strategies with couples may end up being rehashed during dinner-table conversations. Many husband–wife co-therapy teams have felt the need to enter marital therapy themselves, both to understand the process of therapy and to receive help for the stresses their work engenders. Divorces sometimes occur among these married co-therapists, but it is impossible to isolate their co-therapy work together as the sole or even primary cause of their marital dissolution.

Marital Therapists as Individuals

Therapists sometimes need therapy.   The preceding section indicated that when co-therapy is performed by husband–wife co-therapy teams, their own marriages may suffer. The same can obviously occur for a man or a woman practicing alone. Marital therapy for all therapists was advocated earlier in this chapter. The impression should not be drawn, however, that only *beginning* marital therapists may need marital therapy. A career as a marital therapist invariably has important personal implications which can effect changes in an individual. This, in turn, directly affects the therapist's own personal marital system. The therapist is no more immune to needing help with these issues than are the client couples he or she serves. In Chapter Seven changing roles for men and women were discussed at some length. Marital therapists are sensitive to the same issues that affect all other married couples today, and, in addition, they have the added burdens of supposedly being able to treat themselves—an impossibility. They should, therefore, utilize the very help they offer others and seek therapy for themselves when they need it. This might consist of individual psychotherapy, marital therapy, or family therapy, the particular modality being determined by the specific problem being experienced.

Colleagues can help.   Therapy, however, is not the only means by which marital therapists can obtain relief from the pressures their practices create. During most of therapists' careers, they will be regularly involved with supervisors and/or consultants with whom they will be discussing their cases. While these sessions have, as their ultimate goals, better treatment for clients, the therapists' own attitudes, feelings, and experiences in their practices are legitimate aspects of these sessions. In addition, many marital therapists find regular personal and professional interactions with other therapists rewarding experiences. Whether working together on a local committee planning a professional conference or off on the town for an evening of entertainment, professional colleagues ordinarily offer good companionship. They usually understand the special stresses of this practice and are eager to share their own concerns also.

Staying well-balanced. In the final analysis, however, every marital therapist is more than just a therapist. Like all other citizens, the therapist occupies several social roles, his or her profession being only one of these, albeit a very important one. Therapists are members of marital and family units, of their neighborhoods and of their social clubs, of their local governmental units and of their recreational groups. Like anyone deeply emotionally involved in their work, they are subject to "burnout" or loss of motivation in their careers owing to continuous exposure to the demands, responsibilities, and frustrations they encounter. All therapists owe it to themselves, therefore, to get away from their practices on a regular basis and to involve themselves in other activities that take them—at least psychologically—away from their professional concerns. Some prefer physically active pursuits for this purpose, such as running, tennis, or hiking; others enjoy more sedentary activities such as attending the theatre, visiting museums, and reading fiction. Leaving the obvious issues of physical health to one side, the particular activities pursued are not so important as long as they leave individuals with a sense of well-being and relax them from their daily work. Clients don't like dull therapists; neither do marital partners. Marital therapists need to keep both of their "houses" in order, and only they themselves can assume these responsibilities.

APPENDIX A
AAMFT—ACCREDITED TRAINING AND AND ACADEMIC PROGRAMS

TABLE A-1 Accredited Post-Degree Clinical Training Centers

PREREQUISITE	PERSONAL THERAPY	DIDACTIC HOURS	PRACTICUM MINIMUM HOURS	SUPERVISION MINIMUM HOURS	LEADS TO	EXP.
California Family Study Center, 4400 Riverside Dr., Burbank CA 91505 — M.A. in M.F.T. or grad. degree approx. Model Cur of AAMFT	Recommended	150	1500	100 individ. 200 group	Cert.	1983
Family Service of Milwaukee, Box 08434 Milwaukee WI 53208 ... David Hoffman, M.A. — M.A. or prof. grad. degree + 1500 hrs. supervised clinical experience	Recommended	2-4 hrs./wk.	1500 (2 years)	200 (100 individ./ 100 group)	Cert.	1982
Institutes of Religion and Health (Blanton-Peale Graduate Institute), 3 W. 29th Street, New York NY 10001 ... Thelma Dixon-Murphy, Ed.D. — M.A. or prof. grad. degree + 2 yrs. experience	Required (From App. List)	80 credits coursework	Beginners 1350 650 (3 yrs., 8-15 hrs./wk.)—Advanced (2 yrs., 8 hrs./wk.)	350 (180 individ./ 170 group)	D. Min. + Cert.	1984
Marriage Council of Philadelphia, 4025 Chestnut Street, Philadelphia PA 19104 (Affiliated with University of Pennsylvania) ... Ellen M. Berman, M.D. — M.A. or prof. grad. degree & min. of 1 yr. post-degree supervised cslg.	Recommended	10 courses 12 hrs./wk.	500 (12 hrs./wk.)	200 (2 individ./2 grp. per week)	Cert.	1985
CLSC-Metro (Peel Center), Marriage Counselling Service, 3647 Peel Street, Montreal PQ Canada H3A 1X1 ... Dorothy E. Barrier, P.S.W. — M.S.W. + 3 yrs. supervised prof. practice	Recommended	4 full courses	560 (17½ hrs./wk.)	200	Diploma	*1981
M.S.W. (in process)	Recommended	8 half courses	560 (17½ hrs./wk.)	200	M.S.W.	
M.Ed. (in process)	Recommended	6 full courses	1116 (31 hrs./wk.)	210	M.Ed.	

*Renewal application in process.

American Association for Marriage and Family Therapy Commission on Accreditation for Marriage and Family Therapy Education, 924 West Ninth Street, Upland, CA 91786

TABLE A-2 Accredited Graduate Programs

PREREQUISITE	PERSONAL THERAPY	DIDACTIC HOURS	PRACTICUM MINIMUM HOURS	SUPERVISION MINIMUM HOURS	LEADS TO	EXP.
Auburn University, Dept. Family and Child Development, Auburn AL 36849 . . . Sandra M. Halperin, Ph.D.	B.A. and course in abnormal psych	Required	60 quarter hours	600–700	150	M.S.	1984
Brigham Young University, Marriage and Family Therapy Program, Provo UT 84602 . . . Robert F. Stahmann, Ph.D.	B.A.; M.A. in MFT	Some dyadic counseling required	M.S. 30 + Ph.D. 60 + (semester hours)	300-600—M.S. (3 semesters) 600-900—Ph.D. (4-6 semesters)	200—M.S. 300—Ph.D.	M.S. Ph.D.	1981
East Texas State University, Marriage and Family Counseling Program, Commerce TX 75428 . . . Alan J. Hovestadt, Ed.D.	M.A. + counseling experience	Recommended & available	60 + semester hours	1000	200 (1 hr. individ./ 2 hr. grp./per week)	Ed.D.	1984
Loma Linda University, Marriage and Family Therapy Program, Loma Linda CA 92354 . . . Antonius Brandon, Ph.D.	B.A. inc. Human Growth & Dev. Int. & Cslg. Psy. Testing, Stat., Intro. to Personality Theories	Optional but recommended	84 units	500	60 individ. 140 group	M.S. in MFT	*1981
Purdue University, Marriage and Family Therapy Center, CDFS Bldg. Lafayette IN 47907 . . . Wallace Denton, Ed.D.	M.S., M.A. or M.S.W.	Two semester group experience required	60 + semester hours	500	200	Ph.D.	1986
Syracuse University, Dept. of Child and Family Studies, 100 Walnut Place, Syracuse NY 13210 . . . Charlotte Kahn, Ed.D.	B.A. + several yrs. experience	Available; sometimes suggested	36 semester credit hours (45 semester credit hours beg. 5/82)	500	200	M.A.	1980

TABLE A-2 Accredited Graduate Programs (cont.)

	PREREQUISITE	PERSONAL THERAPY	DIDACTIC HOURS	PRACTICUM MINIMUM HOURS	SUPERVISION MINIMUM HOURS	LEADS TO	EXP.
Texas Technological University, Marriage and Family Therapy Program, Dept. of Home and Family Life Lubbock TX 79409 ... Harvey Joanning, Ph.D.	M.A. or M.S. + counseling experience	Recommended & available	65 semester hours	600–700 5 semesters	100 individ. 200 group	Ph.D.	1986
University of Southern California, Dept. of Sociology, Los Angeles CA 90007 ... Carlfred Broderick, Ph.D.	B.A. or M.A.		64 units	1500 (4 semesters minimum, 15 hrs./ wk. total)	200 (1 hr. individ./ 2 hrs. grp. per week)	Ph.D. + Cert.	1985
University of Wisconsin-Stout, Graduate Program in Marriage and Family Therapy, Menomonie WI 54751 ... Charles Barnard, Ed.D.	B.A. or equiv.	Optional, but available	60 semester credits	500	Minimum 200 hours	M.S. in MFT	1982

*Renewal application in process

American Association for Marriage and Family Therapy Commission on Accreditation for Marriage and Family Therapy Education, 924 West Ninth Street, Upland, CA 91786

APPENDIX B
AAMFT—APPROVED SUPERVISION PROGRAM

Note: The following information is reprinted by permission of the American Association for Marriage and Family Therapy, 924 West Ninth Street, Upland, CA 91786

The Approved Supervisor is one who has received advanced recognition for clinical skills and special training and experience in the supervision of marriage and family therapy supervisees and who meets the highest standards of clinical education and practice. The primary purpose of these standards is to identify for students and potential members those who are competent resource persons for the supervision of marriage and family therapy supervisees in keeping with the standards and commitments of the AAMFT.

The AAMFT Board of Directors established standards for Approval of Supervision in 1971. The first Approved Supervisors under this program were designated in 1973.

I. SUPERVISION COMMITTEE

The Supervision Committee, appointed by the President of the AAMFT with the approval of the Board of Directors, receives and reviews applications for the status of Approved Supervisor and recommends to the Board of Directors for appointment those candidates believed to be qualified. The Committee will make available to the Board, as is necessary, documentation adequate to support its recommendations.

The Committee defines and re-defines supervision and makes recommendations to the Board for appropriate standards.

II. MARRIAGE AND FAMILY THERAPY

The development of any professional person embodies (1) the acquisition of knowledge, usually from formal study in an academic degree granting institution, and (2) the application of that knowledge through actual clinical practice of his or her profession under appropriate supervision.

The general requirements for a supervisee in marriage and family therapy are stated in Section IV, RESPONSIBILITIES AND GUIDELINES FOR SUPERVISORS OF CANDIDATES FOR CLINICAL MEMBERSHIP.

From the viewpoint of supervision, the clinical practice of marriage and family therapy is:

A. Understood to be face-to-face sessions with the clients, usually in periods of approximately one hour each.

B. Sustained and intense, and as indicated by the needs of the clients.

C. Considered usually to involve a couple or a whole family. MFT * is distinctly different from group therapy, family life education, marital enrichment, expanding human potential, and/or other group procedures. The AAMFT recognizes the value of these other procedures and that some MFTs occasionally may use them. However, the AAMFT does not consider these procedures to be the foundation of the clinical practice of marriage and family therapy.

D. Understood to deal primarily with relationships, interpersonal interaction, and systems theory. MFT thereby requires special conceptualization as well as procedures which are distinct from the individually oriented therapies. Historically, individually oriented therapists sometimes develop the special skills of MFT, which is a distinctly different procedure. Many MFTs have expertise in both areas. It is the specific expertise in interpersonal relationships, interaction, and systems theory, however, which qualifies a professional as a marriage and family therapist.

III. DEFINITION OF SUPERVISION OF STUDENTS AND ASSOCIATES

Supervision means the oversight and responsibility for the supervisee's *continuing clinical* practice of MFT by an AAMFT-Approved Supervisor.

Supervision of MFT is expected to have the following characteristics:

A. It is face-to-face conversation with the supervisor, usually in periods of approximately one hour each.

B. The learning process is sustained and intense. Customarily appointments are scheduled once a week, ordinarily three times weekly being the maximum and once every week being the minimum. MFT supervision is normally completed over a period of one to three years in blocks of at least twenty (20) hours.

---

*MFT refers to marriage and family therapy wherever used.

C. The total supervision experience should include more than one supervisor, at least one block of twenty (20) hours being with other than the primary supervisor where feasible, preferably one from a different orientation.

D. MFT supervision focuses on the raw data from a supervisee's continuing clinical practice, as this is made directly available to the supervisor through such means as direct observation, co-therapy, written clinical notes, and audio and video recordings.

E. MFT supervision is a process clearly distinguishable from (if in some ways similar to) personal psychotherapy, and is contracted in order to serve *professional/vocational* goals.

F. Supervision by a family member is not acceptable.

G. Peer supervision, a contradiction in terms, is not acceptable. Activities between clinical peers are not applicable for credit toward supervision.

H. In order for a supervisee to receive credit, supervision may be done in a group of no more than six (6) supervisees plus their supervisors for group credit, and of no more than two (2) supervisees for individual credit.

MFT SUPERVISION IS *NOT*:

—administrative supervision—for example, clinical practice performed under the administrative rather than clinical supervision of an institutional director or executive.

—a primarily didactic process wherein techniques or precedures are taught in a group setting, classroom, workshop, or seminar.

—consultation, staff development, or orientation to a field or program.

—role playing of family interrelationships as a substitute for current clinical practice in an appropriate clinical situation.

IV. RESPONSIBILITIES
AND GUIDELINES
FOR SUPERVISORS
OF CANDIDATES FOR CLINICAL
MEMBERSHIP

The Approved Supervisor is expected to make a decision to accept and/or continue a particular supervisee for supervision only if the Approved Supervisor believes supervisee to have the potentiality to qualify subsequently for Clinical membership in the AAMFT.

A. The supervisee accepted should be enrolled in or have already attained the appropriate graduate professional degree.

B. The supervisee is expected to hold Student or Associate membership in the AAMFT.

C. The Approved Supervisor is responsible for the supervisee's familiarity with the important literature in developmental psychology, behavior pathology, personality theory, human sexuality, marriage and family studies, marriage and family therapy, and professional ethics.

D. The major emphasis in supervision of MFT is on the supervisee's work with marital and family processes, including pre-marital and post-marital processes, whether singly, conjointly, or in family groups.

E. It is the Approved Supervisor's responsibility to see that all work being supervised is conducted in appropriate professional settings and with adequate administrative and clinical controls.

F. The Approved Supervisor will provide at least annual and final reports as required when a supervisee applies for AAMFT Clinical membership. These reports should include such information as:

(1) The number of hours spent by the supervisee in different areas of clinical practice.

(2) The number and form of supervisory hours, individual and group.

(3) The number and nature of cases supervised.

(4) An assessment of the applicant's personal and professional readiness for Clinical membership.

(5) Any other information deemed relevant to the evaluation of the application.

G. The Approved Supervisor is expected to be available for consultation with the Membership Committee on any details of the applicant's record, personal adjustment, or clinical competence for membership.

H. The fee for supervision is a function of the private contract between the supervisor and the supervisee, including the amounts agreed to and the collection thereof.

V. REQUIREMENTS FOR APPROVED SUPERVISORY STATUS

A candidate for designation as an Approved Supervisor of MFT is expected to meet the following requirements:

A. Have been in clinical practice as a marriage and family therapist at least five (5) years, two (2) years of which have been as a Clinical Member of the AAMFT.

B. Have received at least 36 hours of individual supervision of his/her supervision of MFT of at least two (2) supervisees who meet minimum qualifications for Student or Associate in AAMFT. This is for a period of one year (academic or calendar). The candidate for appointment as an Approved Supervisor must complete the training for supervision with an AAMFT-Approved Supervisor. (See exception of this requirement at close of this brochure.) Supervision of supervision of two (2) people in a group may be counted as individual.

C. Have at least two (2) years' experience supervising MFT in a clinic or educational setting, or have had at least *three* (3) years of performing private supervision outside of a clinic or educational setting.

THEN THE CANDIDATE SHOULD PROCEED TO DO THE FOLLOWING:

D. Provide the Supervision Committee with a statement of the nature and length of training received for MFT supervision either in formal course work or in AAMFT-approved continuing education.

E. Provide the Supervision Committee with the name(s) and current address(es) of the Approved Supervisor(s) who has *supervised candidate's supervision of*

MFT, from whom the AAMFT will request a professional evaluation, including statistical data and a descriptive commentary on the clinical process and content of this supervisory experience. This should include a description of the candidate's progress while under supervision and a statement concerning his or her achieved level of proficiency.

F. Provide the names and current addresses of two professional colleagues in a position to evaluate candidate's skills and experience in the supervision of MFT (current supervisees excepted).

G. Submit to the Supervision Committee a written summary of the work completed in the past five (5) years with at least one MFT supervisee. The purpose of this summary is to demonstrate knowledge and skill in the supervisory process as outlined in Section IV.

H. Submit to the Supervision Committee a written statement of candidate's personal philosophy of MFT supervision. By "philosophy" is meant one's therapeutic orientation(s) and its implementation in both the therapeutic and supervisory process.

I. Appear in person before the Supervision Committee if requested.

Ordinarily in states which license or certify marriage and family counselors/ therapists, state standards for designation as supervisor will be used in lieu of AAMFT standards, provided they meet minimum AAMFT standards.

VI. RENEWAL AND CONTINUATION OF SUPERVISORY STATUS

Upon application, Approved Supervisor status will be reviewed every five (5) years for an additional five-year period, provided:

A. The Approved Supervisor continues to be actively involved in supervision in MFT for at least one supervisee during the five (5) previous years.

B. She or he continues to fulfill the procedures of Section V.

C. The Supervisor has accumulated the necessary continuing educational requirements which are now established or may in the future be established for Approved Supervisors. (50 hours of CE in supervision, in five years, is the current requirement.)

D. A fee of $50.00 to cover the administrative costs is due on the occasion of initial application and at each subsequent renewal.

Persons are designated as "Approved Supervisor: AAMFT." Appointment is for a five-year period, subject to renewal or discontinuation, beginning on January 1 of the year following appointment. Charges or complaints by fellow members, other professionals, or the public against an Approved Supervisor in reference to supervision practices shall be referred to the Supervision Committee.

After careful consideration, including consultation with the Approved Supervisor, the Supervision Committee may recommend to the Board of Directors the revocation of the supervisory status of a given supervisor. Subsequent reinstatement will require reapplication to the Committee. The Committee may at any time request an up-to-date report of the supervisor's current supervisory activities and procedures.

If a former Approved Supervisor, after the expiration of his or her term, again desires to become a candidate for Approved Supervisor, she or he may reapply and meet the requirements for supervisory status as indicated in Section V.

VII. PROCEDURES FOR CANDIDACY OR APPLICATION

Designation as an Approved Supervisor is by appointment of the Board of Directors of the AAMFT upon recommendation of the Supervision Committee. Such designations will be made at the Fall Board Meeting of the AAMFT and candidates will be notified as to the Board's action following that meeting. Candidates will be processed once a year. The file for each candidate must be completed and in the AAMFT office by *July 1* for action by the Board of Directors at the subsequent annual meeting. New appointments will take effect on the January 1 following.

VIII. FEES

An application processing fee of $50.00 must accompany the completed application form. Upon acceptance, Approved Supervisors will be billed an additional fee of $50.00 to cover the five-year Approved Supervisor designation.

EXCEPTION TO V-B

If an alternate to an AAMFT-Approved Supervisor is to be considered for supervision of supervision, approval for that arrangement must be made in advance. The alternate supervisor shall submit to the Supervision Committee essentially similar documentation required in Section V (A through I) before approval of the alternate can be considered by the Supervision Committee. Contact AAMFT office for appropriate forms.

Applications for Approved Supervisor status are available from the *AAMFT office, 924 West Ninth, Upland, CA 91786.* When the file is complete, including all supporting documentation, the Supervision Committee will receive the candidate's file and make recommendations to the Board of Directors for action. The Committee may first require a personal interview with the candidate.

PLEASE NOTE

July 1 is now the deadline for submitting applications.

Exceptions to provisions contained herein may be considered by the Supervision Committee.

Revision December 1978

APPENDIX C
AAMFT MEMBERSHIP STANDARDS

Note: The following information is reprinted by permission of the American Association for Marriage and Family Therapy, 924 West Ninth Street, Upland, CA 91786

INTRODUCTION

The AAMFT, founded in 1942, serves as the professional association for the field of marital and family therapy. AAMFT membership offers individuals the benefits of membership in a professional association, and serves the public interest through the advancement of the profession. Their brochure describes the requirements and procedures for clinical Members, Associates, and Students.

    The following standards of academic preparation, clinical training, and supervision become effective for applications received after September 1, 1981. These standards are not retroactive and do not affect persons already admitted to any category of membership prior to the above date.

I. CLINICAL MEMBER REQUIREMENTS

A. *Academic Requirements*

    The academic requirement for Clinical Membership is dependent upon the successful completion of a qualifying degree from a regionally accredited institution as defined below:

        Master's degree in Marital and Family Therapy, or a
        Doctoral degree in Marital and Family Therapy, or a
        graduate degree which meets the Course of Study as defined below.

The following areas in the Course of Study below are basic to both Master's and Doctoral level programs. The Course of Study is based on the substantive content in degree programs, rather than specific course titles. The components of the graduate degree in Marital and Family Therapy are as follows:

(1) Marital and Family Systems [2–4 courses]. This is a fundamental introduction to the systems approach to intervention. The student should learn to think in the systems terms on a number of levels across a wide variety of family structures, and regarding a diverse range of presenting problems. The following is a topical list of what is considered appropriate in this area of study:
     (a) Nuclear family
     (b) Marital, sibling, and individual sub-systems
     (c) Family of origin
     (d) External societal influences

(2) Marital and Family Therapy [2–4 courses]. This area is intended to provide substantive understanding of the major theories of systems change and the applied practices evolving from each orientation. Major theoretical approaches to be studied may include:
     (a) Strategic
     (b) Structural
     (c) Experiential
     (d) Neo-analytical—i.e., object relations
     (e) Communications
     (f) Behavioral

Treatment techniques should focus on the following:

(3) Individual Development [2–4 courses].* This area is intended to provide knowledge of individual personality development and its normal and abnormal manifestations. The student should engage in relevant courses in the following areas:
     (a) Human development across the life span
     (b) Personality theory
     (c) Psychopathology—behavioral pathology
     (d) Human sexuality

An attempt should be made to integrate this material with systems concepts.

(4) Professional Studies [1 course]. This area is intended to contribute to the development of a professional attitude and identity. Areas of study may include:
     (a) Professional socialization and the role of the professional organization
     (b) Licensure or certification legislation
     (c) Legal responsibilities and liabilities
     (d) Ethics and family law
     (e) Confidentiality
     (f) Independent practice and interprofessional cooperation

(5) Supervised Clinical Practice [1 year]. This work should focus on the following:
     (a) Individual therapy

*Several of the courses in this category may be required as prerequisites for some degree programs.

        (b)   Marital therapy

        (c)   Family therapy

This work should continue without interruption during the student's academic program or at least one calendar year. Students are expected to spend 8–10 hours in direct client contact.

  (6)   Research [1 course]. This area is intended to provide assistance to students in becoming informed consumers of research in the marital family field. The following content may be included:

        (a)   Research design, methods and instruments

        (b)   Statistics

        (c)   Research in marital and family studies

        (d)   Research in marital and family therapy

Familiarity with substantive finding, together with the ability to make critical judgments as to the adequacy of research reports, is encouraged.

Upon completion of the graduate professional degree plus the required supervised clinical experience, the candidate will be expected to have mastered the important theory in the field of Marital and Family Therapy as defined in the Course of Study.

Graduate and post-degree programs accredited by the Commission on Accreditation for Marriage and Family Therapy Education meet the requirements of the Course of Study.

B. *Clinical Qualifications*

In addition to the clinical requirements in the above academic preparation, the applicant for AAMFT Clinical Membership shall have completed the following:

Two calendar years of work experience in marital and family therapy, following receipt of a qualifying degree, under supervision acceptable to the Membership Committee, such experience involving at least 1000 hours of direct clinical contact with couples and families and 200 hours of supervision of that work, at least 100 hours of which shall be in individual supervision.

C. *Personal Qualifications*

Endorsement by two Clinical Members of the Association attesting to suitable qualities of personal maturity and integrity for the conduct of marital and family therapy.

D. *Licensure/Certification*

Attainment of licensure/certification as a Marriage and Family Therapist in one's state of residence, where the state's standards have been accepted by the Membership Committee as qualifying one for membership.* Currently these states include:

California	New Jersey	North Carolina
Florida	Nevada	Utah
Michigan		

*Applicants who hold a license must possess a qualifying degree earned in a regionally accredited college or university.

II. ASSOCIATE MEMBER
REQUIREMENTS*

A. *Academic Requirements*
   (1) Completion of a qualifying degree from a regionally accredited educational institution, as defined under the section on Clinical Membership.
   (2) Completion of the Course of Study defined in the section on Clinical Membership. Applicants for Associate whose official transcripts reveal deficiencies in content will be required to submit to the Membership Committee a plan which documents how these deficiencies will be corrected.

B. *Clinical Requirements*
   Successful completion of the CLINICAL REQUIREMENTS as defined under the section on Clinical Membership.

C. *Personal Qualifications*
   Demonstration of PERSONAL QUALIFICATIONS as defined under the section on Clinical Membership.

III. STUDENT MEMBER
REQUIREMENTS**

A. *Academic Requirements*
   (1) Current enrollment in a graduate program (master's or doctoral) in Marital and Family Therapy in a regionally accredited educational institution.
   (2) Current pursuit of a course of study substantially equivalent to the Course of Study described in the section on Clinical Membership.

B. *Personal Qualifications*
   Demonstration of PERSONAL QUALIFICATIONS as defined under the section of Clinical Membership.

IV. ADMISSION PROCEDURES
FOR MEMBERSHIP
IN THE AAMFT

Admission procedures for membership (Clinical, Associate, Student) are administered by the Association's professional staff under the direction of the AAMFT Membership Committee. In order to assess the qualifications of the applicants for all membership categories, applicants are required to submit the following:

*Association membership shall be held for a maximum of five (5) years or until satisfactory completion of the requirements for admission as a Clinical Member, whichever comes first.

**Student membership shall be held for a maximum of five (5) years or until satisfactory completion and receipt of a qualifying degree.

A. *Clinical Member*
  (1) An official application for membership, including the names of at least two Clinical Members from whom the AAMFT can request official endorsements.
  (2) Official transcripts of graduate and professional education.
  (3) Proof of licensure/certification, if applicant resides in California, Florida, Michigan, Nevada, New Jersey, North Carolina, or Utah.
B. *Associate Member*
  (1) An official application for membership, including the names of at least two Clinical Members of whom the AAMFT can request official endorsements.
  (2) Official transcripts of graduate and professional education.
  (3) A plan for completion of requisite post-degree supervised clinical experience acceptable to the Membership Committee.
C. *Student Member*
  (1) An official application for membership, including the names of at least two Clinical Members from whom the AAMFT can request official endorsements.
  (2) A statement signed by the coordinator/director of a graduate (master's or doctoral) program in Marital and Family Therapy in a regionally accredited educational institution verifying the applicant's current enrollment in the program.
  (3) A description of the applicant's proposed graduate program, including the coursework to be taken. (This requirement is waived for students enrolled in programs accredited by the Commission on Accreditation for Marriage and Family Therapy Education.)

V. PROCEDURES
FOR TRANSFER OF CATEGORY

A. *Student to Associate*
  Members in the Student category, upon a successful completion of their graduate education, are expected to request advancement to Associate membership. In order for this process to begin, Student members are required to submit:
  (1) An official application for membership, completing those portions of the application which are relevant to the request for Transfer of Category. This application form shall include the names of at least two Clinical Members from whom the AAMFT can request official endorsements.
  (2) Official transcripts of completed graduate and professional studies.
  (3) A plan for completion of requisite post-degree supervised clinical experience acceptable to the Membership Committee.
B. *Associate to Clinical*
  Members in the Associate category, upon successful completion of all academic and clinical requirements, are required to submit:
  (1) An official application for membership, completing those portions of the application which are relevant to the request for Transfer of Category.

This application form shall include the names of at least two Clinical Members from whom the AAMFT can request official endorsements.

(2) Official transcripts of graduate and professional studies completed since entering the Associate category.

(3) Reports of approved supervised clinical practice in Marital and Family Therapy must be submitted by the applicant's supervisor, according to the guidelines in the Approved Supervisor brochure.

APPENDIX D
THE GRADUATE PROGRAM IN MARITAL AND FAMILY THERAPY AT THE UNIVERSTIY OF CONNECTICUT

University of Connecticut
U-117
Storrs, CT 06268

The Graduate Program in Marital and Family Therapy at the University of Connecticut is offered through the Graduate School and the Human Development and Family Relations Program (HDFR). The clinical program is concentrated in the M.A. degree program but may, for those planning careers in research and academic teaching, be added to the Ph.D. program.

The suggested minimum course sequence for the program is as follows:

FALL SEMESTER, FIRST YEAR	CREDITS
HDFR 301—Seminar (Professional Orientation to HDFR)	2
HDFR 303—Research Methods I	3
HDFR 351—Foundations of Marriage and Family Therapy	3
HDFR 365—Human Development Over the Life Cycle	3
	11

SPRING SEMESTER, FIRST YEAR	
HDFR 305—Research Methods II (or Elective)	3
HDFR 353—Introduction to Clinical Practice and Professional Issues	2
HDFR 354—Marriage Therapy	3
HDFR 395—Theory of Family Development	3
	11

SUMMER SESSIONS I AND II
(Between first and second academic year)

HDFR 362—Practicum in Marriage and Family Therapy   6

FALL SEMESTER, SECOND YEAR

HDFR 356—Family Therapy   3
HDFR 362—Practicum in Marriage and Family Therapy   3
HDFR 377—Human Sexuality   3
HDFR 391—Patterns and Dynamics of Family Interaction   3
                                                          ──
                                                          12

SPRING SEMESTER, SECOND YEAR

HDFR 359—Case Seminar in Marriage and Family Therapy   3
HDFR 362—Practicum in Marriage and Family Therapy   3
HDFR 399—Thesis Preparation   —
Elective   3
                                                          ──
                                                           9
                                                          ──
                              Total Minimum Credits   49

Electives recommended include: Psych 311—Psychodynamics, Psych 324—Group Therapy, Psych 309—Psychodiagnostics, Psych 303—Psychopathology, and DRM 264—Legal Aspects of Family Life. Admission to the Practicum is by vote of the Clinical Faculty. Students perform therapy in the Marital and Family Therapy Clinic in the Human Development Center and in selected community agencies and clinics. They are required to *continue*, without interruption, two days weekly, in their Practicums for a minimum of one calendar year.

APPENDIX E
AAMFT CODE
OF ETHICAL PRINCIPLES
FOR FAMILY THERAPISTS

Note: The following information is reprinted by permission of the American Association of Marriage and Family Therapy, 924 West Ninth Street, Upland, CA 91786

PRINCIPLES:

1. *RESPONSIBILITIES TO CLIENTS*

    Family therapists are dedicated to advancing the welfare of families and individuals, including respecting the right of those persons seeking their assistance, and making reasonable efforts to ensure that their services are used appropriately.

2. *COMPETENCE*

    Family therapists are dedicated to maintaining high standards of competence, recognizing appropriate limitations to their competence and services and using consultation from other professionals.

3. *INTEGRITY*

    Family therapists are honest in dealing with clients, students, trainees, colleagues, and the public, seeking to eliminate incompetence or dishonesty from the work or representation of family therapists.

4. *CONFIDENTIALITY*

    Family therapists respect both the law and the rights of clients, and safeguard client confidences as permitted by law.

5. *PROFESSIONAL RESPONSIBILITY*

    Family therapists are honest in dealing with clients, students, trainees, colleagues and, as employees of organizations, remain accountable as individuals for the ethical principles of the profession.

6. *PROFESSIONAL DEVELOPMENT*

    Family therapists seek to continue their professional development, and strive to make pertinent knowledge available to clients, students, trainees, colleagues, and the public.

7. *RESEARCH RESPONSIBILITY*

    Family therapists recognize that while research is essential to the advancement of knowledge, all investigations must be conducted with full respect for the rights and dignity of participants and with full concern for their welfare.

8. *SOCIAL RESPONSIBILITY*

    Family therapists acknowledge a responsibility to participate in activities contributing to a better community in society, including devoting a portion of their professional activity to services for which there is little or no financial return.

REFERENCES

CHAPTER ONE

COOKERLY, J. "The Outcome of the Six Major Forms of Marriage Counseling Compared: A Pilot Study." *The Journal of Marriage and the Family,* 35 (4) (1973), 608–11.
———. "Evaluating Different Approaches to Marriage Counseling," in *Treating Relationships,* ed. David Olson. Lake Mills, Ia.: Graphic Publishing Company, 1976.
SAGER, C. *Marriage Contracts and Couple Therapy.* New York: Brunner/Mazel Publishers, 1976.
SCHOFIELD, W. *Psychotherapy: The Purchase of Friendship.* Englewood Cliffs, N.J.: Prentice-Hall, Inc., 1974.
SHAW, G. *Complete Plays with Prefaces,* Vol. 4. New York: Dodd Mead & Company, 1963.

CHAPTER TWO

ABLES, BILLIE, and JEFFREY BRANDSMA. *Therapy for Couples.* San Francisco: Jossey-Bass Publishers, 1978.
ARD, BEN, and CONSTANCE CALLAHAN ARD, eds. *Handbook of Marriage Counseling* (2nd. ed.). Palo Alto, Cal.: Science and Behavior Books, Inc., 1976.
GURMAN, ALAN, ed. *Questions and Answers in the Practice of Family Therapy.* New York: Brunner/Mazel Publishers, 1981.
HUMPHREY, FREDERICK, and LESLIE STRONG. "Treatment of Extramarital Sexual Relationships as Reported by Clinical Members of the American Association of Marriage and Family Counselors." Paper presented at American Association of Marriage and Family Counselors, Hartford, Conn., May 22, 1976.

MARTIN, PETER. *A Marital Therapy Manual.* New York: Brunner/Mazel Publishers, 1976.

PAOLINO, THOMAS, JR., and BARBARA McGRADY, eds. *Marriage and Marital Therapy: Psychoanalytic, Behavioral, and Systems Theory Perspectives.* New York: Brunner/Mazel Publishers, 1978.

SKYNNER, A.C. ROBIN. *Systems of Family and Marital Psychotherapy.* New York: Brunner/Mazel Publishers, 1976.

STAHMAN, ROBERT, and WILLIAM HIEBERT, eds. *Klemer's Counseling in Marital and Sexual Problems: A Clinician's Handbook* (2nd. ed.). Baltimore: The Williams & Wilkens Company, 1977.

CHAPTER THREE

HUMPHREY, FREDERICK. "Treatment of Extramarital Sexual Affairs," in *Questions and Answers in the Practice of Family Therapy,* ed. Alan Gurman. New York: Brunner/Mazel Publishers, 1981.

HUNT, MORTON. *The Affair.* New York: World Publishing Company, 1969.

LIBBY, ROGER, and ROBERT WHITEHURST, eds. *Marriage and Alternatives: Exploring Intimate Relationships.* Glenview, Ill.: Scott, Foresman & Company, 1977.

NEUBECK, GERHARD. *Extramarital Relations.* Englewood Cliffs, N.J.: Prentice-Hall, Inc., 1969.

VICTOR, JEFFREY. *Human Sexuality: A Social Psychological Approach.* Englewood Cliffs, N.J.: Prentice-Hall, Inc., 1980.

CHAPTER FOUR

ARD, BEN. *Treating Psychosexual Dysfunction.* New York: Jason Aronson, 1974.

CRAWLEY, LAWRENCE, JAMES MALFETTI, ERNEST STEWARD, Jr., and NIN DIAS. *Reproduction, Sex, and Preparation for Marriage* (2nd. ed.). Englewood Cliffs, N.J.: Prentice-Hall, Inc., 1973.

DIAMOND, MILTON, and ARNO KARLEN. *Sexual Decisions.* Boston: Little, Brown & Company, 1980.

GROSS, LEONARD, ed. *Sexual Issues in Marriage.* New York: Spectrum Publications, Inc. (Wiley), 1975.

KAPLAN, HELEN SINGER. *The New Sex Therapy.* New York: Brunner/Mazel, 1974.

————. *The New Sex Therapy. Vol. II: Disorders of Sexual Desire.* New York: Brunner/Mazel, 1979.

LoPICCOLO, JOSEPH, and LESLIE LoPICCOLO, eds. *Handbook of Sex Therapy.* New York: Plenum Publishing Corporation, 1978.

MASTERS, WILLIAM H. and VIRGINIA JOHNSON. *Human Sexual Inadequacy.* Boston: Little, Brown & Company, 1971.

CHAPTER FIVE

BERGER, MILTON, ed. *Videotape Techniques in Psychiatric Training and Treatment.* New York: Brunner/Mazel Publishers, 1970.

SATIR, VIRGINIA. *Conjoint Family Therapy.* Palo Alto, Calif.: Science and Behavior Books, 1964.

VINCENT, CLARK. *Sexual and Marital Health: The Physician as a Consultant.* New York: McGraw-Hill Book Company, 1973.

CHAPTER SIX

BERMAN, ELLEN, and HAROLD LIEF. "Marital Therapy from a Psychiatric Perspective: An Overview." *The American Journal of Psychiatry,* 132, no. 6 (1975), 583–92.

BOWMAN, HENRY, and GRAHAM SPANIER. *Modern Marriage* (8th. ed.). New York: McGraw-Hill Book Company, 1978.

ROLLINS, BOYD, and HAROLD FELDMAN. "Marital Satisfaction over the Family Life Cycle." *Journal of Marriage and the Family,* 32 (1970), 20–28.

UDRY, J. RICHARD. *The Social Context of Marriage* (3rd. ed.). Philadelphia: J. B. Lippincott Company, 1974.

CHAPTER SEVEN

BERNARD, JESSIE. *The Future of Marriage.* New York: World Publishing Company, 1972.

DAVID, DEBORAH, and ROBERT BRANNON, eds. *The Forty Nine Percent Majority: The Male Sex Role.* Reading, Mass.: Addison-Wesley Publishing Company, 1976.

FRIEZE, IRENE H. et al. *Women and Sex Roles: A Social Psychological Perspective.* New York: W. W. Norton & Company, 1978.

HEISS, JEROLD. *Family Roles and Interaction* (2nd. ed.). Chicago: Rand, McNally & Company, 1976.

McCARY, JAMES. *Freedom and Growth in Marriage.* Santa Barbara, Calif.: Hamilton Publishing Company (Wiley), 1975.

PLECK, JOSEPH, and ROBERT BRANNON, eds. "Male Roles and the Male Experience." *Journal of Social Issues,* 34, no. 1 (1978), 1–199.

SAFILIOS-ROTHSCHILD, CONSTANTINA. *Toward a Sociology of Women.* Lexington, Mass.: Xerox College Publishing, 1972.

WELLS, J. GIPSON. *Marriage and the Family* (2nd. ed.). New York: Macmillan Publishing Company, Inc., 1979.

CHAPTER EIGHT

BOHANNAN, PAUL, ed. *Divorce and After.* Garden City, N.Y.: Doubleday & Company, 1970.

BROWN, EMILY. "Divorce Counseling," in David Olson, ed., *Treating Relationships.* Lake Mills, Ia.: Graphic Publishing Company, Inc., 1976.

COOGLER, O. J. *Structured Mediation in Divorce Settlements: A Handbook for Marital Mediators.* Lexington, Mass.: Lexington Books, Div. D. C. Heath & Company, 1978.

FISHER, ESTHER O. *Divorce: The New Freedom.* New York: Harper & Row, 1974.

HUNT, MORTON, and BERNICE HUNT. *The Divorce Experience.* New York: McGraw-Hill Book Company, 1977.

KESSLER, SHEILA. *The American Way of Divorce: Prescriptions for Change.* Chicago: Nelson-Hall Company, 1975.

KÜBLER-ROSS, ELISABETH. *On Death and Dying.* New York: The Macmillan Company, 1969.

LEVINGER, GEORGE, and OLIVER MOLES, eds. *Divorce and Separation: Context, Causes, and Consequences.* New York: Basic Books, Inc., 1979.

WALTERSTEIN, JUDITH, and JOAN KELLY. *Surviving the Breakup: How Children and Parents Cope with Divorce.* New York: Basic Books, Inc., 1980.

WEISS, ROBERT. *Marital Separation.* New York: Basic Books, Inc., 1975.

————. *Going It Alone: The Family Life and Social Situation of the Single Parent.* New York: Basic Books, Inc., 1979.

CHAPTER NINE

CALHOUN, LAURENCE, JAMES SELBY, and H. ELIZABETH KING. *Dealing with Crisis: A Guide to Critical Life Problems.* Englewood Cliffs, N.J.: Prentice-Hall, Inc., 1976.

CUBER, JOHN, and PEGGY HARROFF. *The Significant Americans.* New York: Appleton-Century-Crofts, 1965.

GOLDBERG, MARTIN. *A Guide to Psychiatric Diagnosis and Understanding for the Helping Professions.* Chicago: Nelson-Hall Company, 1973.

GURMAN, ALAN, ed. *Questions and Answers in the Practice of Family Therapy.* New York: Brunner/Mazel Publishers, 1981.

MACE, DAVID, and VERA MACE. *How to Have a Happy Marriage: A Step-by-Step Guide to an Enriched Relationship.* Nashville, Tenn.: Abingdon Press, 1977.

NEUHAUS, ROBERT, and RUBY HART NEUHAUS. *Family Crises.* Columbus, Ohio: Charles E. Merrill Publishing Company, 1974.

SCHILLER, MARGERY. *Personal and Family Finance—Principles and Applications.* Boston: Allyn & Bacon, 1981.

SHULZ, DAVID, and STANLEY RODGERS. *Marriage, the Family, and Personal Fulfillment.* Englewood Cliffs, N.J.: Prentice-Hall, Inc., 1975.

SINGER, LAURA, with BARBARA LONG STERN. *Stages: The Crises that Shape Your Marriage.* New York: Grosset & Dunlap Publishers, 1980.

CHAPTER TEN

ARD, BEN, and CONSTANCE CALLAHAN ARD, eds. *Handbook of Marriage Counseling* (2nd. ed.). Palo Alto, Calif.: Science and Behavior Books, Inc., 1976.

BROWNING, CHARLES. *Private Practice Handbook: The Tools, Tactics and Techniques for Successful Practice Development.* Los Alamitos, Calif.: Browning Therapy Group Publishers, 1981.

INTERNAL REVENUE SERVICE. "Tax Guide for Small Business, Publication #334." Washington, D.C.: Department of the Treasury, 1981.

KILGORE, JAMES. "Establishing and Maintaining a Private Practice." *Journal of Marriage and Family Counseling,* 1, no. 2 (1975), 145–48.

KRUPNICK, ROBERT, and FREDERICK HUMPHREY. "Organizational vs. Private Practice: The Influence of Work Setting on the Practice of Marital and Family Therapy." Paper presented for the American Association for Marriage and Family Therapy, Toronto, Canada, November 7, 1980.

MONDIN, FREDERICK. *The Practice of Private Practice: A Handbook.* Ann Arbor, Mich.: Xerox University Microfilms, 1976.

PRESSMAN, ROBERT. *Private Practice: A Handbook for the Independent Mental Health Practitioner.* New York: Gardner Press, 1980.

SHIMBERG, EDMUND. *The Handbook of Private Practice in Psychology.* New York: Brunner/Mazel Publishers, 1979.

CHAPTER ELEVEN

DEWALD, PAUL. *Psychotherapy, A Dynamic Approach* (2nd. ed.). New York: Basic Books, Inc., 1969.

"Education and Training in Marital and Family Therapy." *Journal of Marital and Family Therapy* (Special Issue), 5 no. 3 (1979), 1–105.

FRAMO, JAMES. "Personal Reflections of a Family Therapist." *Journal of Marriage and Family Counseling,* 1, no. 1 (1975), 15–28.

GULDNER, CLAUDE. "Family Therapy for the Trainee in Family Therapy." *Journal of Marriage and Family Counseling,* 4, no. 1 (1978), 127–32.

LAZARUS, LAURENCE. "Family Therapy by a Husband-Wife Team." *Journal of Marriage and Family Counseling,* 2, no. 3 (1976), 225–33.

MARX, JOHN, and S. LEE SPRAY. "Marital Status and Occupational Success Among Mental Health Professionals." *Journal of Marriage and the Family,* 32, no. 1 (1970), 110–18.

WINKLE, C. WAYNE, FRED PIERCY, and ALAN HOVESTADT. "A Curriculum for Graduate Level Marriage and Family Therapy Education." *Journal of Marital and Family Therapy,* 7, no. 2 (1981), 201–10.

INDEX

Dissolution, marital. *See also* Divorce
    causes of, 142
    theories concerning, 141
Divorce, 32, 34, 39, 57, 140–51
    barriers to, 141, 142
    community, 144
    co-parental, 144
    decision about, 7
    economic, 144
    emotional, 144
    emotional stress and, 146
    etiology of, 141–42
    healthy, 153
    impact of, 146
    legal, 144
    legal issues in, 146–48
    peak time for seeking, 109
    psychic, 149
    psychological process of, 142–44
    and remarriage, 140, 149–50
    right to, 155
    and singlehood, 149–50
    stages of, 144–45
Divorced, pressures on, 149–50
Divorce mediation, 147
Divorce therapy, 6, 140, 144–45, 154
Drug dependence, 168, 172

Ego investment, 114
Ego strength, 34
Ego-syntonic listening, 167
Emergencies, 39–40
Emotional maturity, 14, 169
Emotional support, 8
Empathy, 27, 28
EMS. *See* Extramarital sexual affairs
Ending process, 41–42
Equality, push toward, 129, 142
Ethical codes, and conduct, 211–13, 237–38
Expectations, unrealistic, 107–8
"Expert opinion," 154
Extramarital relationships. *See* Extramarital sexual affairs
Extramarital sexual affairs (EMS), 21, 38, 39, 47–66, 112
    conjoint sessions, 55–56
    emotional disturbance and, 50–51
    fantasies about, 95–96
    nonparticipating spouse, treatment of, 53–55
    "other person" in, 56
    outcomes of, 52, 57–58
    participating spouse, treatment of, 53
    reactions to, 51
    reasons for, 48–51, 53
    treatment of, 51–52, 56–58

Family bonds, loosening, 106–7
Family Coordinator, The, 205
Family Process, 206
Family therapy, 12, 113
    multigenerational, 117

Feedback, importance of, 97–98
Feldman, Harold, 113
Female orgasmic responses, 77
"Fence," 90
Finances, 165–67, 171
Friendship, purchase of, 8

Gender stereotyping, 88–89
Goals, setting, 8
Goodwin, Hilda S., 98n
Graduate program, in marital and family therapy, 235–36
Grief therapy, 151–55
Group marital therapy, 11, 98–99, 131
Groves, Ernest, 4
Groves Conference on the Family, 4

Harroff, Peggy, 170
Humphrey, Frederick, 21, 47, 186, 188

Inadequacy, feelings of, 50
Inclusion–exclusion, 108, 113
Incompatible pairings, 168–69
Individual sessions
    concurrent, 9–10
    individual needs in, 38–39
    need for initial, 21–22
Insight, 34, 35
Intake, and evaluation, process of, 10, 21–22
    background information and questionnaires, 22
Intercourse, sexual
    conditions for positive, 70
    frequency of, 69, 77
    misconceptions about, 68–69
Interpersonal marital system, 14–15, 30
Interviewing, 9
    pacing and guiding, 39
Intimacy, 108, 114
Intrapsychic marital system, 14, 16, 30, 39
    problems, 38
Irretrievable breakdown, principle of, 146

Job satisfaction, 188–89
Johnson, Virginia, 78
Journal of Divorce, 207
Journal of Family History, 205, 206
Journal of Marital and Family Therapy, 204, 206
Journal of Marriage and the Family, Family Relations: The Journal of Applied Family and Child Studies, 205, 206
Journal of Sex and Marital Therapy, 207

Kaplan, Helen Singer, 77–78
Kinsey report, 75
Krupnick, Robert, 186, 188
Kubler-Ross, Elisabeth, 151–52

Labeling, 172
"Let it all hang out" ethic, 94–95
Levinger, George, 141, 142
Liability, 192

Therapist(s)
  academic requirements, 208–9
  as active participant, 38
  as agent of change, 36–37
  anxieties of, 215
  as catalyst, 32, 55–56, 96
  educational role of, 35, 97, 111
  impact of marital therapy upon, 214–18
  as individuals, 217–18
  marital partners as, 216–17
  as mediator, 96
  misusing client, 215
  motivation to be, 214
  need for therapy, 217
  own marriage, impact of marital therapy on, 214–16
  personal standards, 207–8
  personal style of, 28–29
  as positive model, 97
  pro-human, 131–32
  role in ongoing therapy, 27–30
  specific skills and abilities, 207–8
  staying well balanced, 218
Therapy, previous, 24–25. *See also specific type*
Transference, 9, 30
Triangling, therapeutic, 172

Unconscious, dictates of, 12–13

Value congruency, 6–7
Videotaping, 99
Vincent, Clark, 89

Weiss, Robert, 145
Wife
  careers and, 110, 115
  changing role of, 129

Young Parent Syndrome (YPS), 76–77